The 26th "Yankee" Division
on Coast Patrol Duty,
1942–1943

ALSO BY DENNIS A. CONNOLE

*The Indians of the Nipmuck Country
in Southern New England, 1630–1750:
An Historical Geography* (McFarland, 2001; paper, 2006)

The 26th "Yankee" Division on Coast Patrol Duty, 1942–1943

Dennis A. Connole

McFarland & Company, Inc., Publishers
Jefferson, North Carolina, and London

LIBRARY OF CONGRESS CATALOGUING-IN-PUBLICATION DATA

Connole, Dennis A., 1943–
The 26th "Yankee" Division on coast patrol duty, 1942–1943 /
Dennis A. Connole.
      p.   cm.
Includes bibliographical references and index.

ISBN-13: 978-0-7864-3142-7
softcover : 50# alkaline paper ∞

1. United States. Army. Infantry Division, 26th — History.
2. Massachusetts. National Guard. Infantry Division, 26th — History.
3. World War, 1939–1945 — Regimental histories — United States.
4. World War, 1939–1945 — Atlantic Coast (U.S.) 5. World War, 1939–1945 — Naval operations, American. I. Title. II. Title: Twenty-sixth "Yankee" Division on coast patrol duty, 1942–1943.
D769.326th.C66   2008   940.54'1273 — dc22   2007048715

British Library cataloguing data are available

©2008 Dennis A. Connole. All rights reserved

*No part of this book may be reproduced or transmitted in any form
or by any means, electronic or mechanical, including photocopying
or recording, or by any information storage and retrieval system,
without permission in writing from the publisher.*

On the cover: High upon a rock along the New England shoreline, a soldier looks through his field glasses to detect the enemy (U.S. Army Signal Corps photograph); Patches from left the 26th Division patch with the lettering YD worn on the right shoulder; The 1st Coast Artillery, New England, patch worn on left shoulder; Map of duty stations.

Manufactured in the United States of America

*McFarland & Company, Inc., Publishers
Box 611, Jefferson, North Carolina 28640
www.mcfarlandpub.com*

To my mother
Michelina (Mary) Palumbo Connole

Acknowledgments

Along the way, I have received help from many people in the research and writing of this book. Without their time and effort, I could have not completed the project. I would like to thank the following individuals, organizations, government agencies, and libraries.

First, I would like to thank my colleagues at South High Community School in Worcester who answered my many questions about grammar, mechanics, and word usage: Mary Reynolds, Mary Sebring, Tom Nolan, Steven Silverman, Carolyn Martello, and Stu Friedman. I would especially like to thank Michael O'Sullivan, who edited the final draft and recommended a number of valuable changes and revisions that greatly improved and strengthened the manuscript; and Mary Reynolds, who edited several of the chapters and offered advice and support. Thanks also to Cecilia Thurlow who helped with the editing.

My appreciation and thanks to the following: the staff at the Worcester Public Library who were always so helpful, especially Nancy Gaudette, Worcester Room librarian; Lynn Givens, assistant director-adult services librarian, at the McArthur Library, Biddeford, Maine; the staff at the Worcester Historical Museum, especially Julia Barrow and Robyn Christensen; the staff at the National Archives and Records Administration (NARA), College Park, Maryland; the staff at the U.S. Military History Institute, Carlisle Barracks, Carlisle, Pennsylvania, especially the Friends of the Omar N. Bradley Foundation.

A special thanks to Jillian Carle Jakeman of Ocean Park, Maine, a genealogist and volunteer staff member at the Dyer Library in Saco. Jillian was a tremendous help in locating information about the 181st Infantry on coast patrol duty in Maine. She took me on a tour of the Saco-Biddeford-Old Orchard Beach area and showed me many of the places frequented by the GIs. Jillian also introduced me to Talmadge "Ted" Allen, a member of Company A, 132nd Combat Engineers (attached to the 26th Division), stationed at the National Guard Armory in Saco for 11 months from August 1942 to September 1943. Talmadge provided me with much information about the work of his engineering company in Maine.

Next, I would like to thank Brigadier General Leonid Kondratiuk, director, Massachusetts National Guard Museum and Archives in Worcester. Col. Kondratiuk was an immense help during the course of my research and kindly edited several of the chapters. I would also like to thank archivist Kent DeGroodt. Both were always friendly and helpful in locating resource materials about the 26th Division and providing information about the military in general.

Thanks to Edward Michaud, president of Trident Research & Recovery, Inc., Framingham, Massachusetts, and Greg Brooks, president of Sub Sea Recovery of Portland, Maine, for providing information about German U-boat activity in Casco Bay, Maine.

There are a number of veterans from the 26th Division whom I would like to personally thank at this time. First, all the men of Company H, 181st Infantry, including Sulo Ruuska,

Guido Fratturelli, James Carnivale, Richard Brill, Antonio Tata, Romeo LeBlanc, Orlando Vitone, Nicholas Renzetti, George Greenough, Harvey Belluci, and John Gerety.

Others from the 26th Division include Clifford Welcome, Theodore Simmington, Jr., Paul Metcalf, Nathaniel Mencow, Edward Chrobak, Paul Turini, John Judge, Gerald Thibodeau, Edward Griffin, Frank McInnis, Francis Donovan, Philip Leibrock, Werner Schnell, Michael Stubinski and Ross Rajotte (Stubinski and Rajotte both later became members of the 36th Division, like my father). A special thanks to Clifford Welcome, Theodore Simmington, Jr., John Gerety, Ross Rajotte, Nathaniel Mencow, and Sulo Ruuska. I am deeply indebted to all the veterans of the YD whom I have interviewed and corresponded with over the past several years. I cannot thank you enough for all your help, for sharing the great stories of your days in the military, and most of all for your friendship (see Introduction).

I met several times with Dorothy Dineen of Worcester, widow of James Dineen of the 181st Infantry, who told me what she remembered about her husband's days on coast patrol and provided several photographs taken by her husband for reproduction. Thanks, Dorothy. I also wish to thank Mrs. Orlando Orrizzi, Jr., for allowing me access to her husband's photograph collection; several of those photographs are included in the book. Others providing photographs include Karl Ruuska, son of Sulo Ruuska; Dr. Michael Ciaranca, natural resource manager, Massachusetts Army National Guard; the National Archives and Records Administration (NARA), College Park, Maryland (Signal Corps Photos); and the Massachusetts National Guard Museum & Archives. Processing and restoration of photographs from the Sulo Ruuska and Orlando Orrizzi collections was done by Michaels' Photo Center, West Boylston, Massachusetts; processing and restoration of the NARA photos and troops arriving at Camp Edwards, 1941, was done by Robert McMahon Photography, New York, N.Y. McMahon also provided the photographs of the obstacle course at Camp Edwards.

Thanks to Peter Bogdan, editor of the Yankee Division Veterans Association's (YDVA) newsletter, *Yankee Doings*. The story of the men of the 26th Division on shore patrol in New England, previously published in the newsletter in five installments, comprises several chapters of the book.

I would like to thank the members of my family who provided information, my father's sisters Helen Palumbo and Margaret Connole, my sisters Kathy Senior and Deborah Coakley, and my brothers Joe and Rick. Also, my nephew Lt. Col. Kevin Coakley, a career officer in the U.S. Army, who helped me with information about the military.

Finally, to my wife, Joyce; my son, Dennis, and daughter-in-law, Gayle; my daughter, Jill, and son-in-law, Ralph Streete; and my grandchildren, Alexis, Anthony, Sydney, and Dominic Connole, Samantha and Nichole Gambaccini, Jordan, Diana, and Melanie Streete, thank you for your love and support.

Table of Contents

Acknowledgments vii
Preface 1
Introduction 3

1. The 26th "Yankee" Division: Mobilization Period 11
2. Trainees Arrive at Camp Edwards 20
3. Basic Training: March–September 1941 29
4. The "Stovepipe" Platoon 47
5. Time Off from Training: Off Duty Hours 51
6. Public Relations Exercise: Three Day Bivouac in Worcester, Massachusetts 54
7. Advanced Infantry Training: June 16–August 15 59
8. Fort Devens Maneuvers: August 19–September 12, 1941 62
9. Planning Prior to the Carolina Maneuvers of 1941 66
10. The Carolina Maneuvers: October 2–December 3, 1941 71
11. Conclusions of the Carolina Maneuvers 90
12. Return to Camp Edwards: December 6, 1941 94
13. On Shore Patrol in New England and New York: December 1941 to May 1942 98
14. Living Accommodations for Men on Coast Patrol Duty 107
15. Return to Coast Patrol Duty, May 1942: German Spies and Saboteurs Land on American Shores 113
16. U-Boat Sightings and Encounters by the Men of the 181st Infantry 125
17. Problems and Developments 127
18. Saco, Maine — Headquarters, 2nd Battalion, 181st Infantry: May 1942 to November 1943 129
19. Duties and Assignments of the Units on Coast Patrol 139
20. Social and Recreational Activities 149
21. Patrol-Scout Dogs 154

22. Provisional Military Police Unit	162
23. The Rockland Sector	165
Conclusion	175
Appendix A. Organizational List, National Guard of Massachusetts — 1939	177
Appendix B. Organizational List, 181st Infantry Regiment, 26th Division — 1941	182
Appendix C. Station List, 181st Infantry Combat Team	183
Appendix D. History of the 181st Infantry	186
Appendix E. Résumé of Regimental Activities, 181st Infantry, Since Induction on January 16, 1941	190
Chapter Notes	195
Bibliography	205
Index	207

Preface

Presented here is a historical account of the 26th "Yankee" Division (YD) on coast patrol duty along the Atlantic seaboard of the United States from January 1942 through November 1943. The story of the YD troops assigned to safeguard our shores against incursions by Nazi espionage agents and saboteurs during the first two years of the war is a little known, and previously undocumented, chapter of World War II history. My father, Dennis "Joe" Connole, was a member of Company H, 181st Infantry, a regiment of the 26th Division stationed in the city of Saco (pronounced Soco), on the coast of Maine during this period. His involvement was what aroused my initial interest in the subject.

Immediately following the preemptive strike by the Japanese against Pearl Harbor and the subsequent declaration of war against the Axis powers by Congress on December 8, 1941, the War Department implemented a previously prepared "contingency plan" to protect the home front against outside threats to the national security. Given the fear and paranoia of the time, there was great concern among government and military leaders in Washington regarding the threat of a full-scale German invasion, as well as the possibility of U-boats landing spies and saboteurs along deserted stretches and out-of-the-way places along the country's eastern coastline.

Within hours of the Pearl Harbor attack, military officials charged the 26th Infantry Division with securing parts of the coast of New England and Long Island, New York, against enemy infiltration from the sea. In May 1942, the military expanded the division's area of responsibility to include much of the East Coast of the United States, south to the Florida Keys.

Placed under the jurisdiction of the 1st Coast Artillery District (New England), a subdivision of the U.S. Army Coast Artillery Corps (CAC), commanders deployed units at key locations to supplement patrols by U.S. Navy and Coast Guard personnel. The troops of the division bivouacked on the beaches and pulled sentry duty along vast stretches of the coastline.

The role of the Coast Artillery Corps was to protect and defend all major harbors and ports within the continental United States and its territories. The CAC maintained a series of military installations and coastal fortifications at strategic points along the country's maritime frontier, the majority constructed prior to the turn of the century. Coastal defenses included fixed antiship gun emplacements and antiaircraft artillery (AAA) regiments at harbor forts; antiaircraft batteries, both mobile and semi-mobile, strategically positioned in outlying coastal areas at nearby forts, camps, outposts, sub-posts, reservations, and other tactical sites; and searchlight battalions.

Provided is a detailed account of the two highly publicized incidents of saboteurs coming ashore at Amagansett on Long Island and Ponte Vedra Beach near Jacksonville, Florida, in June 1942, which served as a clear indication of the need to be vigilant in guarding America's Atlantic frontier. Following the landings, government and military officials took immediate steps to commit additional men to the patrol and surveillance of the coastline. This decision would have a profound influence on the fate of the 26th Division. The military issued immediate orders for units of the YD to remain on patrol duty for an indefinite period, the effects of which ultimately resulted in a lengthy delay in the combat-ready unit's deployment overseas. Also included are a number of reports of U-boat sightings and encounters with subversive agents by 26th Division personnel who were on beach patrol or manning gun emplacements or positions along the eastern seabord during this period.

Unfortunately, existing histories of the 26th, of which there are only a handful, provide only minimal coverage of the important role played by division forces in the defense of the home front against threats from without during the early days of the war. My intended purpose is to document this important aspect of the country's "home defense." It is important that this unique story, previously neglected by historians, is told to ensure that it be preserved as a record for future generations.

I have spent more than five years researching the story and have based the narrative almost exclusively on primary sources, which include accounts found in division, regimental, and other histories. One of the problems encountered in my research was that the official histories were sorely lacking in specifics regarding the sectors covered by the various units as well as details about the day-to-day operations of the men who carried out the patrols and performed other related duties. Much of the latter information I was able to obtain primarily through numerous personal interviews and correspondence with veterans from the 26th Division.

Also helpful were first-person accounts by veterans published in the *Yankee Doings* newsletter, the quarterly publication of the "Yankee (26th) Division Veterans Association" (YDVA), and elsewhere (see Bibliography). I have, whenever possible, endeavored to present the story from the perspective of the soldiers who were there, much of it in their own words.

Our history begins with the activation of the Massachusetts National Guard, 26th Infantry Division, on January 16, 1941, 11 months before the Japanese attack against Pearl Harbor on December 7, 1941, and chronicles the unit's build-up to "full war strength" during the early mobilization period; continues through basic and advanced infantry training; followed by the unit's participation in the Fort Devens and Carolina Maneuvers of 1941, designed by General Army Headquarters (GHQ) to prepare the U.S. Army for the inevitability of war. The primary focus of the book is on the period spent by the division forces on coast patrol from 1942 to 1943.

In late November of 1943, the War Department removed the last of the YD units from their duty stations, either to train for reassignment to a combat theater of operations zone or to be shipped directly overseas as much needed replacements. At this juncture of the war, the threat to the American mainland had diminished to the point where the military had greatly reduced or eliminated foot and motor patrols and replaced them with "mobile reconnaissance units," stationed at strategic locations, ready to move out at a moment's notice in the event of a threat. The majority of the troops assigned to coast patrol duty went on to serve out the war in combat roles overseas with the 26th and other divisions.

This book is a tribute to the dedicated men of the 26th Division who served on stateside security duty to protect the homeland during this critical early period of the war.

Introduction

In March of 1941, approximately nine months before Pearl Harbor, my father, Dennis "Joe" Connole of Worcester, Massachusetts, reported to the local U.S. Army induction center to begin his one year of active-duty training. After the swearing-in ceremony, the draftees boarded a passenger train for Camp Edwards on Cape Cod to undergo basic and advanced infantry training with the 181st Infantry, a regiment of the recently mobilized 26th Massachusetts National Guard. The companies comprising the battalions of the 181st Infantry were located in Worcester and the surrounding towns of Worcester County in central Massachusetts.

My father's regiment spent approximately 20 months on shore patrol duty in New England and parts of Long Island, New York, from January 1942 until November 1943 (interrupted by three months of combat training at Camp Edwards in March 1942). Stationed in Saco, Maine, the regiment's area of responsibility extended from Machias, near the Canadian border, to Portsmouth, New Hampshire. After relieving the 181st Infantry from shore patrol duty in November 1943, the War Department officially inactivated the regiment in February 1944.

During the winter of 1943-44, the American divisions fighting in Italy suffered heavy casualties and were badly in need of replacements. The majority of the 181st Infantry Regiment's enlisted personnel shipped out to the European Theater of Operations (ETO) beginning in early February 1944 for reassignment to one of the decimated combat divisions.

My father arrived in Italy in early March 1944, landing at Naples, where he received an assignment to the 141st "Alamo" Infantry Regiment, 36th "Texas" Division, a mobilized Texas National Guard outfit. Thus, Joe Connole became a "Yankee" in the "Texas Army."

He joined the regiment at Maddaloni, Italy, during an intensive rebuilding and refitting program out of the line. Many of the replacements were not as fortunate. They had no sooner disembarked from the troop transports at Naples Harbor than officers and NCOs loaded them onto waiting trucks that took them directly to the front lines. Coming under immediate fire or artillery bombardment was a most terrifying experience for the rookie replacements. A considerable number ended up as casualties, sometimes before anyone ever got to know their names. My father underwent his baptism of fire on May 29, 1944, near Velletri, Italy, about 22 miles south of Rome. "The Fighting 36th" was among the U.S. Army's most distinguished and decorated combat divisions of World War II.

Joe Connole earned the Purple Heart for wounds received on June 12, 1944, near the town of Nunziatella, Italy, 60 miles north of Rome, and spent 22 days convalescing in an Army hospital in Naples before returning to his unit to train for the invasion of southern France (Operation Anvil-Dragoon), which took place on August 15, 1944. During his 16 months with the division, he participated in the Rome-Arno, southern France, and Rhineland (Germany and Austria) campaigns.

Shortly after the war ended in Europe (May 8, 1945), the Army determined that my father was eligible for immediate release from the service under the adjusted service rating plan governing discharges for overseas veterans. The new point system, part of the Army's plan for rapid demobilization, went into effect on May 12, 1945. The army awarded points based on four criteria: time overseas, number of days spent in combat, length of service, and number of children. Servicemen with 85 or more points automatically qualified for early separation on a quota basis. In June 1945, Joe Connole returned home to his wife, Michelina (Palumbo), known to friends and family as Mary (her chosen American name) or "Mickey," and children — Dennis, born February 9, 1943, and Richard (born while Joe was overseas) on April 8, 1944.

After the war, Joe Connole led a full life, helped raise five children, and had eleven grandchildren and two great-grandchildren. In early 1948, he went to work for the Boston & Maine Railroad as a conductor and later a brakeman. He worked his way up the ladder and, in the mid–1960s, the railroad promoted him to the top management position of yardmaster for the Worcester Freight Terminal. He held this important position until he retired at age 64 in 1983, after 35 years of service.

His loving wife, Mary, passed away in 1980, at age 58, a victim of cancer. The couple was happily married for 38 years. After doctors first diagnosed my father's cancer at age 69, he finally quit smoking. My father died of lung cancer one year later on August 9, 1990. Both my parents were victims of a lifetime addiction to cigarette smoking, unable to give up the habit. Throughout the 1930s through the early 1960s, smoking was highly glamorized by the media in movies and magazines, and later on television, and became not only acceptable, but even desirable.

* * *

Shortly after my dad passed away, family members were going through his personal effects and found several campaign and other medals, including a Bronze Star, Combat Infantryman Badge, and the Purple Heart in a bureau drawer. These were replacement medals, which my father obtained from the U.S. Army's Military Awards Branch in the mid–1980s. The originals were long since gone, most likely lost, or accidentally discarded during a family move from one home to another over the years. My younger sister Kathy told me that she remembered the day the replacement medals arrived in the mail. My father placed them on the kitchen table to show her. "He acted so proud," she said, as he explained the significance of each award and told her of the campaigns in which he had participated.

A certificate from the War Office accompanied the Bronze Star Medal authorizing the award "by executive order 24 August 1962," to Pfc. Dennis J. Connole for "meritorious achievement in ground combat against the enemy during World War II in the European-African-Middle Eastern Theater of Operations." The certificate is dated "30 November 1984."

In early 1944, General George C. Marshall suggested to President Franklin D. Roosevelt in a memorandum that the Bronze Star decoration be awarded to "any person serving in the military" who "distinguishes, or has distinguished, himself in combat, ... particularly the Infantry riflemen who are now suffering the heaviest losses ... and enduring the greatest hardships." Marshall and others in the military bureaucracy viewed the measure as a means of "raising the morale of combat troops." The president authorized the medal on February 4, 1944, retroactive to December 7, 1941.[1]

In 1948, President Harry S. Truman approved "the retroactive award of the Bronze Star Medal to soldiers who had been awarded the Combat Infantryman Badge or the Combat Medical Badge during World War II."[2]

The sight of the medals brought me back to the time I was about four years old, when I first discovered the originals along with a large collection of war souvenirs in a nightstand drawer in my parents' bedroom. Stacked neatly inside the drawer were several large packets of what I learned later were German marks, two cigar boxes with lids, along with several smaller boxes.

One of the cigar boxes contained all kinds of German Army pins, medals, insignias, emblems, ribbons, badges, and other decorations of all sizes and shapes—souvenirs from the war. There was also a beige or khaki-colored armband with a black swastika. I distinctly remember a small, thin black wallet, or billfold, approximately 3 × 5 inches, that held a picture of a young-looking German in uniform on one side and an identification card on the other covered in clear plastic.

The other cigar box contained loose paper money and coins of all different shapes and sizes, presumably from the countries to which my father had traveled while overseas. There were different denominations, some very colorful with pictures of kings, queens, presidents, and other government officials. The coins were silver, copper, and steel. Most were round; a few were hexagonal or octagonal while others had holes in the middle. The second box contained my father's identification, or dog tags, on a chain, his brass "ruptured duck" pin, several Army patches, one the YD patch of the 26th Division and another of the 1st Coast Artillery District (see front cover), a tarnished brass U.S. Army belt buckle, and numerous other items.

There were a number of smaller boxes that contained my father's campaign and other medals. The only one I remember in any detail was the Purple Heart, because of the pretty purple ribbon and pendant heart with gold border and profile of General George Washington. My mother told me that my father received the medal because of wounds he received in Italy. "Did he get shot?" I asked. "No," she said, "it was from shrapnel." "What is shrapnel?" She replied, "They are pieces of metal from an exploding shell." "What is a shell?" was my next question, and on and on. The questions were endless, but she patiently answered each one as best she could.

For a kid my age, it was like discovering a treasure chest. I spent countless hours sitting in my parents' bedroom playing with the war souvenirs, examining them closely and lining them all up neatly in rows. I would play with the fasteners and clasps and would pin several of the medals to the front of my shirt. Fascinated by the colorful ribbons, gold pendants, and other items, I would play with the souvenirs for hours at a time. This, of course, was in the days before television.

Also found among my father's effects after he died was a copy of his discharge papers along with several pictures of him in uniform, one as a military policeman with a .45 caliber sidearm and holster, nightstick, and black MP armband with white letters. It was at this time that I made a promise to myself to check into his service records.

* * *

Over the years, my father was reluctant to discuss the war with anyone, myself included. He belonged to the Vernon Hill American Legion Post No. 435 in Worcester and it is possible he would talk on occasion with other ex-servicemen, but I have no way of knowing for sure. This attitude was typical of many veterans who, upon discharge, made the conscious decision to forget the war, and move forward. Many, like my father, spent the rest of their lives trying to put the violence and horror of their days in combat behind them.

Occasionally, when I was younger, my dad might mention the war in passing, a place he had been or, on rare occasions, tell a brief story about a particular incident, usually a humorous one. At no time did he ever mention any of his experiences under fire.

One time, when I was 13 or 14 years old, the family went on a day trip to Hampton Beach in New Hampshire during my father's two-week summer vacation. We were sitting on the beach alone while the rest of the family was cooling off in the water, when he mentioned to me that while serving in the Army he had been stationed nearby in Maine on "submarine watch." He said his outfit patrolled the beaches to prevent the Germans from landing agents and that he later became a member of a military police unit. I remember asking him a bunch of questions about his job as an MP.

My father was aware of my interest in the war, most definitely because of his involvement, and I had read many books on the subject. When I was older, whenever I approached him about his part in the war, he would become upset, sometimes angry. I stopped asking. If he was going to relate his experiences, it would be on his own terms.

* * *

Even though the promise to check on my father's military background occasionally crossed my mind, I never seemed to be able to make the time to begin. In the end, it was a book that provided the impetus for me to take that initial step. In 1998, after completing *Goodbye, Darkness* by William Manchester, I decided it was time to begin my search. Manchester's memoir of the Pacific War is, in my opinion, one of the most superbly written and extremely moving books about one man's combat experiences. This also coincided with the first year I had access to a computer and the Internet, which I would soon discover is an incredible resource for doing research of this type.

My father's discharge papers indicated he was a member of the 141st Infantry Regiment, 36th Division. Armed with this meager amount of information, I sat down at the computer one day in October 1998, and went on the World Wide Web. I typed in the name of his regiment, not knowing what to expect. Much to my surprise, a web page for the 36th Division Veterans Association appeared on the screen. The site contained a wealth of information about the division and attached units. And so began my journey to discover all I could about my father's time in the service of his country.

At the same time I was doing research about the 36th, I was also gathering information about the 26th Division. I joined the division veterans association as an associate member and began receiving the quarterly newsletter, *Yankee Doings*. The editor of the magazine published my letter asking if anyone from the division remembered my father or could provide information about the unit on patrol. I wrote letters to the editor in every city and town in Worcester County that had an armory affiliated with the 181st Infantry, seeking information about the unit on duty in the state of Maine between 1942 and 1943. I also wrote a letter to the "In Search Of" column of the *American Legion Magazine*.

The first reply came from Clifford Welcome of Orange, Massachusetts, a veteran of Company F (181st), who said he would be more than happy to help with my quest. We began corresponding by mail and occasionally talked on the telephone. He provided me with a brief history of his company as well as a great deal of information about the regiment on coast patrol in Maine. Mr. Welcome answered my many questions and sent me a picture of himself (see p. 144) on sentry duty along with several pictures of the company headquarters and barracks in

High Pine (Wells), Maine. He enthralled me with stories of the regiment's days on patrol in New England. I cannot thank him enough for all his help.

Mr. Welcome later sent me his brass infantry insignia, displaying crossed muskets, worn on the left lapel of the Class A uniform, which is a very unusual item. Mr. Welcome said that no one in his family was interested and he wanted me to have it. His kind gesture moved me. The two-piece pin, issued prior to the war, is made of solid brass. Later lapel pins were made of pressed metal and were brass-coated. It has, above the crossed muskets, the number of the regiment, 181, and is the type my father would have worn. I treasure this small piece of World War II memorabilia.

Here is the letter I received from Mr. Welcome that accompanied the lapel pin:

> February 20, 1999
> Orange, MA 01364
>
> Dear Mr. Connole,
>
> I am sending you several pictures of Company F, 181st Infantry. They are the best I have.
>
> I enjoyed the article you sent me [Richard P. Taffe (Lt. Col. AUS Retired), "As War Clouds Gathered," Army Magazine (December, 1991)] — it was about the way we ate, lived, etc. We had good times and bad times but I met a lot of good fellows that I will never forget — many of them are gone.
>
> I am sending you a lapel insignia of the 181st, which we wore on our dress uniform.
>
> I am glad you are taking such good interest in the 26th Division — thought everyone had forgotten us World War II veterans. It does my heart good to know some people think of us.
>
> Sincerely yours,
> Clifford Welcome

As a result of my request for information through the local newspapers, several other veterans of the 181st contacted me, including Theodore Simmington, Jr., of Company K and John Gerety of Company H. Gerety was my father's commanding officer while a member of the MP unit in Maine. These men, in turn, provided me with the names and telephone numbers of other veterans to contact, and so on.

At the Worcester Public Library, I found a copy of *The History of the 26th Yankee Division*, originally published in 1955, which provided information pertaining to the division's pre-war training period, but unfortunately only touched upon its 20-month stint on coast patrol duty along the East Coast in 1942 and 1943. The YDVA reprinted the history in 2000, and I purchased a copy for my collection (Turner Publishing Company).

During the summer of 2001, my wife and I visited the four sites that served as headquarters for units of the 2nd Battalion (Companies E, F, G, and H), 181st Infantry, while on coast patrol duty, three in Maine — High Pine (Wells), Old Orchard Beach, and Saco — and one in Portsmouth, New Hampshire. We located the old High Shoe Factory building occupied by my father's company in Saco, and one of the office workers gave me a brief tour of the first and second floors. The building had changed little in 60 years.

My sister Debbie remembered that several times my father had mentioned the name Fratturelli, his platoon sergeant when he was a member of Company H, 181st Infantry (originally from Fitchburg, Massachusetts). A colleague at South High School, Charles Favreault, had a copy of the *Historical and Pictorial Review: National Guard of the Commonwealth of Massachusetts* (26th Division) published in 1939 that had belonged to an uncle, which he let me borrow. I found the name Guido J. Fratturelli along with his picture in the Company H group photograph.

It was a long shot, but I dialed Information, and to my complete surprise, the operator found a listing in Fitchburg. My heart raced. I decided to write a letter as a means of introducing myself. This was in July of 1999. I wondered if, after all these years, he remembered my father. As it turned out, he was well acquainted with him. Several days later Mr. Fratturelli sent a very nice letter of reply. We later talked on the telephone and he provided me with a great deal of information about the company and the mortar platoon.

He informed me that the company held a reunion every year on the second Tuesday of September at 1 o'clock in the afternoon and invited me to attend. I was thrilled and honored. The group was to meet at the Froshin Club in nearby Shrewsbury, a suburb of Worcester. The prospect of meeting many of the men in my father's outfit was very exciting and I waited for the next meeting, only a few months away, with great anticipation.

The first gathering of Company H took place in 1947, and the group had met every year since at a Worcester or Fitchburg-Leominster area club or restaurant, until the last in 2003. The number of attendees had dwindled over the years, from a high of 75 to between 15 and 20 in recent years. Richard W. Brill, the former first sergeant of Company H, helped organize the first reunion two years after the war ended. He grew up in Leominster and joined the Massachusetts National Guard in 1936 when he was only 17 years old.[3]

I was fortunate to have attended five reunions of Company H, from 1999 to 2003, and had a chance to meet a number of men who knew my father well. Several of the veterans have graciously provided me with pertinent information about the company, as well as many wonderful, sometimes moving, and heart-warming stories.

In an interview in the Worcester *Telegram & Gazette* in 2001, Brill informed the reporter he believed that Company H "could have a record for reunions." Most of the men who attended "were from central New England," he said, "reflecting the original makeup of the division." Brill reminisced, "Those first years we all got drunk. None of that any more. We're all a bunch of geezers now, but we have a lot of fun. I look forward to it all year."[4]

I corresponded with Mr. Brill after our first meeting and he provided me with much information on the company's days on patrol and also the MP unit, of which my father was a member. At the 2002 reunion, the former first sergeant presented me with his personal copy of the 26th Division *Historical and Pictorial Review* of 1939. It was indeed an honor. Mr. Brill had signed the yearbook on June 15, 1939, along with the officers of Company H. It is one of my most treasured pieces of memorabilia from the era.

Dr. Romeo LeBlanc, a retired dentist from Shirley, Massachusetts, had organized the reunions in recent years. LeBlanc, a native of Fitchburg, joined the division in 1939, upon graduation from high school. A few of the men "come in wheelchairs," he said in the *Telegram & Gazette* interview. "We have dinner and shoot the breeze and start reminiscing. Many of these men saw some of the fiercest fighting in Europe, but war is not what occupies their collective reverie. We don't remember the bad things very much," Dr. LeBlanc said. "Mostly we talk about the funny guys we had in the unit and the funny things that happened. There was plenty of both."[5]

I was deeply saddened when, in August 2004, I received a telephone call from Dr. LeBlanc informing me that he had to cancel the upcoming September reunion. Two members of the company had passed away during the year and a number of others were in ill health and could not attend. There would be no more reunions. One of the deceased was Sulo Ruuska of Quincy, with whom I had become very close over the past several years, corresponding regularly and occasionally talking on the telephone. Sulo provided me with many of the stories found in the book. He passed away at age 85 on August 4, 2004.

I remember my first Company H reunion in 1999. I felt a little out of place at first. Mr.

Ruuska came over with a friendly smile, shook my hand, and introduced himself. He welcomed me to the reunion. I felt at ease almost immediately. I told him I was the son of Joe Connole. Sulo said he knew my father well. He took me around, introduced me to the other veterans as Joe Connole's son, and stayed with me throughout the gathering. Many of the men said, "Oh sure, I remember Joe," and said a few kind words. Sulo had the wonderful ability to make a person he had just met feel like he was an old friend. When the reunion broke up, we exchanged personal information and agreed to keep in touch.

While conducting research for the book, I made numerous telephone calls and wrote dozens of letters and e-mails seeking information and asking questions. Each day I could not wait for the replies to arrive — each day I learned more and more about my father and the units in which he served. All of the men I contacted were very friendly and accommodating. They took the time to speak with me at length and answer my many questions, for which I am eternally grateful.

1

The 26th "Yankee" Division: Mobilization Period

On August 23, 1939, Joseph Stalin "shocked the world" by signing a non-aggression pact with Adolf Hitler, in which both countries "agreed not to go to war against the other." In the early morning hours of September 1, 1939, a state of war began when German forces invaded Poland across a wide front. Sixteen days later, on September 17, Soviet troops crossed the Polish border and attacked the beleaguered country from the east. During the offensive, the German High Command introduced a new concept of offensive warfare called the blitzkrieg, or lightning war, which stressed speed and surprise. Blitzkrieg tactics employed a combination of air power, tanks, and subversive warfare to break through or outflank enemy defenses, get into rear areas and create disorder. Military leaders had tested and refined the tactics during the Spanish Civil War (1936–1939).[1]

Highly mobile panzer units followed by infantry troops pushed across the borders, blasting holes in the Polish defenses. Poland maintained a large army, but lacked modern armament and equipment. The blitzkrieg tactics threw the Polish army into complete confusion. "From the skies," German dive-bombers and fighters "destroyed the Polish air force, damaged communications lines, and prevented the Poles from moving reinforcements, supplies, and ammunition to the front lines." The Poles fought bravely against insurmountable odds. When the Red Army attacked on September 17, "the Poles' situation, already desperate, became hopeless." By late September, the Polish government and military high command escaped into exile. Hitler and Stalin partitioned the country, with the Soviets occupying the eastern third.[2]

Hitler's powerful war machine in turn easily crushed the defenses of Denmark, Luxembourg, the Netherlands, Belgium, Norway, and France. On June 10, 1940, Italy entered the war on the side of Germany and declared war on Great Britain and France. One month later, on July 11, 1940, Herman Goering's Luftwaffe began an all-out attack on British ports, airfields, and industrial centers, thus commencing the Battle of Britain. Beginning in August 1940, Luftwaffe bombers carried out a series of "attacks on the population and air defenses of major British cities, including London by day and by night." The Blitz, from blitzkrieg, the British name for the sustained attacks, lasted until mid–May 1941. The fighting soon spread to Greece and North Africa.[3]

At this time, a majority of the people in the United States believed the country should remain neutral. President Roosevelt and other interventionists urged support of the nations fighting the Axis powers, "short of war." Isolationists, opposed to any kind of U.S. aid to the nations fighting against Germany, accused the president "of steering the nation into a war it was not prepared to fight." On March 11, 1941, Congress approved the Lend-Lease Act proposed by Roosevelt, empowering the president to supply raw materials, equipment, weapons, and food "on a cash-and-carry basis" to "any nation deemed vital to U.S. security," principally to the United Kingdom, Soviet Union, and China. As German victories continued to mount, isolationist sentiment, originally strong, began to evaporate. Following the Japanese surprise attack against Pearl Harbor the movement ceased to exist altogether.[4]

During the late 1930s, the U.S. military was woefully undermanned and unprepared. America needed men and materials to bring the army up to strength in the event circumstances forced the country to enter the war. In 1939, the army totaled approximately 190,000 regulars — "only the 17th largest army in the world — just behind the Rumanian Army." In June 1940, at the behest of President Roosevelt, the Senate began debate on the Burke-Wadsworth bill, pro-conscription legislation to reintroduce the World War I Selective Service Act (or Selective Draft Act) of 1917 (Sen. Edward R. Burke, D–Ind., and Rep. James W. Wadsworth, D–NY, co-sponsored the bill). On September 16, 1940, the Congress passed a revised version of the act, the Selective Training and Service Act of 1940, the first peacetime draft in the history of the United States. Roosevelt signed the bill into law on the same day. The first of the conscripted men entered the Army on November 18, 1940.[5]

The legislation required all male citizens between the ages of 21 and 36 to register with one of 6,443 local draft boards, manned by unpaid civilians from individual communities, before October 16, called R-Day. The act imposed a penalty for draft dodgers of up to five years imprisonment and a $10,000 fine. The period of service was initially set for one year, which the legislature extended in August 1941 to 18 months. Officials exempted registrants with dependent children, as well as those "with occupations essential to the health, safety, and welfare of the country." Initially, the Selective Service Agency granted students a deferment, but eliminated the exemption in July 1941. The bill also contained a provision for conscientious objectors, exempting them from military training and service provided they serve the country in another capacity under civilian direction. "To the relief of Selective Service officials, the registration was massive and smoothly executed," Kennett wrote.[6]

Government officials held a national lottery in Washington, D.C., on October 29, 1940, to select "the first batch of draftees" for training and service. Secretary of War Henry Louis Stimson "plunged his hand into what looked like a giant fish bowl, plucked out a blue capsule, and handed it to Franklin Delano Roosevelt." The president announced to a national radio audience, "The first number drawn by Secretary of War Stimson, is serial number 1-5-8." The drawing continued for the next 17 hours and 31 minutes. When the bowl "was finally emptied at 5:47 A.M. the following day," it "had yielded 8,994 capsules containing the pre-assigned draft numbers of 17 million American men from 21–35 years old." Of the 6,175 men from across the nation that held the first number 158, eight were from the city of Worcester, Massachusetts, and 13 others were from Worcester County. The first group to be called up would be men with one of the first 25 numbers.[7]

The first Selective Service draftees, later referred to as selectees, short for Selective Service trainees, and inductees (the terms were used as synonyms for draftee), entered the Army on November 18, 1940. Part of the Selective Service Act of 1940 "enjoined" employers to restore jobs to former conscripts after the required one year of military service, unless it was "impossible or unreasonable" to do so. If an employer failed to comply, it would be liable to court action. The inductee would then be able to return to his old job, to essentially pick up where he left off and get on with his life. That is, if the United States did not end up going to war.

One day after the draft, President Roosevelt toured the northeast by train as part of his reelection campaign and made a whistle stop at Worcester's Union Station en route to Boston for a major speech at the Boston Garden. The "crowd, variously estimated at between 5,000 and 10,000, ... waited nearly an hour in a chilly drizzle before the Presidential special pulled into the station at 3:34 P.M., 49 minutes behind the scheduled arrival," wrote Raymond A. Fitzpatrick of the *Worcester Telegram* staff. The throng, which included a number of large groups from Democratic organizations and delegations from labor unions, "roared a welcome as the train pulled in and cheered the President at pauses in his brief talk." Addressing the crowd from the back of his specially equipped railroad car, Roosevelt spoke "of the need for Americans to prepare for war." He "turned his guns against the Republicans in Congress who voted against New Deal 'reform' measures." Fitzpatrick reported that the "cheers were frequent and unrestrained."[8]

When the president "referred to the fear in Sweden, Switzerland, Greece, and Ireland, the crowd booed briefly." When Roosevelt finished his "short talk," he stood on the rostrum for several minutes as the crowd chanted enthusiastically, "We want Roosevelt." Radio station WTAG, owned by the *Worcester Telegram* and *Evening Gazette*, broadcast the speech to the local listening audience.[9]

* * *

On August 27, 1940, the Congress declared a "national emergency," authorizing President Roosevelt to call the Army Reserve and National Guard into active federal service for a period of one year, "as part of the national mobilization for defense." The avowed purpose of the call-up was to engage the troops in a one-year period of intensive training to prepare them in the event the country went to war. The War Department ordered the first of the National Guard and other reserve units to active duty status on September 16, 1940. According to military historian Lt. Col. Michael D. Doubler, "Four Guard Divisions, four observation squadrons and 18 Coast artillery units were included in the first callup." By October 1941, "more than 300,000 Guardsmen in 18 Divisions, 28 separate regiments and 29 observation squadrons [had] entered federal service, doubling the size of the Army."[10]

The War Department set the mobilization date for the 26th "Yankee" Division, Massachusetts National Guard, to take place on January 16, 1941. Major General Roger W. Eckfeldt, the 26th Division commander, received notification of the intended date in early October. In anticipation of the call up date, units stepped up training and increased the number of drills (prior to this date the number of annual paid drill periods was 60). Division "intensified schooling programs" for commissioned and non-commissioned officers, brought records "up to date in accordance with active duty standards," and shipped "high ranking officers ... to Service Schools by the dozens."[11]

Headquarters staff members spent the next several weeks making the necessary preparations for the move to Camp Edwards on Cape Cod, located in Barnstable County, within the townships of Sandwich and Bourne, Massachusetts. The military reservation, named after General Clarence R. Edwards, the division commander who served during World War I, covered an area of approximately 24 square miles.

Units around the state ordered key personnel in the headquarters section to report for duty to their individual armories on a full-time basis. In an article titled "As War Clouds Gathered," Lt. Col. Richard P. Taffe, AUS Retired, wrote, "We spent three months converting personnel records from state to federal forms, chasing men all over the state for signatures, conducting retirement ceremonies for those we were losing or parties for those who were being promoted or transferred." Taffe was a member of Headquarters Company, 3rd Battalion, 181st Infantry, of Natick, Massachusetts. He later served with the 81st Infantry Division in the Pacific Theater. At the time of federalization, "Company and battery units were individually at about fifty man strength." The full complement for a company was between 185 and 200 men.[12]

In anticipation of going on active service, the division "cleaned its ranks." The first members dropped from the rolls, the Yankee Division historian says, were "minors [those under the age of 18] and the physically unfit." Before the guardsmen's official induction, each man had to undergo a rigorous physical examination "to determine whether they measured up to Regular Army requirements." This took place at the armories during the first ten days of activation (January 16–25). The *History of the 104th Infantry* noted that 112 of its members failed to pass the physical examination.[13]

John D. Turini (T/7) of Clinton, Massachusetts, a cook with Company G and later Headquarters Company, 2nd Battalion, wrote that when the time came for him to take his physical examination, his company commander was concerned that he and another member of his unit "were way underweight." On the day of the exam, the CO "took the two of us to a restaurant and made us eat a big meal and then top it off with banana splits and big glasses of milk—felt I was ready to bust." A couple of hours later, Turini took his physical. "The doctor said I was a little underweight but it was better than being overweight." Turini's final comment, "It took a little time and several trips to the bathroom before we were back to normal."[14]

A number of others, "who had previous service in the Regular Army and those who had completed six or more with the National Guard were also eligible for discharge," Taffe wrote. Many members of the YD "had served during World War I or during the 1920s and were immediately discharged because of age." Also included among the list of waivers implemented by the guard were men with "critical job skills and family responsibilities," wrote Doubler.[15]

A high percentage of the remaining sergeants who had completed "the '10-series,'" an Army correspondence course, or "a course of study at the Massachusetts Military Academy, ... appeared before examining boards, and if qualified, were commissioned." This eliminated many of the "senior NCOs ... and other key personnel" within the units. The losses and promotions created numerous vacancies within the non-commissioned officer ranks. Because of the immediate need, the regiments instantly promoted a number of men to fill open slots. Taffe said that he went from being a private first class to first sergeant in one day. One corporal became the battalion sergeant major and two other privates first class took over as supply sergeant and communications sergeant. Having been a member of the guard for more than four years, this "did not bother us in the least," commented Taffe, as "having so many years and hours available to us, we literally had memorized the infantry drill regulations and could do every job in the company."[16]

For the purpose of filling the large number of vacancies occasioned by the discharges, the regiments of the division conducted recruiting drives. Companies introduced contests and awarded prizes "to individuals and groups who brought in the largest number of recruits." Units held rallies and "pitched recruiting tents" on the commons in their home city or town.[17]

At this time, the 26th was a square division, consisting of two infantry brigades, the 51st and 52nd, each made up of two regiments, the 101st and 182nd, and the 104th and the 181st, respectively. This would soon change. American divisions would become triangular, having three regiments (see next chapter). Headquarters for the Worcester element of the 181st Infantry Regiment was located at the National Guard Armory, 44 Salisbury Street near Lincoln Square in Worcester. This included Companies A, B, C, and D, which comprised the 1st

Battalion, approximately 500 officers and enlisted men. On January 16, members of the 1st Battalion, and Company D, 101st Medical Regiment, assembled at the armory to begin their active duty period. The men spent Monday through Saturday at the armory preparing for activation and returned home nights and Sundays.

* * *

At eight o'clock on the morning of Saturday, January 25, 1941, the troops of the 1st Battalion, 181st Infantry, and attached units, under the command of Colonel Roy W. Smith, marched out of the National Guard Armory on their way to Worcester's Union Station for the train ride to Camp Edwards on Cape Cod. "Snow from the winter's worst storm carpeted their path but a bright sun beamed on them in the chilly morning air as they swung smartly along, keyed to the music of their 181st Infantry Band," wrote a reporter for the Worcester *Sunday Telegram* in an article (unsigned) titled, "City Bids Farewell to Parting Troops." My uncle, Matthew J. "Mitt" Palumbo (Band-181), who enlisted (such men were called enlistees or volunteers as opposed to selectees or inductees) in the Massachusetts National Guard on December 3, 1940, was a horn player in the regimental band.[18]

The marching troops "chanted to the rhythmic beat: 'I'll be back in a year little Darling, Uncle Sam has called and I must go, I'll be back in a year little Darling, you'll be proud of your soldier boy I know.'" Less than two weeks earlier, the citizen soldiers had been working as letter carriers, milkmen, police officers, lawyers, or one of a hundred other occupations and professions.

At the head of the column, were "Spanish American War veterans, members of Veterans of Foreign Wars' posts, Legionnaires and delegations from various other military organizations." The old soldiers, many on "the portly side and not a few with medals pinned on overcoats, ... plodded along." The reporter of the "Farewell" article wrote, "The ceremonies served to recall the scenes of '98 and '17 and the youth of those wars were the escorts yesterday."[19]

As the soldiers marched up Main Street in the direction of City Hall, "an estimated 20,000 to 30,000 residents lined sidewalks, snow banks, and office and store building windows, waving and cheering as the boys trudged through the slush of the recent snowstorm." Parents and friends called out names and nicknames and shouted farewells to the boys they recognized in the ranks, wishing them Good Luck. There were "silent nods of recognition ... accompanied by such parting words as 'take care of yourself' and the all but whispered 'God bless you.'" Many among the crowd, some World War I veterans, and those who lost loved ones in the Spanish-American War and the Great War, stood with tears streaming unashamedly from their eyes.[20]

In accordance with new Army regulations, the men marched three abreast, led by an honor guard carrying national and regimental banners that waved in the morning breeze. The men wore "full winter regalia," long overcoats, with overseas caps crowning their heads and galoshes protecting their feet. On their backs were light packs with the "old doughboy" style steel helmets from World War I attached.[21]

Slung over their right shoulders were "new rifles," the recently acquired .30 caliber semi-automatic M-1 Garand. The 1st Battalion, 181st Infantry of Worcester, was one of the first units in the country to receive the Garand, produced at the Harrington & Richardson Arms Company plant on Park Avenue in the city. The company manufactured more than 500,000 of the weapons during the ensuing war years.[22]

The guardsmen turned left on Front Street to Washington Square, where they passed in

National Guard troops arriving at Camp Edwards, 1941 (Massachusetts National Guard Military Museum and Archives, Worcester).

review before acting mayor John M. Toomey surrounded by a number of city government officials, members of the City Council Military Affairs Committee, and other dignitaries. The mayor delivered a five-minute speech, wished the outfit "God-speed," and "assured" the men "of the city's continuing interest in their welfare."[23]

At Worcester's Union Station platform, parents, wives, sweethearts, and friends bid farewell to the young men in uniform. Just as the NCOs called for them to board the special ten-coach New York, New Haven & Hartford Railroad (commonly referred to as the New Haven Railroad) troop train, the parting soldiers received goodbye hugs and kisses from relatives, friends, wives, and sweethearts. As the soldiers boarded the train, members of the Worcester Chapter, American Red Cross Canteen Corps handed each man two packs of cigarettes. Once the troops settled in, corps volunteers served hot coffee and sandwiches.[24]

The special troop train departed Worcester at 1 P.M. The train halted briefly in Framingham to pick up the 181st Antitank Company of Hudson, and arrived at Camp Edwards at approximately 4:30 P.M. Fitchburg area units of the regiment left that city the following day. Other 181st units in the northern and eastern part of the state (3rd Battalion) left on Monday, January 27. At this time, the 181st Infantry Regiment consisted of 1057 enlisted men and 23 officers.[25]

* * *

Basic training for the guardsmen of the 1st and 2nd Battalion, 181st Infantry, began bright and early on Monday, January 27. The 1st Battalion, which included the Worcester companies

(A, B, C, and D), had arrived on Saturday, and the 2nd, comprised of the companies (E, F, G, and H) from Fitchburg (2 companies, E and H), Clinton, and Orange, on Sunday. The companies of the 3rd Battalion (I, K, L, and M), from Natick (Hq.), Milford, Marlborough, Webster, and Gardner, were scheduled to arrive later that day.

Reveille was at 6 A.M. "with first call five minutes before." Breakfast was served beginning at 6:30. The day's program, set to begin at 7:30 A.M., "called for eight hours of drilling on the parade ground." A 3-inch snowfall on January 24 blanketed the camp. The soldiers "swung into today's program with overshoes and rifles," wrote Joseph H. Gauthier, a staff reporter for the Worcester *Evening Gazette*. After breaking for lunch at 11:30 A.M., it was back to the parade ground area at 1:00 P.M. for four more hours of march and drill. Training went on for seven days a week, with the soldiers answering "16 calls a day [bugle calls—first call, reveille, mess, drill, guard mount, etc.], week days and the same number Sundays, but they're one hour later," Gauthier wrote.[26]

"Though the schedule may be hard, the men are comfortably situated in warm barracks with their own foot lockers and with iron cots covered by a four-inch mattress with four blankets and sheets and pillow cases with pillows," wrote Gauthier. The troops were well fed. The "mess schedule, copied off a company bulletin board," listed the meals for the day: "corn flakes, fresh milk, French toast and syrup, a fresh orange and toast and coffee" for breakfast; "pork roast, mashed potatoes, gravy, creamed corn, apple sauce, canned peaches, bread and butter, and hot coffee" for dinner; and for supper, "beef stew, pineapple pudding, bread and butter and tea."[27]

* * *

At Camp Edwards, the regiments of the division had to prepare for the arrival of incoming selectees, scheduled to begin in March. Cadres (training personnel consisting of officers and NCOs), had to be organized. Regimental Headquarters balanced units by shifting personnel. Units had to requisition equipment and supplies and make ready the unfinished barracks for the new arrivals. "Floors and windows were washed and the hue and cry went out from the old soldiers that they were becoming housemothers and that the new compliment would be spoiled by so much initial attention," wrote the historian of the 26th Division. Schools "for staff and field company and non commissioned officers" were set up and run by qualified instructors. Training of the regiments progressed rapidly, and by the end of February, staff personnel were about ready for the arrival of the scheduled influx of recruits.[28]

The Army had accelerated construction of the camp, which began in mid–1940, to meet the requirements of "M," or Mobilization Day. Many of the barracks and other buildings were in various stages of completion. Interior walls were nothing but bare studs and remained that way for some time. Private rooms on the first and second floor for cadres had yet to be finished. "Soldiers, in addition to their training, became carpenters, painters, riggers, laborers, and landscapers," the 26th historian wrote. The men were required to keep the buildings clean of carpenters' debris and sawdust while the work was in progress. Several weeks passed before guardsmen made the barracks a comfortable and livable place.[29]

* * *

On January 6, 1941, Local Selective Service Board #167 in Worcester notified Joe Connole of his draft status and shortly thereafter, he received his letter of induction from the president, which read in part, "Greetings, You have been selected to serve in the U.S. Army." Following the salutation, the induction notice contained instructions on when and where to report.

Dennis Joseph Connole graduated from St. John's Catholic High School in June 1938. There were seven children in the Connole family: Catherine, the oldest; Albert; Margaret "Peg"; Helen; Elizabeth "Bette"; my father, Dennis; and the youngest, Rita. Albert was a petty officer in the U.S. Navy during the war and served on a cruiser assigned to convoy duty in the North Atlantic. Seaman 2-c Bette Connole was a member of the Coast Guard Women's Reserve, stationed in Palm Beach, Florida, and later in New York City as part of an intelligence unit. My father's sister Helen was married to Matthew "Mitt" Palumbo, my mother's brother. Mitt was a member of the 181st Infantry Regimental Band.

Upon graduation in 1938, Dennis, or "Joe" as his friends knew him, went out to find a steady job. Very few, if any, young men or women in my father's working-class neighborhood on Providence St. went on to college in the 1930s, unless it was on a sports scholarship. College was never a consideration.

Right after graduation in 1938, Joe Connole found employment with the New York, New Haven & Hartford Railroad as a laborer with the title of shipping checker. His duties included "loading and unloading freight cars; sorting incoming packages for delivery; following up on lost freight; checking merchandise, and assisting the shipping clerk." Although the job was an entry-level position, the railroad was an excellent place to work during the pre-war Depression years. The work was steady, the companies paid a decent wage, and even more important, there was always a good chance for advancement.[30]

On March 12, 1941, Joe Connole reported to the U.S. Army Induction Center at the Lamartine Street (elementary) School building a short distance from Kelly Square in Worcester. Personnel at the center had the inductees fill out a registration form with their basic information and then called each man up for a personal interview. Next, the inductees had to undergo a physical examination followed by psychiatric screening by the medical staff to determine whether they met the minimum standards for military service. Physicians rejected a number of the men for various health reasons or physical defects such as cardiovascular disorders, vision problems, asthma, chronic diseases, or other conditions, which in their professional judgment or opinion would prevent the individual from performing satisfactorily.

After signing their induction papers, the draftees and enlistees were fingerprinted and given a service number. A lieutenant lined the men up, called the group to attention, and conducted the administration of the oath of allegiance, the final step in the process.

Nathaniel "Nate" or "Gus" Mencow from Worcester enlisted in the Army in 1941. He reported to the induction center at Lamartine Street School on March 21, 1941, nine days after my father. Mencow, who was attending Boston University at the time, "volunteered" for the draft because, as he said, "I had a high draft number, but I wanted to get my service time out of the way sooner rather than later so I could finish my education without interruption.... On this particular day," Mencow remembered, "there were about two dozen guys who went through the process."[31]

During an interview with Nate, a colleague in the Worcester Public School System, he related that after the swearing-in ceremony, the officer in charge took everyone out to lunch at a Chinese restaurant on Southbridge Street, across from the old Post Office (where the Federal Building now stands). The officer then escorted the group to Union Station where they boarded a New Haven Railroad passenger train bound for Camp Edwards on Cape Cod. Nate received an assignment to Company M, 3rd Battalion, originally from the north Worcester County town of Gardner.[32]

* * *

The first of the "filler replacements" began arriving at Camp Edwards in early March. Throughout the remainder of the month, and into April and May, trains arrived on a daily basis with the trainees, described by the 26th Division History as "the finest cross section of American manhood available." All were single men between the ages of 21–35, in "top physical condition ... selected principally from Massachusetts to serve for a one-year period." The trainees were drawn from every walk of life, there were "principals, college professors, policemen, chefs, salesmen, politicians, mechanics, barbers, ... the youngsters who hadn't yet started on a vocation in life"—and one 21-year-old "shipping checker" from Worcester.[33]

2

Trainees Arrive at Camp Edwards

I have based many of the following descriptions and accounts depicting the various phases of basic and advanced training conducted at Camp Edwards during this period on information provided by the "History of the 104th [Infantry]." The History Committee for the 104th Infantry, headed by Capt. Robert M. Mackintosh, "assembled, evaluated, and elaborated on the source material that served as a basis for the ... composite history," which covers the period from 1939–41. According to the Acknowledgements, company historians provided histories for the respective companies and Pvt. Francis Kirley of Holyoke provided the statistical data. The schedule and types of training for the other three regiments of the 26th Massachusetts Division, the 101st, 181st, and 182nd, was the same.

When my father and the other Selective Service draftees (also referred to as inductees and selectees), still in their civilian clothes, disembarked from the passenger trains at Camp Edwards on Cape Cod in early March 1941, a waiting cadre lined them up in some semblance of a formation. An officer called the group to attention and gave the men a brief welcoming speech. The majority of the trains pulled in at the siding during the late afternoon and evening hours, the exact time depending on their point of origin within the state.[1]

Inductees arriving at Edwards looked out over a bleak wilderness and saw a barren landscape with no grass or trees. Construction at the camp, established in 1933, was undergoing a rapid buildup. Row upon row of unpainted barracks and other buildings lined both sides of the outer road that surrounded the parade ground, approximately three-fourths of a mile square. Patches of snow and ice covered the ground and a cold, fierce wind swept viciously across the unprotected flatlands of the camp. There had been a recent thaw and the men marched the mile or so from the railhead to their billets, in many places up to their ankles in mud. Here and there, large puddles of standing water obstructed their path.

One historian of the 104th Infantry, who arrived at the camp in January, provided his first impressions: "We left the train and carried our heavy packs the mile to the new barracks through much snow. So this was to be [our] home: What a desolate place; no sidewalks; snow everywhere; all buildings unpainted; seemingly a dreary, forlorn, out-of-the-way place."[2]

The winters of New England could be harsh, especially for the draftees from warmer areas of the U.S. who later joined the division. A few days after the attack on Pearl Harbor, Robert B. "Bill" McCarter, who had just finished basic training at Camp Shelby, Mississippi, boarded an Army train "with covered windows and traveled for 2½ days, not knowing where he was going." When the train arrived at its destination, there was six inches of snow covering the ground. McCarter "asked the conductor where he was and was told, 'Iceland.'" He soon discovered that "he was at Buzzard's Bay, Cape Cod, better known as Camp Edwards." McCarter became a forward observer with the 180th Field Artillery (FA), 26th Division.[3]

Main gate—located on Route 28 in Falmouth, Massachusetts (W.R. Thompson & Company Publications, Richmond, Virginia).

Upon arriving at their temporary quarters, the men were pleasantly surprised to find the buildings warm with mess help serving hot chocolate and fresh doughnuts. After refreshing themselves, an NCO instructed the men on how to make a bed — the Army way — with square corners, referred to as an "envelope fold," and a top blanket tight enough to bounce a quarter. The spare blanket was used to "hood" the pillow so that no part of the sheet was visible (the pillow is exposed only during inspection). Many of the recruits had never made a bed in their lives, although most would never admit to it.

After satisfactorily completing this task, the group was off to the mess hall for a meal of "frankfurts and beans, tomato salad, rice pudding and coffee" before retiring. This would be the recruit's first taste of Army chow. During the first couple of weeks, there was a lot of bitching and complaining about the food. There were some who absolutely hated it, declaring that they missed their mothers' home cooking. But there were also a large number of men who enjoyed the meals. No matter what the trainees thought about the food initially, after completing several days of strenuous training and exercise most could not wait to get to the mess hall. Many even tried to coax the servers on kitchen police (K.P.) into giving them extra portions. After eating as if they had never seen food before, there was not a scrap left on the trays and they were usually looking for seconds. Historian Lee B. Kennett says, "The new soldier gained from six to nine pounds in the first few months in uniform."[4]

During the trip to Cape Cod, smoke and cinders from the locomotive had seeped into the passenger cars and covered the men's skin and clothing. Before retiring, the recruits assembled in the washroom for a required "90 second shower en masse — 30 seconds under the taps to get wet, 30 seconds outside to soap up while another group went in, and 30 seconds back in to rinse off." Non-coms stood by with watches to time each shift and then blew their whistles when the allotted time was up. This measure was necessary to ensure there was enough hot water for everyone.[5]

Above: Camp Headquarters building, although still standing, is presently abandoned. *Below:* Camp Edwards had five service clubs — this was the main club. The facility was a place for off duty soldiers to congregate and relax. There was a canteen, library, lounge, smoking area, a game room with ping pong and pool tables, etc. Paid hostesses (senior, junior, and canteen hostesses) worked with community volunteers to coordinate camp dances and other programs for soldiers and schedule entertainment (both photographs from W.R. Thompson & Company Publications, Richmond, Virginia).

Camp Sports Arena which housed the gymnasium, track, exercise rooms, etc. (W.R. Thompson & Company Publications, Richmond, Virginia).

After spending the better part of the day at the induction centers in their hometowns completing the necessary paperwork, undergoing their preliminary physical examinations, and then a long train ride to camp, the men were ready to crawl between the sheets for a good night's sleep, retiring about midnight.

Lt. Col. Richard P. Taffe, AUS Retired, Headquarters Company, 3rd Battalion, 181st Infantry (Natick), described his barracks building and company area, which was typical of all the others:

> The barracks were still not quite completed, and the exposed two-by-fours on the interior walls stayed that way for some time. There were bare squad rooms on the first and second floors, a latrine complete with stainless steel mirrors and signs warning of the boiling water, which could scald one. An orderly room and sleeping quarters for the sergeant major were the only small rooms on the first floor, and on the second, a room for the first sergeant and company clerk, and a room in which the communications sergeant and a supply sergeant slept.

Each two-story barracks building could comfortably accommodate approximately 65 men. Across the "paved regimental street in front of the barracks," there were two "smaller buildings—the supply room and mess hall," he wrote.[6]

No sooner had their heads touched the pillows than the bugle call for reveille sounded at 6 A.M. and the non-coms roused them from their bunks. Taffe says, "We did not learn about the 24-hour clock until much later." For the next several days, the men had very little time to call their own.[7]

After breakfast, the group was off to the station hospital for a battery of medical tests, chest x-rays, and a series of inoculations. Standing by were a group of medics, mostly inexperienced, ready to try out their recently acquired "needle techniques." The men received shots to prevent every disease imaginable—typhoid, diphtheria, smallpox—and several others they never even knew existed. The Company M, 104th Infantry, historian wrote facetiously,

"We were inoculated against everything except slipping on the soap in the shower room and breaking our necks."[8]

That night, the barracks resounded with a chorus of moans and groans as men rolled over on their sore arms. Some of the men suffered from an acute reaction to the vaccination shots. They failed to answer reveille and the barracks sergeant declared them sick in quarters. In a few cases, those with very high temperatures returned to the hospital for treatment. For days afterwards, the men suffered from stiff arms and had to help one another putting on their field jackets and packs. One witty young man from Company M, 104th Infantry, quipped "that he had to give up drinking beer because he had leaked from all the places he was jabbed."[9]

Later in the day, the men marched to the Recruit Reception Center, located near the railhead, for their initiation into the Army's mysterious way of issuing uniforms. Non-coms herded the selectees into a long warehouse and ordered them to strip to their underwear. They then filed down a long counter where a line of supply clerks attended to their military clothing needs. The clerks quickly sized each man up, threw various items of clothing in their general direction, and shouted, "Next." The men quickly learned that "there were two sizes of clothing in the Army, too big and too small."[10]

Bugler sounding reveille — believed to be my Uncle Matthew J. "Mitt" Palumbo, a member of the 181st Infantry Regimental Band. His wife, Helen, confirmed that he was a bugler (courtesy Massachusetts Army National Guard).

The historian for Company M, 104th Infantry, described one group of new arrivals as looking "more like a crew of ship-wrecked Nazi seamen, rather than U.S. Soldiers." Actually, they were the victims of sadistic supply clerks at the reception center. Many had shoes that "were sizes too large, and some sets of underwear that could pass as pajamas." "GI overcoats" issued to some of the shorter men were 10 sizes too big, and dragged along the ground. Others received "raincoats large enough to be used for rubber life-boats." After a while, the long and short, or those with items too loose or too tight, got together to swap various items of clothing for another with a more reasonable fit. Occasionally, a few of the men, by chance, ended up with the correct size.[11]

One young man, Arthur R. Mullin (M-104) from Lowell, Massachusetts, described as "a modest lad of some 250 pounds," was the "supply sergeant's despair." The

2. Trainees Arrive at Camp Edwards

Above: View of main Service Club from northwest water tower with barracks in background. At the height of the war, the camp housed 34,108 enlisted men and 1,945 officers. *Below:* Typical Post Exchange (PX)—a version of a department store for base military personnel (both photographs from W.R. Thompson & Company Publications, Richmond, Virginia).

26th Division Headquarters area located on the east side of the camp near the airfield. The building in the left middle appears to be one of the four movie theaters on the base. Division Headquarters is probably the building above and just to the right of the theater. If you look closely, you can see the flagpole and flag on the right side of the building (W.R. Thompson & Company Publications, Richmond, Virginia).

only item of clothing that fit was the necktie. After Supply Sergeant Frank Wetkowiecz made a few alterations to the pants and shirt, Mullin managed to squeeze into the uniform. Providing Mullin with a means of holding up his trousers was yet another matter altogether. "No Army belt would even come close to encircling his waist." In what the historian for Company M called "a moment of genius," Wetkowiecz "spliced two belts together and the fit was perfect."[12]

Historian Lee B. Kennett noted some of the "extremes" among the men in the Army that *Yank*, the soldier's weekly, pointed out: "The biggest foot in the Army belonged to a private who wore a specially made shoe in size 18½ EEEEE" while the "heaviest man ... weighed 407 pounds"; "the oldest," a sergeant, "was seventy-four, having enlisted in 1895 and "the youngest ... was fifteen — though he was discharged soon after the Army learned his true age."[13]

The uniforms had changed very little since World War I; in fact, most items were from that era. These consisted of "itchy" olive-drab wool shirts, with button down collars, and "breeches, that smelled faintly of mothballs." It was not unusual for a man to reach into one of the pockets and find a Post Exchange (P.X.) receipt dated 1918. Wrap leggings, called puttees, extended from just below the knee ("two fingers below" was regulation) to the ankle, "with the end-tie tucked back into the wrap just below the tops of the high brown shoes." If the men wound the wrap too tight, it would cut off the circulation, and if too loose, it would, in time, slide down to their ankles.[14]

On a long march, the end of the wrap would occasionally come loose and begin to unravel. Those following next in the column would step on the wrap further pulling it undone to trail several feet behind the marcher, who was usually too exhausted to stop and fix the problem. Some of the men "got smart" and used safety pins to secure the ends. The Army later replaced the wrap leggings with canvas ones. Non-coms taught the new soldiers "to put the hooks on the outer side of the legs so they wouldn't snag as they tried to walk," wrote Taffe. "All of us envied the paratroopers, who were allowed to wear the new combat boots."[15]

The men also received a World War I issue dress jacket with its familiar "choke collar" (called a "monkey jacket" because it resembled the coat worn by an organ grinder's monkey); a heavy, wool "GI overcoat," and raincoat. A "Montana peak" style campaign hat, similar to that worn by some state troopers, topped off the uniform. Near the end of 1941, fatigue clothes replaced the wool uniform for training.[16]

Once the recruits received their standard clothing allowance, supply issued each man his individual weapon and other equipment, including World War I steel helmet, referred to a "tin hat," pack, web belt, ammunition pouches, bayonet, entrenching tool, canteen, gas mask, etc.

Above: Unknown soldier — typical uniform worn during training (courtesy Massachusetts Army National Guard). *Below:* Pvt. Dennis "Joe" Connole (December 22, 1941) — home on Christmas leave.

* * *

Next came several days of testing, interviews, and classification. The basic aptitude test given all GIs was the Army General Classification Test (AGCT), which "consisted of 150 multiple-choice questions with a forty-minute time limit." The questions were of three types, block counting, the matching of synonyms, and simple mathematic problems. "The test was machine graded, and the results were used in the placing or classifying of the new soldier." Kennett says, that the "men usually tried their best on the AGCT," in the hopes that "a high score would help them find a better Army slot."[17]

There were five classes, determined by score. Class I was 130 or over; Class II from 110 to 129; Class III from 90 to 109, considered average; Class IV 70 to 89; Class V was below 69. For admission to Officer Candidate School (OCS), a man needed a score of 110 or better. In addition to the AGCT, there were a number of special-

View from water tower looking south (W.R. Thompson & Company Publications, Richmond, Virginia).

ized aptitude tests administered when soldiers indicated a prior line of work or training on their initial assessment questionnaire, such as radio repairman or having clerical skills. These tests determined a soldier's competency in these areas.[18]

The first sergeant of each company, called the "top kick," or "top" for short, hovered about taking copious notes in an attempt to identify early on some of the best and the brightest selectees that "they would like to get their hands on." Also identified at this time were some of the "oddballs" the sergeants prayed "they wouldn't be stuck with." The sergeants personally interviewed each of the men and checked his qualifications and backgrounds for possible placement into a key job or position. As they became better acquainted the recruits, a number of lateral moves were made within each unit, as well as transfers from one unit to another. "One state police officer," for example, "initially assigned to a rifle company, was identified as a perfect chauffeur for the colonel." A "couple of college students and newspapermen moved out of the rear ranks into headquarters assignments," Taffe wrote.[19]

3

Basic Training: March–September 1941

After completing the induction process, the men received an assignment to one of the companies (185–200 men each) of the division's four regiments (101st, 104th, 181st, and 182nd). Richard P. Taffe (Hq. Co., 3rd Bn.-181) noted that enlistees received preferential treatment as to which company they would like to join, and usually chose a unit as close to their hometown as possible so they would be among old friends. On the other hand, non-coms "arbitrarily assigned" the draftees, "one company at a time, to flesh out the regiments." Pvt. Joe Connole ended up in Company H, 181st Infantry, originally from Fitchburg, Massachusetts.[1]

Non-coms selected those men who had some type of previous military training, such as military school or ROTC, for example, for appointment as acting squad leaders. These men wore armbands with the three stripes of a buck sergeant. If the company needed additional men for this purpose, usually the biggest and toughest got the assignment.

Francis D. Donovan of Battery C, 211th Field Artillery Battalion, wrote, "The 181st was located next to the 101st Infantry at Edwards, and we [211th] were on the easterly side of the 101st. The 67th 'Rebel' AA [antiaircraft] outfit was near the [main?] gate, and the officer's club was adjacent. The canteen was located on the north side of the muster field [parade ground], near headquarters."[2]

In his memoirs, John D. Turini (G-181 and Hq. Co., 2nd Bn.-181) of Clinton, Massachusetts, provided a description of what it was like at Camp Edwards when reveille sounded:

> Early every morning the band would march up and down the street to get everyone in the mood. Then it was get dressed and out in formation for morning roll call. After roll call, we had time to get our bunks made up. We would shave and shower if there was hot water. And this part of barracks living I really hated. The barracks had a shower room, 6 lavatories, and 5 or 6 toilet stools. These toilets were exposed and in the open. So if you had to go there were people on either side of you, which made it kind of uncomfortable to do your thing, as it was impossible to relax.

Turini's final comment, "And because all of us were in the same boat getting used to this new life you had to do what you had to do."[3]

Former T/Sgt. Lorenz F. Bading of Braunfels, Texas, a member of the 36th Division Band stationed at Camp Edwards from October 1942 to April 1943, remembers "the band playing for Reveille every morning before daylight; it was so cold that the valve and slide instruments promptly froze up, leaving only drums and a few squeaking reed instruments to provide the music — pitiful sound." Bading, with his wife and one-year-old daughter, lived off base in a "summer cottage," which was extremely drafty and expensive to keep warm. He also remembered, "Those who commuted to and from Camp with cars, shoveling snow, and more snow, snow chains, etc."[4]

Victor Quaranta, Dominick Cialone, Orlando Orrizzi, Company H, 181st Infantry, Saturday inspection, 1941 (Dorothy M. Orrizzi Collection).

During the period from reveille to retreat, the men folded mattresses and bedding in half and placed them at the foot of the bed. Every item of a soldier's clothing and equipment on display in the barracks had to be standardized. Every Saturday morning, the company held a full-field inspection. The men had to arrange every item of military gear as well as all personal items in a precise manner. After a fashion, most of the men "could look at a full-field inspection layout on the bunks and spot every error instantly," Taffe wrote. "We knew which way the knife blade should face (to the right) and where the shoelaces went."[5]

Footlockers had to be neat and orderly, with socks, underwear, towels, toothbrush, shaving gear, comb, etc., all uniformly arranged. Shoes and boots were placed neatly under the bunks, and clothing — raincoat, overcoat, field jacket, fatigue jacket, spare shirts, and trousers (wool and cotton) — hung on a wall rack behind the bunk, carefully spaced approximately one inch apart so that the air could circulate between.

Anyone "who got too many gigs, regardless of how many stripes they might be wearing," had weekend passes cancelled, wrote Taffe. Too many gigs might result in an extra detail. More than just a few of the men, who did not want to take a chance on being restricted to base, got up at three and four o'clock on Saturday morning just to prepare for the weekly inspection.[6]

As was the custom in the 26th "Yankee" Division, each regiment held an orientation meeting on the day after the recruits' arrival at the camp. Non-coms gathered the rookies in one of the camp theaters. The regimental chaplain opened the ceremony with a few brief remarks followed by a prayer. Next, the executive officer (XO) introduced the commanding officer, his staff, and the three battalion commanders to the assembly. The CO stood at the podium, welcomed the new men, and gave a brief talk on the history and traditions of the regiment.[7]

Above: 2nd Lt. Donald Haynes, 1st Sgt. Louis DeStefano ("our old first sergeant"— Guido Fratturelli), 2nd Lt. Walter Harvey, Company H, 181st Infantry, Saturday inspection, 1941. *Below:* Sulo O. Ruuska, Orlando Orrizzi, Oscar Erickson, Bernie Dymek, Company H, 181st Infantry, Saturday inspection, 1941 (both photographs from Dorothy M. Orrizzi Collection).

After the colonel finished addressing the men, the non-coms issued each man a blue colored card displaying the regimental coat of arms. The coat of arms for the 181st Infantry was a blue crest showing a colonial powder horn, above which was an arm clothed in blue with a ruffled white cuff and a hand grasping a broad sword. The motto of the regiment, printed below the crest, read, "KEEP YOUR POWDER DRY." On the back was an explanation of the powder horn emblem, which symbolized the earliest days of the regiment as a Minuteman organization during the Revolutionary period.

Following the welcoming ceremony, the 1st sergeant addressed the group. His speech was brief and to the point. He spoke of the regiment's responsibility in making soldiers out of civilians and preparing them for the possibility of war, and also of the responsibility of each man present. "The program of training you are about to undergo, will be intense, rigorous, and difficult," he stressed. "We are all part-time soldiers; we all want to go home just as soon as this job is done, but not one day before." The sergeant closed with, "All we ask of each man is that he do his best and be a good soldier."[8]

The author of the introduction to the "History of the 104th [Infantry]" wrote, "These were called 'Orientation Meetings;' but I felt they should have been more plainly called 'let's understand each other' or 'here it is' meetings, for we certainly heard the facts plainly stated." Following the ceremony there were refreshments for all.[9]

* * *

For the next 13 weeks, the recruits would undergo the full basic training cycle. Taffe says that those weeks "were agonizing for all of us," as everyone, including the "old timers," the guardsmen who had been in the outfit prior to activation, were required to complete the full

Sgt. Paul "Whitey" Garganigo, Company H, 181st Infantry, .30 caliber heavy machine gun, 1941 (Dorothy M. Orrizzi Collection).

3. Basic Training: March–September 1941

cycle. During the first three weeks of basic, the day consisted primarily of "marching practice, close order drill, and calisthenics classes." The troops also took part in a number of "regimental conditioning hikes and parades." The first hikes during the months of March and early April took place over icy roads with bitter winds and flying sand that stung the men's faces. Heavy, cold rains are typical April weather in New England. The selectees soon accustomed themselves to the rigors of military life and began to settle into the daily routine.[10]

Periods of exercise and drill were interspersed with two hours of classroom instruction, which included lectures on military courtesy and discipline, articles of war, care of clothing and equipment, military sanitation, first aid, the nomenclature of various weapons, care and use of arms, manual of arms, and a wide variety of other subjects.

The men always displayed a "keen interest" when Lt. Abdon F. Guidette lectured on "Sex Hygiene," wrote the historian of Company C, 104th Infantry. Medical personnel conducted periodical "short arm inspections" (the examination of a man's penis for venereal diseases), which he says, "was a great embarrassment for some of the boys." Army physicians conducted "sex morality lectures," and "sometimes concluded [their] remarks with the admonition, 'Flies spread disease, so keep yours buttoned,'" wrote Kennett.[11]

Cadres assigned men to work details as needed — the men shoveled snow, dug trenches, and later, during the spring thaw, built hundreds of miles of duckboard walks. The recruits pulled K.P. for sometimes as long as 16 hours, rising at 4 A.M. Men scheduled for K.P. (kitchen police) tied a white towel around the rail at the foot of their bunks to identify themselves for early wake up call. Two jobs dreaded on K.P. were pots and pans or peeling potatoes. Every meal in the Army included potatoes, home fries, boiled, mashed, French-fried, etc.

Interior guard duty lasted for one 24-hour period, two hours on and two hours off. Every man had to memorize the 12 General Orders for guard duty: 1. To take charge of this post

Stanley Toczko, Arnold Washburn, Joe Lariviere, Alex Berman, Company H, 181st Infantry (Dorothy M. Orrizzi Collection).

Dominick Cialone, Bob Gibson or Bernie Dymek, Leonard Riley, Company H, 181st Infantry, Cape Cod Maneuvers, 1941 (Dorothy M. Orrizzi Collection).

and all government property in view; 2. To walk my post in a military manner...; etc. "To the second one," Robert W. Brickman (D-141) wrote, "we added to ourselves 'Taking no s--t from the commander.'" Occasionally, the officer on duty or the sergeant of the guard would approach a man standing guard to inspect his appearance and question his orders. If satisfied, he ordered the soldier to carry on. The man walked around the perimeter of the ammunition dump, or one of the camp's other vital installations, with live ammunition and orders to "shoot to kill" anyone who did not respond to a challenge. Taffe wrote, "We learned just how dreary and cold it could be on an Army post doing interior guard at night with the wind and snow swirling across the parade field."[12]

To the non-coms, the task of transforming the recruits into first-rate soldiers initially looked like a lost cause: men falling asleep in class, sloppy uniforms, and others continually out of step during drill. There were always at least one individual in the outfit who just could not seem to get the hang of it. When the sergeant shouted left face, he would turn right, and vice versa. When participating in calisthenics classes, he was always out of sync. He was late falling out for morning reveille and always compiled the most gigs during Saturday morning inspections. It took him forever to strip his rifle, let alone put it back together. Very often, some kind soul would take the person under his wing and help him get through the training period.

Each company had its share of goldbricks, men who shirked their duty or who always tried to duck out of doing their share of the work. This, of course, meant that someone else had to pick up the slack. There were also a number of guys who would break the rules— that is, do something against orders. Sometimes the entire company would suffer the consequences of one "fuck up." The other men had ways of dealing with guys like that and they either straightened themselves out or spent some very sorry days and nights in basic. Clifford P.

3. *Basic Training: March–September 1941*   35

Above: The M1 75mm howitzer, designed for rapid movement across difficult terrain. Replaced in 1942 by the M1A1 75mm standard light howitzer (W.R. Thompson & Company Publications, Richmond, Virginia). *Below:* The M114 155mm towed howitzer is a type of medium field artillery piece first introduced in 1942 (Harrison Photos, Monument Beach, Massachusetts).

Welcome (F-181) of Orange, Massachusetts, said, "If one guy screwed up, everyone paid. We took care of the guy who screwed up." Gradually, the patience of the teachers began to bring results. Each week inspections improved and the company began to shape up and work as a cohesive unit.[13]

Everyone soon learned "when and how to salute, how to report to the company commander, the customs of the service, how to count in cadence, the position of a soldier at attention, the secrets of K.P. and what went into the food" and "that the 1st Sergeant wasn't as tough as he looked." They also learned where most rumors originate — in the latrine. Thus, the men referred to them as "shit-house rumors."[14]

The training staff conducted only a minimal amount of training indoors, the theory being that exposure to the elements would harden the troops. Long hikes to distant training areas, frequently through rough terrain and deep snows, built toughness and stamina. As basic training progressed, the marches became progressively longer. Hikes of as much as 15–20 miles or more with a full field pack, weighing an average of 55 pounds, and a 9.8-pound rifle became routine. Early on in the training, as many as half the men might drop out from exhaustion or heat prostration.[15]

It made no difference what the weather was like; the troops marched in rain, heavy snow, or sub-freezing temperatures. Conditions were especially grueling with snow and ice on the

Rail Fence, Obstacle Course — Camp Edwards. "Several soldiers execute perfect steeplechase form, as they fling themselves over the five-foot rail fence" (U.S. Army Signal Corps/RMP Archives —1942).

ground. On any incline, for every two steps forward a marcher would slide one step back. The Yankee Division historian wrote, "Hikes to training areas were distant and frequently through heavy snows." There was a lot of grumbling, but once the men were in top physical shape, morale soared. The unusually high spirits "produced the famous 'dipsydoodle' hiking step developed by the men of the division."[16]

Learning to interpret the standard 30-inch march step proved difficult for many of the recruits at first. The men in the column would gradually start to stretch out farther and farther along the route of march. Soon the drill sergeant was shouting to the men in the rear, "Come on you guys, close it up, close it up." Of course, it seemed as though all the big, tall men were positioned at the beginning of the marching column and the shorter fellows at the back. The little guys, who were stuck in the rear, had to keep running to catch up. No sooner would they get caught up and catch their breath when inevitably they would be forced to start running again.

After a few weeks, some of the boys in the company became well acquainted and formed fast friendships. The historian of Company D, 104th Infantry, related that soon the barracks became a "very hazardous place" with everyone trying to outdo one another pulling the most mischievous pranks and practical jokes. The high jinx sometimes strained new friendships to the limit. The men had to be on their toes at all times, lest they fall victim to some prankster.

Horizontal Ladder, Obstacle Course — Camp Edwards. "Determined soldiers swing across fifteen feet of horizontal ladders" (U.S. Army Signal Corps/RMP Archives —1942).

It got to the point where most guys would, as a matter of routine, make a quick reconnaissance of their bunk before getting under the covers. There were short-sheeting incidents, crackers or sometimes even small animals placed between the sheets. Most victims failed to complain, knowing it would only bring a chorus of laughter and more harassment later. Some guys in the company always seemed to be on the receiving end of most practical jokes, while others, nobody dared to mess with.[17]

* * *

The 3rd Battalion of the 104th Regiment had a very unusual configuration, in that, for a time, it consisted of five companies instead of the usual four. Shortly after the regiment arrived at Edwards, Col. John J. Higgins, known as "J.J.," commander of the 104th Infantry, added a fifth, designated "J" Company — the reason for which I will explain following a few brief preparatory remarks as to how this happened to come about. Normally, the U.S. Army does not use the letter "J." The 3rd Battalion of each regiment usually consists of Companies I, K, L, and M. Historian Maj. Mark M. Boatner III, in his book *Military Customs and Traditions*, explains that "the American Army started lettering companies in 1816," and "since the script 'J' looked so much like 'I' the letter was not used." Boatner noted that "J is the most recent

Asparagus Patch, Obstacle Course — Camp Edwards. "Depicted training exercise is called the 'asparagus patch,' consisting of pine logs stuck in the ground, is an obstacle that looks easy but is an extreme of body and mind" (U.S. Army Signal Corps/RMP Archives — 1942).

addition to our alphabet and when first adopted was used interchangeably with I." He added, "Remember also that the Army of that day relied entirely on handwritten orders and correspondence which made the likelihood even greater that the [cursive] I's and J's would be confused." The standard regiment of the new 1816 system consisted of 10 companies, A–K, less J.[18]

At Camp Edwards during this period, many specialists worked at their particular jobs full-time and were unable to train as regular soldiers. This group "included the Mess and Supply sergeants, Company Clerks, Cooks, Artificers [skilled mechanics], and Headquarters Clerks." Because these men did not participate in regular fitness and arms training or instruction, regiment felt it deprived them of "the opportunity of being good all round soldiers." In early February, Col. Higgins "inaugurated a plan" to "expedite" this problem. The colonel founded Company "J" and placed the outfit under the command of Lt. Richard G. Risley and Lt. Klemens Kalva, both natives of Springfield.[19]

The unit, which had its own staff of non-commissioned officers, trained as a group for two or three hours every afternoon, participating in regular fitness training, which included drill, calisthenics, and conditioning marches, as well as taking classes "in subjects such as the School of a Soldier, Sanitation and First Aid, Hygiene, Scouting and Patrolling, Combat Principals, Interior Guard Duty, Nomenclature and use of Weapons, etc." The company historian praised the members of the new outfit: "Good results were obtained and the new men were willing students." There is no record of the participants' opinions, which likely differed markedly since, before the company's formation, they were free from this physically demanding and often boring training.[20]

The new outfit "was often the butt of many friendly jokes but," the historian wrote, "considerable esprit de corps was built up." Company "J" became "known jestingly as Risley's Rangers or Kalva's Kavalry." The February 1941 issue of *The Torch*, the regimental newsletter, carried the following poem about the unit, written by one of its members, "which," the company historian commented, "had almost a complimentary tone to it":

> Today I write of Company "J,"
> The lost battalion as some might say;
> With company clerks and K.P.s too,
> It's like part of a mulligan stew,
> You should have seen them when they began,
> They made me laugh to beat the band;
> With bobbing up and bobbing down, I swore to myself that they'd all fall down.
>
> With some good hard toil in a noon-day's hike,
> The boys got ready for the regimental hike,
> And you should see them march with their shoulders back,
> Like the Colonel's best and that's a fact.
>
> Take a lesson, boys, in how it's done,
> It was only hard when they begun,
> You can do it too, if you find the way,
> To do it right on the very first day.

The outfit was such an oddity that the Springfield newspaper "published a picture of the company lined up in formation." "J" Company "marched as a unit in several parades and made a fine showing on every occasion." "The company was an unusual undertaking and Colonel Higgins received much favorable comment," the historian wrote.[21]

Company "J," it turned out, was short lived; Col. Higgins disbanded the unit at the start of regimental exercises in June 1941, "in order that these men might be released to their own companies for full time duty."[22]

Wall Training, Obstacle Course — Camp Edwards. "Enlisted men along with Officers, are required to train rigorously on the anti-aircraft training center's obstacle course to stay in peak condition" (U.S. Army Signal Corps/RMP Archives — 1942).

* * *

From the fourth to the seventh weeks of basic, the men moved to the known distance firing ranges for training with the .30-caliber rifles. The majority of the troops of the 181st Infantry were equipped with the old World War I Enfields (M1917) or .03 Springfields (M1903). Some of the companies, including the Worcester companies (A, B, C, and D) as well as Company F of Orange and Company G of Clinton, had received the new Garand M-1 semi-automatic rifles. Many hours of "dry shooting" preceded the range firing.[23]

Training staff also instructed the men in the different firing positions — standing, sitting, kneeling, and prone — until perfected. Statistics showed that this preparatory procedure increased scores appreciably. During this phase of training, all members of a .30-caliber light machine gun (air-cooled), or .30-caliber heavy machine gun (water-cooled) crew, and those men armed with the Browning Automatic Rifle (BAR), were required to fire the official courses.[24]

Beginning in the fourth week, the troops ran the newly constructed obstacle course designed to train soldiers in full battle gear under simulated field conditions. The rugged 500 yard course, a troop training strategy developed at Fort Belvoir, Virginia, incorporated walls to climb, hurdles to jump and dodge, a section with 20 staggered automobile tires to high-step through, barbed wire entanglements to negotiate, trenches and water hazards to traverse using rope swings or narrow log bridges, steep slopes to climb, pipes to crawl through, horizontal ladders to swing hand over hand across, and other challenging obstacles.

The army training staff at Fort Belvoir designed the timed course, popularly known as the Steeplechase, to test the speed, balance, agility, and endurance of the troops. Nate Mencow remembered, "We ran the obstacle course once or twice a week. It was located next to the parade grounds and was a very difficult course. By the end of training our time improved tremendously."[25]

During the fifth week of training, the regiments took part in the first of a series of night marches and operations, observing strict march discipline with no lights allowed. The troops marched to the objective and took up a defensive posture. Each company moved and operated separately during the movement.[26]

Unknown soldier at rifle range with U.S. Model 1903 Springfield Rifle (courtesy Massachusetts Army National Guard).

Two battalions organized and defended the main line of resistance (MLR), with the third stationed at the rear in reserve. The reserve battalion reconnoitered both flanks for routes of advance and for counterattacks. The Regimental CO positioned the antitank company at the rear of the column, ready to move forward and defend against motorized and mechanized attacks, which was standard operating procedure early in the war. Later, this policy would change. These preliminary operations were the forerunner of much more complicated problems that the regiment was to participate in during maneuvers held later at Fort Devens and in North Carolina.[27]

Shortly after the men retired on the first night, the long anticipated tear gas attack occurred. Non-coms, standing up-wind, released several canisters, sending a cloud of gas toward the bivouac area. Everyone leaped out from under their blankets and scrambled to get their masks on. Men who had trouble locating, or fumbled with, the mask, choked and gasped for breath. They rubbed their watery eyes in an attempt to relieve the stinging sensation, further aggravating the problem. Some men managed to get the mask on but, in their haste, forgot to clear it (exhale sharply to force any gas inside the mask out) and, as a result, breathed in the toxic fumes. Many of the men became violently ill and vomited, some into their masks.[28]

Gradually, the boys toughened up. They learned to get by on a minimum of sleep. When

Wall Training, Obstacle Course — Camp Edwards. "Seven fully equipped trainees, go up and over an eight-foot wall of the anti-aircraft training center. The ropes are used only by the shorter participants who cannot otherwise reach the top" (U.S. Army Signal Corps/RMP Archives —1942).

the sergeant shouted "Take 10," they would be out in a matter of seconds. They hiked so much, "the average life of a pair of shoes was about three weeks." Sleeping in the open on hard rocky ground became routine. A 20-mile hike with full packs became a stroll. After a time, it was common for many to return to the barracks after a long grueling hike, get dressed, and go polka dancing, or "Polish hopping," as the GIs called it, forty miles away in Taunton.[29]

Joe Connole was member of Company H, 181st Infantry, a heavy weapons company. There were four platoons in the company, two .30-caliber machine guns, one .50-caliber machine gun, and one 81mm mortar platoon. Later, after the 26th became a triangular division, this changed, and the .50 cal. machine gun crew became part of the battalion's newly formed antitank company. At this point in the training, the men in the weapons company soon learned what their future job was to be — a .30 cal. or .50 cal. machine gunner or 81mm mortar gun crewmember, or driver, messenger, etc. My father ended up in the mortar platoon (see below).

During week six, the men of Company H began training on their assigned crew served weapons, heavy machine guns, or mortars. From this point on, training became a matter of each squad member becoming familiar with the nomenclature and learning the capabilities of their weapon, as well as their particular job assignment.

An 81mm mortar crew about to fire a round. Notice scrub vegetation typical of the Cape Cod environs. (Harrison Photos, Monument Beach, Massachusetts).

* * *

The 26th Division history states that in the spring of 1941, a serious AWOL problem began to develop. An unusually high number of soldiers began "leaving the training area without permission." With the advent of warmer weather, the young men, who had been training for several months with out letup, "became restless." Many of the men had not been home for some time and suffered from homesickness. Then there were a few "who by nature or upbringing" constantly resisted authority. There existed a number of "disadvantageous factors" that helped contribute to the overall situation. First of all, it was peacetime, not war; second, the men were all within a day's travel of their homes; and last, the history concluded, "the winter training period had developed the men to such an advanced state of physical well-being that some emotional outlet was almost a certainty."[30]

"Initial AWOL cases in a newly activated division are a very serious problem for any division commander," wrote the 26th Division historian. Under normal circumstances, such cases are dealt with "expeditiously" and treated "with maximum jurisprudence" to prevent the situation from getting out of hand. In this case, however, it was the "general consensus of opinion" between Major General Roger W. Eckfeldt and other high-ranking officers to adopt a policy of leniency. Division leaders made a direct appeal to the troops of the division to honor their commitment not to shirk their duty. They asked the troops "to respect [their] obligation to train and prepare [themselves] for possible war." This unusual strategy, the history claims, met with a high measure of success. "There was, however," the author concluded, "a small segment of soldiers that took advantage of the leniencies in the policy and resisted this appeal to the extent that they became chronic AWOL'S and were for the duration a source of annoyance."[31]

***

During weeks eight and nine of basic training, the regiments fired at the rifle ranges for record. Infantry companies qualified at the 200- and 300-yard ranges. At the "1,000-inch range," troops fired the .30 cal. heavy and the .30 cal. light machine guns. Qualification for the BAR and pistol also took place on the 1,000-inch range. The rifle companies returned to the target ranges for week ten to fire by battalion.[32]

To qualify on the rifle range a man had to receive a minimum score. Each circle on the target had a numerical value, five for a bulls-eye, four for the next circle, etc. Robert Brickman (D-141) wrote, "After firing your quota of bullets in the allotted time, the pit crew pulled the target down and counted the hits." The crew then held up numbered placards to indicate the score for each hit. If the shooter "missed the target completely," the crew "waved a red flag"—one wave for each miss. "The flag was laughingly referred to as 'Maggie's drawers,'" he said.[33]

The GIs had to qualify on both the M1 and the 03 Springfield rifle. The trainees qualified in the prone position. There were three qualifying ratings, expert, sharpshooter, and marksman, and the men were awarded badges accordingly.

"If a man failed to qualify, he was said to have 'boloed.'" Brickman said, "I only boloed on one weapon, and strangely enough it was the .30 caliber water cooled heavy machine gun which I eventually was destined to lead into combat."[34]

During the eleventh and twelfth weeks, the training staff conducted numerous demonstrations, presented to each company separately. The first was "a test of the powers of observation; something which is vital to the making of a good scout." For the demonstration, the troops occupied a vantage point on the side of a hill. The instructor chose a number of volunteers from among the audience to participate in the demonstration. First, he removed a blanket covering a table situated on a platform with a number of military articles laid out and asked the class to look at the various items and memorize them, allowing the men ample time to do so. Then he replaced the blanket and asked the men one by one to give the total number and to name each one. Not one person could correctly name them all.[35]

Next, the instructor "told the men to look over the terrain" to their front and tell how many soldiers were concealed in the area. The group could only detect about one-third of the men hiding there. The purpose of the demonstration was two-fold, to show the men "just how observant a scout must be in order to be of any use to his own forces," as well as the use and benefit of camouflage.[36]

Next was a demonstration of the correct manner of passing through a barbed wire entanglement, followed by the incorrect and then correct method of crossing an open field by a squad sent out on scouting mission.

The training staff conducted several night demonstrations over a three-day period. One included a presentation on how far light and common sounds can travel at night. Instructors "had the cooperation of the moon because the nights were as dark as pitch," which increased the effect of the demonstration dramatically. The flare of a match, adjusting the sights on an M-1 rifle, the cutting of barbed wire entanglements, and the firing of a rifle shot (a combination of noise and light), as well as several other examples, occurred at timed intervals from known distances. The instructor asked several members of the group to estimate the distance of each from its source, which the men grossly underestimated. According to the history of the 104th Infantry, when the men were told how far these sounds had traveled, "ejaculations of surprise were heard." The author commented, "It seemed unbelievable that noises,

3. Basic Training: March–September 1941   45

"Artillery Soldiers training on an obstacle course at the anti-aircraft training center at Camp Edwards — 1942" (Office of War Information).

common every-day sounds, would carry over such long distances during the still of the night."[37]

The second demonstration covered the proper safety measures troops needed to take to prevent detection in the event a flare went off in combat while scouting or patrolling.

It was on one of these nights that the troops of the division participated in one of their longest marches of the year to Lawrence Pond in Sandwich, northwest of Camp Edwards, a distance of approximately 11 miles. The purpose of the march was to attend a demonstration by combat engineers, "to show the use of assault boats in the night crossing of an un-fordable stream by an infantry battalion." Following the demonstration, the troops of each battalion had to successfully complete the training exercise. The engineers had prepared a number of inflatable rubber boats, each with a capacity of nine individuals, eight infantrymen, plus one engineer to maneuver the craft for the trip across.[38]

From concealed places on the shore, the troops, crouching low to prevent detection, carried the boats to the water's edge. The men loaded their equipment, pushed off from the shore, and climbed aboard. The occupants proceeded to paddle silently to the opposite side, whereupon the lead man jumped out and pulled the raft up on dry land. Upon landing, the initial party seized the nearby high ground to protect the crossing by the next group, and so on. One 104th Infantry historian described the exercise, carried out "under cover of a smoke screen and with machine gun fire [every fifth bullet a tracer] all about us," as "particularly thrilling." Shortly after the crossing exercises, "the long march back to the base camp was begun and a more tired group of individuals never existed than the regiment when they arrived back at the barracks," he wrote.[39]

During week twelve, all members of the regiment received instruction in the use of the bayonet and the art of grenade throwing. "Grenade throwing has proven a popular phase of training with the American doughboy," wrote one historian for the 104th Infantry. All men armed with rifles from the antitank company, the three heavy weapons companies, Service Company, Headquarters Company, and Battalion Headquarters Detachment, together with all rifle units, fired on the known distance ranges in a daylong exercise. Qualification with the .45-caliber pistol took place on the 1,000-inch range at the end of the 12th week.[40]

In the thirteenth and final week of basic, the regiment conducted combat, practice firing with the BAR, light machine gun, and the .30 cal. rifle on the "musketry range." Squad and platoon problems followed the combat firing exercises. There was no let-up at the end of the basic training cycle, and on June 16, the units started right in on advanced training exercises.[41]

4

The "Stovepipe" Platoon

As mentioned in the previous chapter, Joe Connole ended up a member of the mortar platoon of Company H, 181st Infantry. The 81mm mortar is a smoothbore, muzzle loading, high angle fire weapon weighing 136 pounds. The mission of the battalion heavy weapons company is to provide close and continuous fire support to the infantry companies. Standard procedure was for the company commander to attach one or more machine-gun or mortar squads to each of the rifle companies for support. The job of the machine-gun squads is to lay down fields of fire in the attack or in defense of a position. Heavy mortars serve as the battalion commander's own personal artillery.[1]

Cartoonist Bill Mauldin, in his book *Up Front*, had this to say about mortars:

> Mortars [60mm and 81mm] are the artillery of an infantry company. Outside of the bazooka, they carry more viciousness and wallop per pound than any weapon the infantry has. The guys who operate them are at a big disadvantage. Because of the mortar's limited range, they have to work so close to the front that they are a favorite target for snipers, patrols, shells, and countermortar [retaliatory] fire. Knocked-out mortar positions earn Iron Crosses for ambitious young herrenvolk.

Mauldin bemoaned the fact "that the Germans make them too," and that is "the worst thing about mortars," he complained. Hogg wrote, "Mortars were heartily disliked by the infantry, since they were quick to come into action and deadly in their effect."[2]

Unlike the machine guns, which provided direct sweeping fire, the mortar is used for high angle, or indirect, fire only. Mortar crews utilize the weapon to "throw shells over hills, into gullies, and other places," referred to as targets in defilade, that the infantry could not reach using direct fire from small arms and machine guns. The weapon fires a shell high into the air, which "then drops almost straight down on top of the enemy." Mortar fire is invaluable against dug in enemy troops and entrenched positions, such as a bunker or dugout with overhead protection.[3]

The Mortar Gunnery Field Manual (FM 23–91) states that the "immediate objective" of the mortar team "is to deliver a mass of accurate and timely fire so that the maximum number of casualties are inflicted" and that "the number of casualties in a target area can be increased in most instances by surprise fire." The team can achieve the "greatest demoralizing effect on the enemy ... by delivery of a maximum number of rounds from all the mortars in the mortar section in the shortest possible time." The battalion commander may employ the mortar platoon "to neutralize or destroy area or point targets, to screen large areas with smoke for sustained periods," or "to provide illumination."[4]

The mortar consists of three main parts, the barrel, the base plate, and the bipod. All three units are easily dismantled. Broken down, the gun's component parts form separate loads, the weight of which is manageable enough for one man to carry, but by no means an easy task. The weight of the various parts is as follows: barrel, 44.5 pounds; bipod, 46.5

pounds; and the base plate, 45 pounds. The barrel is 49.5 inches long, with a base cap that has a removable firing pin threaded into the center.[5]

Set at an elevation of between 45 degrees and 85 degrees, the weapon has a range of between 250 and 3,290 yards (approximately 2 miles). An 81mm mortar can fire 30 to 35 rounds per minute for short periods and 18 rounds per minute for a sustained period.[6]

The 81mm projectile is a "tear-drop shaped bomb with fins at the rear to give stability in flight." Mortar ammunition is classified into three basic types: high explosive (HE), chemical (smoke), and training. There were two types of high explosive rounds: HE light, for use against personnel, and HE heavy, for use in the demolition of enemy shelters and defenses. HE shells weigh between 6.87 and 15.05 pounds, depending upon the size of the charge. The "lethal radii" of a mortar shell, "based upon standard 1939–45 HE bombs," was 49 feet (a diameter of 98 feet) at an angle of 70 degrees. This figure, Hogg points out:

> can be considered the "worst case"; the actual distribution of [steel] splinters resembles a figure eight with the bomb in the center and the two loops at each side. Very little goes forward or backward. The greatest area of risk being at the side, and that is what [this figure] represent[s]. The area [of splinter distribution] immediately in front of the bomb is a matter of 4–5 meters (13–16 ft.) at the most.[7]

A mortar squad consists of a squad leader (sergeant) and seven or more enlisted men: one gunner (corporal), one assistant gunner (a Pfc. or Pvt.), a base plate man, and five or six ammunition bearers (a Pfc. or Pvt.). The Table of Organization & Equipment (TO&E) identifies each man in the squad by number, 1, 2, 3, and so on. The gunner was No. 1; the assistant gunner No. 2; the base plate man No. 3, and the ammunition bearers, No. 4, 5, 6, etc. Each ammo bearer usually carried six rounds of ammunition, called a clove. Normally, it was the gunner's job to carry the barrel and his assistant the bipod.[8]

Guido Fratturelli of Fitchburg, Massachusetts, the mortar platoon sergeant of Company H, 181st Infantry, said, "Carrying the base plate was by far the worst job in the mortar platoon." At a reunion of Company H in 2002, I asked Mr. Fratturelli who carried the base plate. Sulo Ruuska interrupted the conversation with, "Whoever Guido was mad at," and everyone laughed. To which Fratturelli replied, "No, no, no. At first, the number 1, 2, and 3 man in the squad carried the barrel, bipod, and base plate respectively," he said. "Later, I made everyone take a turn equally."[9]

The bipod at 44.5 pounds and the mortar barrel at 46.5 pounds, were also bulky and cumbersome to carry. Fratturelli said, "I always tried to get a ½- or ¾-ton weapons carrier to transport the guns." Most of the time, however, battalion denied the request, he reported, because vehicles were always in short supply.[10]

One of the gunner's duties was to set up the mortar and align it to hit the target. The assistant gunner assisted in mounting the weapon and, once the weapon was ready to fire, loaded the rounds upon orders from the gunner. Just before firing, the assistant gunner removes the safety wire (cotter pin) from the fuse, which is located in the nose. Ammunition bearers saw to it that the gun crews had an ample supply of shells.

Under ordinary circumstances, mortar crews used jeeps towing ¼-ton trailers to transport weapons, ammunition, and equipment any distance. The TO&E for 1941, indicates that the mortar platoon had seven jeeps and six trailers assigned to it. Fratturelli said that during the training period of 1941–1942, the men hand carried the weapons everywhere they went. He claimed that the TO&E may have called for a specific number of jeeps and trailers, but that his platoon had none. "We never had that luxury."[11]

Members of the mortar squad followed a regular training schedule of instruction and drill. This was necessary due to the high number of replacements. A number of the new men had received some prior training, but others had none at all. The purpose of mortar drill was to teach each member of the team his regular assigned duty in executing movements with equipment and serving the weapon during firing. Training began with preparatory instruction, geared to teach the individual soldier to perform in a prescribed manner. Training personnel conducted a series of demonstrations eventually followed by hands-on exercises.[12]

Initially, each soldier performed the required exercises without regard to time. Development of accuracy was the most important consideration during the training exercises. Once crewmembers attained the habit of exactness, they practiced for speed until they were able to perform each test with the required accuracy in the allotted time.[13]

The platoon sergeant familiarized the trainees with the duties of the other crewmembers by rotating assignments. This way, if the squad lost one or more of its members in battle, the others could step right in and take over. Once the crewmembers became proficient in drilling exercises, they began live fire training.[14]

As the rifle companies advanced rapidly in a fast action, it was sometimes necessary for the crew to move the weapon to a new position as quickly as possible to provide continuous fire support. Platoon sergeants trained the crews to carry out this part of their job with the utmost speed and efficiency. The drill consisted of setting up the weapon, sighting it, and then dismantling it and moving to a new position. The crew repeated this exercise over and over, grumbling all the time as they did so.

During the course of training, non-coms impressed upon the men of Company H the importance of the heavy weapons company in support of the rifle companies, as well as the mission of the unit in the overall scheme of battalion tactics and maneuvers. Section and squad leaders emphasized that the success of the weapons team depended upon the coordination and cooperation of each crewmember.

Sergeant Fratturelli pushed the men and worked them hard, and like all new trainees, including my father, they bitched long and loud. "There was a possibility the country might be at war soon, and I was responsible for getting the men ready," he explained.[15]

* * *

In a letter to the author in May 2000, Fratturelli related the particulars of an interesting story about the 81mm mortar platoon that occurred while the 181st Infantry was on shore patrol duty in Saco, Maine. He began, "Believe it or not, in the three years of training [prior to the deactivation of the 181st in December 1943] the mortar platoon fired a live ammo exercise on only one occasion" (due to a shortage of ammunition).[16]

"During the summer of 1943," Fratturelli continued, "the 1st Army Commanding General [Lt. Gen. Hugh A. Drum] was conducting a tour of the 26th Division units stationed along the east coast in Maine. On a set day, the general came to the 2nd Battalion Headquarters in Saco to inspect the troops." While there, for reasons unknown, "he requested that the 81mm mortar platoon perform a live fire exercise." The intended target was a "small island in Saco Bay near the mouth of the Saco River, roughly 2,500 yards from shore" (approximately one and a half miles away).[17]

An experienced mortar fire team should be able to hit any target within three rounds, but the mortar platoon of Company H had never fired the weapons, which was of great concern to Sergeant Fratturelli. A large group of dignitaries was present to view the demonstration, including the general and his entourage, the battalion commander and several staff officers, as well as a number of men from the companies. With all of the brass hats looking on, Fratturelli was under intense pressure to succeed.

Through his binoculars, the sergeant estimated the range and relayed the grid coordinates to the fire direction center (FDC). From the mortar position, the island appeared a tiny speck in the far distance. "Judging distance over water was very difficult to do," Fratturelli said. FDC personnel plotted the data then forwarded the firing instructions to the gun crew. The gunner made the necessary adjustments to elevation and traverse and the squad leader issued the command to "fire one round."[18]

The assistant gunner dropped the round down the tube detonating the charge that propelled the shell out of the muzzle in a high arching trajectory on its way toward the distant target. Several of those in attendance caught a faint glimpse of the projectile streaking skyward before it disappeared into the clouds. After several seconds elapsed, the first round fell short and exploded in the water about 30 yards in front of the island.

Sergeant Fratturelli corrected the range and relayed the changes to the FDC. The gunner made the necessary change in elevation. The squad leader again shouted "fire one round" and the shell headed for the target exploding about 30 yards or so beyond. The disappointment was evident as a collective sigh could be heard from the crowd of anxious onlookers.

As Fratturelli made what he hoped would be his final range adjustment, the tension continued to build. The gunner indicated the weapon was set to fire and the squad leader gave the command. The mortar coughed and round three was on its way. The crowd waited anxiously in great anticipation of the outcome. This time, the shell made a direct hit and a loud cheer went up from the audience. "Of course the boys and I were elated and congratulated each other at our success," Fratturelli wrote. "The General gave our crew a job well done."[19]

5

Time Off from Training: Off Duty Hours

At the end of a day's training, if the men had some time off, many would often head for the base canteen, where they could "ease the parched condition of their throats" drinking 3.2 beer "and prepare for the next dry spell." Others might take in the latest movie at one of the many theaters at the camp.[1]

There were nightly boxing matches in the middle of the huge quadrangle that were very popular among the men. Members of the audience had to be very careful they did not "leave the ring area in the wrong direction," especially if the person preceded the event by having a "few beers," otherwise, a person could very easily get himself lost. Such a mistake, Richard P. Taffe (Hq. Co., 3rd Bn.-181)) explained, "could require a considerable walk; moreover, it could require a considerable explanation, even a fight, should you have walked into the wrong barracks in the middle of the night and tried to take over someone else's bunk." After losing their way a few times, the men learned to orient themselves to the location of their barracks area in relation to the water tower located adjacent to the camp's warehouse.[2]

Unless scheduled for duty or restricted to camp, the men had weekends off from noon on Saturday until 6 A.M. on Monday morning. On Saturday nights, many went to the local bars or clubs in one of the many towns and villages surrounding the camp. One very popular nightspot was the Coonamessett Club in Falmouth, until division headquarters declared the place off limits to the enlisted men because of the frequent brawls that ensued after some elbow-bending by the servicemen. The club featured dining and dancing and served up as fine a steak dinner as could be found anywhere on Cape Cod. There was music in the lounge by the Bistany's Bombardiers, and other "native talent." Another favorite at the club was Charlie Mack, who sang while accompanying himself on the accordion and piano. Frank "On the Bubble" McEvoy emceed the popular nightclub shows.[3]

The regimental athletic officer formed baseball or softball and basketball leagues—with inter-battalion competition between companies. At the end of each season, there was a playoff among the best teams for the division championship.[4]

Company morale officers arranged for truck convoys "each weekend and Wednesday afternoons to transport the boys to the beaches, ball games, and various dances" held in many of the cities and towns "within a 70 mile radius." During the warm summer months, large numbers of the men enjoyed "many happy hours at Nantasket Beach with the bathing beauties outnumbering the men bathers at least three to one." The GIs also spent many "Thursday and Saturday evenings in the popular Roseland Ballroom in Taunton dancing the 'polka' to the well-known music of Jan Zmuda."[5]

The historian for Company K (104th) listed numerous other social events and excursions enjoyed by its members, which were typical of most companies: "outings and parties; clam-bakes on the shores of Cape Cod; get togethers in the mess hall, with food, songs and chatter; boat rides to the islands around Martha's Vineyard; mass migrations to sporting events of the season; and dinners at nearby roadhouses, where entertainment provided by the members [of the company] rivaled that of professionals."[6]

As often as possible, the servicemen would head directly home for the weekend. A few, who were lucky enough to possess their own vehicles, used them to transport themselves and their buddies home. Everyone chipped in for gas. My Aunt Helen Palumbo said that my Uncle Matthew J. "Mitt" Palumbo (Band-181) came home from Camp Edwards every weekend while they were going together. One of his Army buddies, Peter Loconto of Worcester, had his own car. About 1 or 2 A.M. on Monday a group from the city who were returning to camp would meet at the Boulevard, an all night diner on Shrewsbury Street, and head back, arriving just before reveille.[7]

Some men took the train home. One company historian from the 104th Infantry says that the railroads lowered their rates for servicemen, "permitting us to go home for less than one cent a mile." Company morale officers arranged for "excursion trains, for dances, for shows, for concerts, and for sightseeing trips." Nathaniel "Nate" or "Gus" Mencow (M-181) said, "the train to Worcester took four to five hours, with many stops along the way." There was also a bus from Camp Edwards that went to Fall River; Providence, Rhode Island; and then on to Worcester and points beyond. Others, who wanted to get home quicker, thumbed a ride. People would not hesitate to stop and pick up a serviceman in uniform.[8]

Mencow had a good friend named Dick Smith, who was married to Frances Gordon. Her family had connections to the Wyman-Gordon Company, a large manufacturing plant in Worcester that produced airplane parts for the government. The family's chauffeur driven black Cadillac limousine would pick up Smith and his pals at the base on Saturday morning after inspection and drive them home in comfort. "We went over the old Route 140, a very long trip through many small towns. It took about three to three and a half hours."[9]

* * *

The United Services Organization, Inc. (USO) Club on Main Street in Falmouth was a very popular place with the GIs from Camp Edwards. Every week, the club provided a slate of organized activities for the men. A number of Junior Volunteers and U.S.O. girls were always on hand to entertain the boys or help out when needed. The hostesses provided warm conversation over coffee and doughnuts; did mending; wrote letters; and socialized with the servicemen at regularly scheduled events.[10]

The USO, founded on February 4, 1941, sponsored "nearly 3,000 clubs and services ... in this country and overseas in the western hemisphere." This number included "more than a thousand 'hometown USO's' conducted by local communities in affiliation with the national organization." In 1941, President Franklin D. Roosevelt challenged private organizations around the country to provide morale and recreation services to U.S. military personnel. In response, six civilian agencies—the YMCA, YWCA, National Catholic Community Service, the National Jewish Welfare Board, the National Traveler's Aid Association, and the Salvation Army—pooled their resources to "form a new organization, United Services Organizations, or USO." The goal of the organization since its inception has "been to provide 'a home away from home' for men and women in the armed services." "Clubhouses" were the "heart of the USO," but "other services" included: "USO Camp Shows, mobile service units, station lounges, USO Travelers Aid Centers, [and] aid to troops on maneuvers."[11]

Saturday night dances were a regular feature at the clubs, with music provided by the regimental orchestra or band from Camp Edwards. The orchestra or band, or one of the three or four piece combos formed by some of the musicians, also furnished music for numerous dances at the Service Club, Officer's Clubs, and regimental get-togethers. My uncle, Matthew "Mitt" Palumbo, was a horn player in the 181st Infantry Band. He was also an accomplished guitar player and regularly played in one of the combos. Every Wednesday evening, two student instructors from nearby Hyannis State Teacher's College held dancing classes. There was also a regular program of "vocal solos, instrumental music, and movies" to keep the boys entertained.[12]

What started out as a half-dozen 26th Division soldiers wanting to sing Christmas carols in December of 1941 turned into one of the biggest regular social gatherings at the Falmouth USO Club. An article in the September 18, 1942, issue of the *Falmouth Enterprise* titled, "Soldiers Bring Songs of the West and South to Song-fests at U.S.O.," reported that every Sunday at 7:30 P.M., anywhere from 25 to as many as 600 boys filled the USO auditorium. Miss Leona Wilson, a USO staff member, led the singing and accompanied on the piano.[13]

Mrs. Fred S. Howard also played accompaniments on her violin. As soon as Miss Wilson struck the first chords, the boys got up out of their seats and maneuvered for a spot around the grand piano. "Surefire openers," were "'Home on the Range,' 'Red River Valley,' and 'Jeannie with the Light Brown Hair.'" Before the first song ended, there might be several hundred boys clustered around Mrs. Wilson at the piano.[14]

Every week several very talented young men got up to sing solos, much to the delight of the crowd. The weekly program varied. "Songs of the deep south and the far west, songs of the cities and of the country and the plains, all had their turn." Several USO volunteers passed out songbooks as well as "a collection of favorites on mimeograph sheets" to help the singers with some of the words, but they all knew the tunes. Favorite songs included "I'll Take You Home Again, Kathleen," "There is a Tavern," "Loch Lomand," "Alouette," and "Cielito Lindo." A close second were several songs from World War I, such as "My Buddy," "Tipperary," "Over There," and "I Don't Know Where I'm Going But I'm On My Way."[15]

As more and more soldiers from around the country came to Camp Edwards to train, "regional songs that are kin to folk songs" became increasingly popular with the boys and began taking up a greater portion of the program. After the 36th "Texas" Division arrived in August 1942, the boys from Texas added a segment of songs from the Lone Star state. In "the past few weeks," Wilson said, "the rafters have rung with 'The Eyes of Texas are Upon You,' ... 'Deep in the Heart of Texas,'" and a rousing rendition of "Home on the Range." "It doesn't sound like the same song you hear on the radio or glee club programs," she pointed out. "It belongs to these boys."[16]

Some of the veterans from the 26th Division remember that when the Texans began singing "The Yellow Rose of Texas" every one had to stand up or a fight would ensue. It was explained that, "The boys from the Lone Star State considered 'Yellow Rose' the anthem of Texas."

The singing usually lasted until between 10 and 10:30 P.M., sometimes later. Mrs. Wilson had her troubles trying to end the show at 10 P.M. because so many of the boys did not want to go back to camp until they heard every one of their favorite songs. But, reveille came mighty early on Monday morning.[17]

6

Public Relations Exercise: Three Day Bivouac in Worcester, Massachusetts

On Friday, August 1, 1941, the 181st Infantry Regiment, approximately 3,500 officers and men, traveled the 106 miles from Camp Edwards to Worcester for a three-day bivouac at Institute Park near Lincoln Square. The 450-vehicle convoy, "in 12 march groups," each consisting of 40 to 50 vehicles, left Edwards at 7:30 A.M. at 15-minute intervals. The first contingent arrived in the city at 10:45 A.M., and the last at 1:45 P.M. "By 3 P.M. Institute Park was covered by more than 1,700 tents, wrote Frank J. Boyce, staff reporter for the *Worcester Telegram*. The regiment "turned the park into an Army camp — a city within a city." He predicted the event would be "the most colorful homecoming since World War days."[1]

During the regiment's stay, the city council's Military Affairs Committee and civic authorities arranged "a Homecoming of Entertainment." Officials turned over all proceeds from the slate of events to the regimental fund. One of the main events was a night baseball game between the 181st Infantry baseball team and the Norton (Company) Abrasives, "an outstanding semi-pro team" of the New England League, scheduled for 9 P.M. at Fitton Field on the Holy Cross campus. The Abrasives were in second place in the league standings. The price of tickets was 50 cents, "plus 25 cents to park inside the college grounds." Planners expected an "overflow crowd" to attend.[2]

Other events on the weekend program included "a concert of martial airs" by the 181st Infantry Band at 7:30 P.M. on the steps of the Worcester Memorial Auditorium. A formal dance followed the concert from 8 P.M. until midnight. The price of admission for a civilian was 50 cents, 25 cents for soldiers, and no charge for women. The "181st Infantry Rhythm unit" provided the music and the money from the dance would "benefit the band's music fund." "One of the features of the evening" would be "the selection of a 'Regimental Queen'" by a panel of judges headed by Brigadier General Francis V. Logan, commander of the 52nd Brigade.[3]

"The bivouac," explained Boyce, "gives the home folks an opportunity to see at close range what the Army has done with its sons, and provides a practice maneuver for the soldiers as well." Advance officers informed Boyce that both the road movement and the Worcester festivities would be "strictly regulated." The safe movement of such a large contingent of men, vehicles, and equipment required a great deal of skill and "taxed" the "ability of transportation officers ... in keeping traffic unsnarled and [moving] at an even pace." Military officials considered the Friday evening parade "part of the close-order drill" of an infantry regiment "necessary for the development of discipline and perfection."[4]

Division authorities, in co-operation with police officials, pre-planned the logistics of crowd control and assigned 110 MPs, 60 from regiment, "50 regular YD Military Police from other regiments," plus 200 city police officers, "to help direct traffic and keep order." A picture of my father, believed taken at this time, shows him in the uniform of an MP.[5]

"Each company in the problem set up its own little city according to plan," wrote Boyce. The companies brought their own kitchen equipment by truck. A 2 ½-ton carrier, containing "three stove units heated by white gasoline," towed "a new ice-box trailer" capable of holding "enough perishables to feed" the unit "for an entire day." Kitchen personnel set up field kitchens, and completed arrangements for sanitation and supply. Mess sergeants used nearby hydrants to supply their water needs. Water waste was "poured down street catch-basins." The city's Public Works Department scheduled trucks to pick up the garbage twice during each day. Each unit was responsible for the disposal of their own rubbish.[6]

Men on K.P. duty set up large tables "for serving the mess" and placed three 30-gallon corrugated garbage cans with immersion heaters nearby for washing mess kits, "two with hot soapy water and the other with plain hot water" (known as "the three container method"). "For mess prior to the parade, soldiers had filet of haddock, mashed potatoes, spinach, salad, bread and butter, ice cream and coffee." Latrines "were dug and screened ... at least 100 yards from company kitchens." City officials arranged for the use of the nearby Boy's Club for showers and swimming.[7]

Beginning at 7 P.M., the regiment marched in parade through the streets of the city to Fitton Field, approximately two and a half miles away. A contingent of military police led the column followed by Col. Roy W. Smith, commander of the 181st Infantry, and his staff officers. Next in line, was the 181st Regimental Band, "conceded the best in the Yankee Division." The three battalions of the regiments were next in order. Steel helmeted troops marched with "full pack and equipment," including weapons with "gleaming bayonets" slung over their right shoulder.[8]

Behind the infantry troops came a long line of vehicles and equipment that included 2 ½-ton troop carriers, ½-ton weapons carriers, ambulances, jeeps—some towing anti-tank weapons (37mm guns)—"field artillery trucks hauling 75s [75mm antitank guns], vicious looking guns used to support the infantry," and staff cars. The parade extended for some 10 miles, "six miles of trucks and four miles of soldiers." Boyce says, "The entire movement of men and trucks took exactly 45 minutes to pass City Hall." An estimated 40,000 people lined the parade route to view the procession.[9]

City officials, along with Gen. Logan and Col. Smith, and other military leaders stood in review on a platform in front of City Hall on Main Street, as the troops marched smartly past. "Chorus upon chorus of applause went up as each helmeted company 'strutted its stuff' for the home folks." City workers hung stars and stripes banners on light poles, and businesses, stores, and offices in the retail district decorated their establishments "with flags and other patriotic emblems." Three gleaming new Air Corps fighter planes from the Boston Army Base (now Logan Airport) "swooped low" making pass after pass over the long procession.[10]

The long line of troops entered the stadium, marched around the perimeter running track for review before the game, and then seated themselves on an "embankment" on the right field side of the baseball diamond. John F. Houlihan, a reporter for the *Worcester Telegram*, wrote, "The right field embankment looked like a solid slope of brown as the 3,500 soldiers took up residence there." Drivers broke from the column and turned down nearby Middle River Road, closed to civilian traffic, where they parked their vehicles.[11]

A capacity crowd of 15,000 civilian and soldier spectators, "the largest ever to watch a semi-pro game in the city," looked on as the Norton team beat the 181st nine by a score of 11–4 under the floodlights on Fitton Field. Houlihan wrote that the crowd "overflowed the stands." The 181st Infantry team, coached by Pvt. John Whalen of Worcester, a former Holy Cross catcher, held its own until the eighth inning, when the Abrasives scored five runs. Boyce reported that it was the first time the team had played under floodlights and were "troubled by distance judgment."[12]

Houlihan wrote that the 181st Infantry team "gave it the old college try and was hot on the heels of the Abrasives until flattened under the impact of a five-run eighth inning." The *Telegram* reporter said "circumstances played a large part" in the loss. After giving up four runs in the first inning, "the soldiers fought an uphill struggle." They "pecked away at the variety of Norton pitchers and were yipping at the heels of the leaders" when, in the last of the eighth inning, "the fatigue of a tough week of maneuvers and drilling, not to mention the traveling in army trucks yesterday, took its full and costly toll."[13]

After the game, trucks transported the troops back to Institute Park. Regiment allowed the soldiers to go home, but they had to report for roll call by 6:30 A.M. Colonel Smith scheduled a full field inspection to take place from 8 to 11 A.M., which was open to the public. With "$85,000 in fresh pay jingling in their pockets," a happy group of soldiers headed out on the town with friends and family for a night of revelry. "Military police details roamed the city, keeping a watchful eye on fellow soldiers." The MP unit was quartered at the Precinct 1 Police Station on Waldo Street near the Central Business District, "prepared to rush out on a moment's notice of trouble."[14]

Following roll call the next morning, the troops prepared for the field inspection, described by Boyce as "rigorous." When the inspection of each unit began, the soldiers stood aside their pup tents with equipment laid out neatly on the ground before them. As the inspecting officer stopped in front of each man, the soldier came smartly to attention and brought his rifle up to inspection arms. Boyce wrote, the purpose of the "inspections of each soldier's equipment and tent was "to make sure each man is ready to go into combat." Following the inspection, the troops had the remainder of the day off. "Ideal weather" brought out a crowd of 25,000 visitors.[15]

On Saturday afternoon, the soldiers gave friends and family a tour of the temporary camp. Children stared wide-eyed at the sight of the M-1 Garand rifles, machine guns, and other armament on display. Visitors inspected an 81mm mortar set up by members of the heavy weapons platoon. "Pretty young women tried on the boy friend's gas mask, inspected the tents, drank from canteens, and even wore steel helmets," Boyce wrote. Clifford P. Welcome (F-181) remembered "nosey people poking their heads into the tents while the men were changing clothes."[16]

The 1st Battalion, 102nd Field Artillery, "with its 16 75-millimeter guns," set up camp "in the vacant lot between [Institute] Park and League Park [?] on Park Avenue." The big guns were towed behind 2½-ton trucks. First Battalion consisted of four batteries, A, B, C, and D, each with four guns. The artillerymen set up one of the guns and placed it on display for viewing by the crowd. Several guides stood by ready to answer any questions the spectators might have concerning the weapons.[17]

Company D, 101st Combat Engineer Battalion, constructed a 216-foot long pontoon bridge with rope handrailing across Institute Pond (Salisbury Pond today). "Known as a model 1935-footbridge, and built on floats, the construction takes exactly 12 minutes for the engineers to build," Boyce wrote. The bridge attracted much attention and most of the visitors took a stroll across. "Each approach was guarded by a sentry with a rifle who admitted only a few persons at one time to cross the narrow span," wrote William H. Moiles, a *Telegram* staff reporter. "One way traffic was in force and as a stream of people completed a crossing in one direction, another stream would start in the opposite directions." The engineer battalion also demonstrated the use of several "assault boats," capable of carrying nine infantrymen and two engineers.[18]

No sooner had the bridge been put up when a World War I veteran, who claimed to be "a member of the old 504th Engineers, approached Col. Roy W. Smith and asked permission to be the first to cross. The old veteran got about half way across, lost his balance after leaning too heavily on one of the rope guides and fell into the water. He managed to maintain his grip on the rope and was hanging half in and half out of the water. Several of the engineers went to his aid "and hauled him to safety — very wet in one area," wrote Boyce.[19]

"Soldiers living in the county were given passes to leave town" and "hundreds of parents drove to the park to pick up their sons and drive them home," Boyce wrote. Other members of the regiment, "who lived too far from here to make home trips, spent the day catching up on sleep," and "swimming at Lake Quinsigamond and the Worcester Boy's Club."[20]

The caption on the back of this picture reads, "Victor Quaranta [H-181], Worcester, Mass." I believe it is a picture of the three-day bivouac at Institute Park — August 1 to August 3, 1941. Notice pond in background (Dorothy M. Orrizzi Collection).

That evening, 4,000 soldiers and civilians attended the regimental dance at the Worcester Memorial Auditorium. During intermission, Gen. Logan, who headed the panel of judges, crowned 17 year old Miss June Perreault of Worcester regimental queen, and presented her with a "gold loving cup." Judges "selected Miss Perreault, a finalist in the 'Miss Massachusetts'" pageant of 1940, "from about 25 young ladies." Pvt. Winthrop E. Annetts of Company A "presented the queen a floral bouquet on behalf of the enlisted men."[21]

On Sunday morning, the regimental chaplains held Protestant and Catholic services. After the noon mess, the troops boarded transport vehicles and the long convoy rolled out of the city, "piped out by the regimental band," amidst "tears mingled with cheers." "Many touching scenes marked the departure as parents said goodbye, sweethearts embraced and husbands parted with wives and children."[22]

The outfit began pulling out for Camp Edwards at 4:30 P.M., "prepared to 'go to war' on Monday morning." After the soldiers departed, "it was impossible to determine that 3,500 men had lived in the park, for the area was perhaps even cleaner than before they came," praised Boyce. "Like a huge fan, the men of each company spread out over their territory and advanced the entire length of the unit's area" picking up "every bit of paper and debris, even cigarette butts and match sticks." It was not until 8:30 P.M. before the last vehicle cleared the city limits.[23]

7

Advanced Infantry Training: June 16–August 15

The first phase of Advanced Infantry Training (AIT), weeks 14 through 17, began on June 16. The training program consisted of brigade field exercises, involving the use of the regimental combat teams (RCTs) as a whole, with supporting antitank, artillery, and engineering units participating. For the 104th Infantry this series of problems included, among others, "repelling enemy [Red Forces] landing attempts along the coast from New Bedford westerly"; "establishing a beachhead along Old Silver Beach [in North Falmouth] and Monument Beach [in Bourne]"; and attacking, capturing, and occupying a number of enemy held positions, including the village of Mashpee, the Cape Cod Airport, and the Canal.[1]

In several of the scheduled exercises, "all movements were made under the cover of darkness." Throughout the advanced exercises, umpires decided the outcome of each problem and graded each unit's overall performance.[2]

The second phase of advanced training, weeks 18–19, which took place beginning in August, involved the introduction of new "Blitz[krieg] tactics" being employed by German forces in eastern Europe. For the first time, armored units brought up light tanks and other armored vehicles, described as "Blitz wagons," for use against the infantry units. During the exercises, Red [enemy] Forces incorporated the use of parachute troops, amphibious tanks, and observation aircraft. The RCTs were subject to simulated combat situations involving "active gas attacks, air attacks, scout-car attacks, and other obstacles and harassing agencies."[3]

During the last week of the exercises, Brigade staged several problems involving the division as a whole. The primary purpose was "to stress security, surprise, reconnaissance and discovery of the enemy situations" during the execution of each of the exercises. The final problem called for the 26th Division to "envelop the left flank of the enemy, a triangular division reinforced by heavy bombardment aviation," and "cut off reinforcements." The advanced exercises ended on August 15, five days before the commencement of scheduled maneuvers at Fort Devens in Ayer, Massachusetts.[4]

* * *

The majority of the time, the ordinary soldier had absolutely no idea what was going on during a particular exercise or maneuver. Company-grade officers (captain or lower) rarely informed the soldiers under their command of the bigger picture. This was typically true during combat as well. Usually, officers gave the non-coms and enlisted men their assignment and told them only what they needed to know for the short term. The military taught the enlisted men never to question orders. Instead of running smoothly, many problems appeared to be an exercise in organized chaos. There were mix-ups and much confusion. Units were in the wrong place at the wrong time, or failed to show up at all as expected. Richard P. Taffe (Hq. Co., 3rd Bn.-181) wrote that "many times" during the maneuvers planners "halted extensive maneuvers in place" so that officers could rearrange troops "to fit the scenarios."[5]

The 26th Division historian wrote, "The individual soldier knew little of what was going on higher up and generally felt that the whole show was completely SNAFU — situation normal all fouled [fucked] up." Paul Fussell noted in his book *Wartime* that there was a "widespread employment of acronyms and abbreviations" by both the Allies and Axis during the war, citing numerous examples. "As usual," he continued, "American troops seemed especially fertile with insult and cynicism ... devising SNAFU, with its offspring TARFU (Things Are Really Fucked Up), FUBAR (Fucked Up Beyond All Recognition, and the perhaps less satisfying FUBB (Fucked Up Beyond Belief)." These he listed among a group, he says, that "became delightful, funny fresh idiom."[6]

When a screw-up occurred, the men chuckled and blamed it on the officers in command. Many wondered, sometimes aloud, "Do these guys have any idea what the hell they're doing?" The author of the YD history stated, "If it were possible to give [the individual soldier] an insight into the mechanics of the higher echelon, he would probably develop a profound respect for the tremendous task of launching an army into attack at the proper time, in the correct place, and with the necessary support." A few officers would take the time to explain the overall situation to the men under their command. The GIs had a greater respect and admiration for these individuals.[7]

* * *

During the early days of training at Camp Edwards and throughout the maneuvers that followed, the YD was equipment poor. Nate Mencow (M-181) says, "In those early days we used broomsticks for rifles." Heavy weapons crews had to use wooden machine guns, while a length of stovepipe (hence the name "Stovepipe Platoon") attached to a wooden base plate served as a mortar. "We had a few mortars in the regiment that looked like logs and a few vehicles that had signs showing what they should have been," wrote Taffe. Troops advanced behind deuce-and-a-half trucks displaying white oilcloth signs on the side, with the word "TANK" in three-foot high black letters. Paul Metcalf (G-101) wrote in the *Yankee Doings*, "Our antitank guns ... were a 2 × 4 mounted on the wheels of a 'Model T,'" and that "pick-up trucks" (½-ton weapons carriers) served as tanks.[8]

(Captain) C. Lincoln Christensen, a munitions expert with the U.S. Army's Ordnance Department, who served as an observer for the War Department during the Carolina Maneuvers, wrote that as he conducted his duties "our nation's unpreparedness became more and more evident.... Sticks in the hands of troops often served as rifles, stove pipes as mortars, wooden cannons were found on tanks, and trucks sometimes masqueraded as tanks." The abundance of "make-believe weapons" in use during the war games resulted in the widespread circulation of jokes and wisecracks among the troops. "A supply sergeant, tending a wooden-barreled tank gun, would say with a straight face that he was waiting for the anti-termite stuff he had requisitioned; others would complain that they had not received the paint and varnish for their stick rifles."[9]

Piper Cubs posing as "fighter-bombers," would zoom in low and drop bags of flour simulating bombs. When the bags hit the target, usually by accident, they would explode into a large white dust cloud. Judges considered men hit by the flour bags casualties and removed them from the exercise. Over time, more and more new weapons, armor, vehicles, including the versatile jeep and peep (a larger version of the jeep later phased out by the army), and other equipment began to arrive.[10]

8

Fort Devens Maneuvers— August 19–September 12, 1941

Just before the end of the advanced training exercises, the 26th Yankee Division received orders from 1st Army Headquarters to take part in the VI Corps maneuvers; a tactical affair scheduled from August 20 to September 12, at Fort Devens in Ayer, Massachusetts, in northern Worcester County. The Devens Maneuvers were the precursor to the upcoming large-scale Carolina Maneuvers that were to take place from October 2 until early December, in which First Army also scheduled the division for participation. The primary purpose of the Devens exercises was to coordinate mechanized attacks—those carried out by armored vehicles, including light and medium tanks, half tracks, and scout cars—with infantry tactics in a two-sided maneuver.

The field exercises, which extended over the terrain north of Fort Devens into New Hampshire to a point just south of the city of Nashua, marked the beginning of a "very rugged" three weeks for the troops of the division. The late summer weather was hot and dusty and the training strenuous. In this chapter, I have once again based all descriptions and accounts of the activities of the 26th Division during this period on those found in the *History of the 104th* [Infantry].[1]

On the morning of Tuesday, August 19, units of the division, approximately 6,000 troops, entrucked and headed for Fort Devens. "The movement from Camp Edwards to Fort Devens was in the form of a tactical problem." Tactical operations en route included the movement of division troops "in four CT [regimental combat teams] on multiple roads," reconnaissance, communication control, and security. Corps scheduled all four regiments to be in position at their assigned assembly areas no later than noon on the 20th. Upon arrival, orders called for commanders of each regiment to make a reconnaissance of their respective areas, establish an MLR (main line of resistance) and reserve area, position artillery batteries and other supporting fire, as well as to post security elements.[2]

Troops spent the overnight bivouac of August 19 at the Upton State Forest (Upton, Mass.) "with orders not to unroll packs and be ready to move out at a moment's notice." The soldiers slept on the bare ground without cover. No sooner had the men bedded down when the clouds opened up with a deluge of rain. It poured hard and steady throughout the night. The men were "positively drenched to the skin," and "sloshed around" on the wet ground all night long. Above the sound of the unrelenting rain, one could hear the muttered curses of the angry, uncomfortable men as they tried unsuccessfully to get some sleep. The historian for Company C, 104th Infantry, wrote, "At first we were miserable, but after getting wet we became silly and laughed and joked all night long."[3]

The following day was extremely hot and all the men "were wishing for cooler weather." They did not have to wait very long for Mother Nature to grant their wish. That night was unseasonably cold for New England, with temperatures dropping below the freezing mark. The next morning, the troops "had to break the ice in the water containers in order to wash."[4]

On the trip to Devens, many of the boys had a "novel way of making friends" with the people in the various towns along the march route. They did so "by dropping notes," with their names and military addresses on them, stating that they were lonely soldier boys away from home, followed by a request asking the finder to become a pen pal. For some weeks afterwards, the men received "hundreds of 'fan' letters in answer to the notes." More "than a few love affairs" began "as a result of correspondence between note-throwers and young ladies who picked them up."[5]

A weary and bedraggled group arrived at Fort Devens on the afternoon of August 20th. MPs directed the convoys to their assigned area on the old artillery range, situated about three miles west of the fort proper, where the troops first set eyes on the pyramidal tent city, set up by an advance detail. This would be their home for the next 23 days.

The location of the site was very disheartening to everyone. One soldier of the 104th Infantry described the bivouac area "as a terribly dusty, hot place" and dubbed it "the dust bowl." The Company C historian remembered "getting off the trucks amidst a veritable cloud of dust and unbearable heat." The troops "lived, ate, and slept in dust," he wrote. Heavy troop and vehicular traffic pulverized the dry soil into a fine black powder that clung to skin and clothing and seeped into the soldiers' belongings. The men complained about the taste and objected strenuously about having to eat it. In addition to the heat and dust, the soldiers battled hordes of annoying flies and mosquitoes.[6]

The "lack of water and bathing facilities" was most upsetting. The water, heavily chlorinated and disguised with lemon juice, made the men wonder what it was they were drinking. Most could not force it down. Supply had to haul potable water daily from the fort to the campsite. While out in the field on maneuvers, a few of the units encamped near streams and small ponds where the men were able to bathe regularly. Shower points were also set up near creeks and ponds with gasoline motors operating the pumps.[7]

The men complained about sleeping on the hard earth, claiming "the difference between the Camp Edwards ground," which is predominantly sandy, "and the Fort Devens terra firma" was "comparable to the difference between a beauty-rest mattress and a hardwood floor."[8]

Much to everyone's chagrin, the men discovered numerous unexploded artillery shells at various locations within the confines of the camp area. Corps Headquarters had to call in a detail of demolitions experts from the engineers to defuse and dispose of the duds, which were still potentially dangerous. The situation was ripe for a serious accident; fortunately, one did not occur. Eventually, Corps attached several explosive ordnance specialists to the division to handle any future problems.[9]

* * *

The VI Army Corps war games, scheduled from August 27 to September 11, pitted the Red Army against the Blue Army. During the period of August 21 to August 25, the regiments participated in a number of small-unit problems. The Massachusetts-New Hampshire boundary separated the Red Army on the north from the Blue Army on the south. On August 26, both sides began concentrating troops at their respective jump off points, with the first exercise beginning the following day. The first maneuver, "#1 Meeting engagement," called for the Blue force to advance against the Red Army, make contact, and drive them northward. Units were to stress "security on the march, reconnaissance, advancing by infiltration."[10]

Other scheduled corps maneuvers included "#2 Pursuit and withdrawal," "#3 Enveloping armored attack and Defense," "#4 Penetrating armored attack, defense." Maneuvers one to four lasted two days each. Maneuver "#5 Reconnaissance, attack and defense" was a four-day affair. A critique for officers followed problems No. 1 and 2, No. 3 and 4, and No. 5, in one of the camp theaters. For one mission, a regimental combat team (RCT) might be part of the Red Army opposing the Blue Army, and for the next, the two sides would reverse roles.[11]

Of the "problems and maneuvers" participated in by the 104th Infantry, the historian for Company C admitted that "most of us understood little." Comments to this effect were quite common. "The men soon learned that it was nothing unusual if on some of the maneuvers no one seemed to know what it was all about," reiterated the Company D historian.[12]

During the maneuvers, a number of major problems occurred, the most prevalent being units getting lost and roadways becoming clogged with vehicles during an advance, halting or delaying the exercises. Another common problem, most annoying to the troops, was that "the kitchen truck kept getting 'captured,'" which meant the men had to go without hot meals for long stretches. Fortunately, apples from nearby orchards were plentiful and the crop ripe and delicious. Handouts from friendly town and farm folks also helped a great deal. Some of the veterans remember the Good Humor man stopping along the roads where they could buy a cool, refreshing drink or a cold, chocolate covered ice cream bar.[13]

The troops trained all day during the week and usually had nights and weekends off. On Friday nights, the base camp cleared out. Men who lived close enough went home. The soldiers visited clubs and nightspots in Ayer, Fitchburg, Worcester, or one of the other nearby cities and towns seeking entertainment and female companionship. One local attraction frequented by the men of the division was the Whalom Water and Amusement Park in nearby Lunenburg. At 7:30 P.M. on Saturdays, the soldiers headed over to the park's main ballroom for a night of dancing to music featured by some of the area's well-known bands. Occasionally, some of the men traveled to Boston for a weekend excursion.[14]

The Fort Devens maneuvers closed on Wednesday, September 10. At exactly 11 A.M. on the 11th, the division broke camp "to the notes of the bugle" and made ready for the return trip to Camp Edwards the following day. That night, all officers and men slept in pup tents. At 8:30 A.M., the convoy began the 120-mile trip back to Cape Cod. No one was sorry to leave. In fact, a few of the guys were so happy to be back that, upon arrival, they "kissed the barracks." The historian for the 104th Antitank Company wrote, "We were glad to be able to sleep in cots, have cool buildings, better meals in our new mess hall [constructed while the unit was in the field] and plenty of hot water for showers." Division awarded every man a nine-day furlough, promised to the troops before they left for Devens.[15]

* * *

Demobilization of the first National Guard units ordered to active duty was set to begin on September 15, with the first of the draftees scheduled for release from the service beginning in October, as their one-year commitments expired. Following Hitler's invasion of the Soviet Union in June 1941, "General George C. Marshall, Army chief of staff, pressed Congress for an extension of the draft and Guard active duty." On August 12, "after divisive congressional debates," the House of Representatives renewed conscription extending the National Guard call-up for six months by a one-vote margin. The Senate quickly followed suit and President Roosevelt "signed the bill into law; the Guard would remain on active duty until at least April

1942." This did not sit well with those affected by the change. The men felt that they had fulfilled their commitment and wanted to go home and get on with their lives. Military historian Christopher R. Gable says that the extension "seriously depressed morale" and that "some enlisted men regarded them as but the latest of many injustices perpetrated by the Army."[16]

The discontent started as a low grumble of protest. During various exercises and events, shouts of "'OHIO,' meaning over the hill in October" could be heard from small numbers of the selectees "that first protected themselves against detection." This slogan became the "war cry" of men "expressing their intention to desert." Dissatisfaction with the situation began to grow and whenever a group of high-ranking guard officials came within hearing range, a chorus of disgruntled men would howl "OHIOOOOOOOHIOOOO," which the 26th Division historian claims, "was extremely embarrassing" to the officers.[17]

In the days between the division's return to Camp Edwards and early October, units spent their time cleaning equipment and preparing for the long trip south to the Carolina Maneuvers area.

On September 15, 1941, the division received a large shipment of the new M1 Garand semi-automatic rifles, enough to equip all units still using the old Springfield and British made Enfield weapons dating to World War I. The job of cleaning the cosmoline (a thick grease coating used to prevent rust) covering the rifles fell to the skeleton crew that remained back at the camp while everyone was away on leave. These men had taken their leaves prior to the Devens maneuvers. Within a "few short days, all rifles were ready for firing at the range." When the furlough period ended, all units of the division participated in "range work."[18]

9

Planning Prior to the Carolina Maneuvers of 1941

The main purpose of the Fort Devens maneuvers was to prepare the 26th Division for the U.S. Army war games (General Headquarters or GHQ maneuvers) scheduled for the Carolinas from October 2 to December 3, 1941. For the first time, division forces would be taking part in large-scale simulated combat exercises involving troops and units from other divisions. The "fundamental goal" of GHQ planners "was to make the maneuvers as much like real war as possible in order to test and train under near battle conditions." The training exercises conducted by the War Department in Louisiana and the Carolinas during the summer and fall of 1941 were the largest mass maneuvers and gathering of troops since World War I, with "nearly half" of the Army's total manpower, approximately 500,000 troops (fighting men plus support personnel), participating "in these enormous field exercises."[1]

A history of this pre-war training program, which was an integral part of the Army's mobilization period between 1939 and 1941, can be found in military historian Christopher R. Gable's excellent work titled, *The U.S. Army GHQ Maneuvers of 1941*. The author outlines the precedents that shaped the thinking of military leaders in the years following the First World War, which set the stage for the formation of new doctrines that would change the structure and composition of the U.S. Army prior to America's entry into World War II.

Brigadier Gen. Harold W. Nelson, who provided the Foreword to the book, wrote:

> The 1941 Maneuvers, ... served to test emerging assumptions about doctrines, organization, as well as equipment. Equally important, they allowed the service's leaders to take the measure of the rising crop of field grade officers who would soon direct the fortunes of the largest military force the nation ever raised. The training tests ... also helped develop the combined-arms doctrine, with infantry-artillery teams supported by independent tank battalions as its centerpiece, that prevailed during the war.

Gen. Nelson praised Gable's book, stating that the work "provides an important and useful addition to the emerging body of historical literature on military training" and, he concluded, "I especially urge our young officers and noncommissioned officers to read and reflect on this important milestone in our Army's victory in World War II."[2]

At the outset of World War I, the U.S. military lacked proper training and was therefore unprepared for modern warfare. "Doctrine was out of date, experience in the command of large forces was nonexistent, and the coordination of arms and services was largely a matter of theoretical conjecture," wrote Gable. "Once war was declared, it took a year and a half to create an American field army capable of mounting an offensive on the Western Front." Lt. General George C. Marshall, then a colonel on the staff of the American Expeditionary Forces (AEF) during the Meuse-Argonne offensive, the last major operation of the war (the war ended on November 11, 1918), "noted with dismay the 'stumbling, blunderings, failures, appeals for help, and hopeless confusion' that characterized the initial phases of the Meuse-Argonne campaign."[3]

Gable provides a list of the major blunders by commanders at this late stage in the war: overoptimistic planners, who underestimated the strength of the enemy, set unrealistic objectives; high-ranking officers proved inept and had to be relieved of command; and last, logistics and communications, vital to the success of any operation, foundered. Tactical commanders who, because of a lack of training and experience, "had never mastered the use of supporting weapons ... resorted instead to ruinous frontal attacks by their brave but artless infantry." This was probably one of the most disturbing aspects of the entire campaign, and the war. On September 1, 1939, the same day Germany attacked Poland, President Franklin D. Roosevelt appointed General Marshall to the position of army chief of staff. Marshall did not intend to allow history to repeat itself.[4]

One week later, on September 8, the president proclaimed a limited national emergency. The purpose of the declaration, Roosevelt reported to the press, was to strengthen "our national defense within the limits of peacetime authorizations." Before the new chief of staff lay the monumental task "of readying the United States Army for another world war."[5]

One of Marshall's first official acts was to place Lt. Gen. Lesley J. McNair in charge of the Army's training program. McNair came to GHQ "following a tour as commandant of the Army's Command and General Staff School at Fort Leavenworth, Kansas." Gable says that McNair held the reputation of being "the brains of the Army" and would in time win acclaim as "the chief architect of the Army's ground forces in World War II." McNair appointed Lt. Col. Mark W. Clark, an ambitious young officer who had rapidly moved up through the ranks, as his deputy director. In 1940, McNair assigned Clark the task of "formulating concrete plans for the next year's training activities." McNair wanted to use the scheduled maneuvers "to give small units experience in teamwork and combined arms." The primary objective of the training program was to weld all of the arms and services of the U.S. Army into a single unified whole.[6]

One important aspect of the planned maneuvers was to evaluate the performance as well as to test the leadership skills of the officer corps of the Regular Army and National Guard units. Marshall referred to the planned maneuvers as the "combat college" for the rising crop of field grade officers who would eventually lead the troops into battle. The 26th Division historian wrote, "This type of large-scale training is the yardstick by which senior officers are measured and marked. And by the length of their mark are they known and permitted to command.... With human lives at stake, the short marked leaders must be purged." He closed, "The military is a ruthless profession in some aspects."[7]

The Army's chief of staff wanted assumptions about emerging doctrine, leadership, and tactics tested and perfected before going into combat. Theoretically, if field commanders made mistakes, Corps Headquarters could detect them early and make corrections and adjustments to ensure they did not happen under actual battle conditions. "Equally important," Marshall stressed, "was the utilization of maneuvers as field laboratories for the armored, antitank, and air forces that had come of age since 1918."[8]

During the German campaigns of 1939 and 1940, Hitler's powerful military machine, spearheaded by panzer divisions, easily rolled over the defenses of Poland and France. German forces used blitzkrieg tactics, a combination of air power, tanks, and subversive warfare to break through or outflank enemy defenses. The destruction of the "once proud French Army" in a span of 10 days during May 1940 "made it clear to all that mechanization had established a new era in warfare." Gable defined mechanization as "the large-scale employment of armored fighting vehicles."⁹

* * *

On May 25, 1941, the last day of the Louisiana maneuvers, Brig. Generals Adna R. Chaffee and Bruce Magruder, the Army's mechanized brigade commanders, met in the basement of the Alexandria, Louisiana, high school to discuss the creation of an autonomous American mechanized branch, independent of the infantry. Also present at the meeting were a number of other interested officers such as Col. George S. Patton, Jr. and Brig. Gen. Frank Andrews, assistant chief of staff. Patton, a tank brigade commander in World War I, was at the time one of the Army's leading experts in tank warfare. General Andrews, acting as a spokesman for the self-appointed committee, delivered the group's recommendations to Marshall.¹⁰

On June 6, 1941, Marshall informed branch chiefs of his decision to create an American mechanized branch of the U.S. Army having independent status. The Army chief of staff named General Adna R. Chaffee, a cavalry officer, as chief of the experimental Armored Force. Gable says, "*Armored* was chosen for the new force because it avoided the Cavalry's *mechanized* as well as the Infantry's *tank*." The newly formed Armored Force comprised the I Armored Corps, strictly a headquarters organization, and two armored divisions, the 1st and 2nd, "the real fighting force of the armored command." Chaffee's first order of business was to field the two armored divisions by bringing together units from existing armored brigades. The War Department officially activated the independent Armored Force on July 10, 1940.¹¹

Marshall placed Major General Bruce R. Magruder (Infantry) in command of the 1st Armored Division and Maj. Gen. Charles L. Scott (Cavalry) in command of the 2nd. In December 1940, recently promoted General George S. Patton, Jr. (Cavalry), considered one of the Army's leading experts on tank warfare at the time, succeeded Scott. Patton promptly named his division "Hell on Wheels." Magruder spent considerable time trying to find an appropriate name for his new command, finally settling on "Old Ironsides." Reportedly, he was impressed with the parallels between the development of the tank and that of the famous Navy fighting ship U.S.S. *Constitution*, known as "Old Ironsides." During the late summer of 1941, the armored force trained to perfect the blitzkrieg tactics used by the German army in its sweep across Europe.¹²

The armored division of 1940, as devised by Chaffee, contained the same basic elements of the German panzer division. It consisted of an armored brigade made up of three armored regiments and one artillery regiment; an infantry regiment of two battalions; an additional artillery battalion; a battalion of engineers; and reconnaissance, supply, and command echelons. Chaffee set the wartime strength of each division at 11,200, with 3,243 vehicles of all types, including 287 M3 light and 120 M2 medium tanks. Like its counterpart, the entire command was fully motorized.¹³

"The role of an armored division," as expressed by Chaffee before the U.S. Congress in 1941, "is the conduct of highly mobile ground warfare, particularly offensive in character, by a self-sustained unit of great power and mobility, composed of specially equipped troops." Massed armored units would be utilized on missions, "either strategical or tactical, whose accomplishment will effect to the maximum the total destruction of the enemy." Chaffee, Gable says, "was unswerving in his advocacy of massed armored units, even to the level of armored armies."¹⁴

* * *

Another major problem that the U.S. Army faced in the prewar period was finding a way to defeat enemy armored operations. An infantry division's "sole defense against armor at

The 37mm M3 Antitank Gun, introduced in 1940, became the first weapon of its type fielded by the U.S. Infantry. Replaced in 1943–44 by the more powerful 57mm Antitank Gun. (Hamlet Publishing Company, Brooklyn, New York).

the end of 1940" was the 37mm antitank gun, first developed in 1936. Most experts deemed the weapon, "a direct copy" of an obsolescent German model, totally inadequate for its intended purpose. The U.S. Army's "Ordnance Department insisted the 37-mm gun had been obsolete from the day it was accepted," wrote Gable. The antitank gun, supposedly, had an effective range of 1,000 yards against light tanks and 500 yards against medium tanks.[15]

The June 1941, issue of *Time* magazine reported that tests conducted by ordnance personnel, showed that the weapon "failed to penetrate even one inch of armor at 100 yards." The protective armor plate carried by an M3 light tank was a maximum of 1.5 inches thick. Only 60 of the pieces were in service, scattered among the infantry regiments and artillery battalions.[16]

General McNair, whom Gable called "perhaps the Army's keenest student of antitank matters," studied various "means of stopping the tank throughout the 1930s, but received little encouragement from superiors." In 1939, as commandant of the Command and General Staff School, McNair initiated a review of antitank measures used to neutralize enemy armor, which culminated in the publication of a field manual written for instructional purposes titled *Antimechanized Defense*. This comprehensive study "proposed that each infantry division should possess a battalion of antitank guns to serve as a highly mobile antimechanized reserve in support of the regimental antiank companies." When faced by an armored attack force, infantry units could call up the antitank reserves to neutralize the threat, which would enable the infantry troops to continue the offensive operation.[17]

In April 1941, General Marshall instructed the Army's G-3 Section (Operations and Training) "to study the feasibility of establishing highly mobile antitank units [battalions], such as those proposed in *Antimechanized Defense*." In less than two weeks, G-3 returned with an affirmative recommendation "for the establishment of divisional antitank battalions to reinforce the regimental antitank companies" (Note: when the army ordered the divisions to triangularize in early 1941, the reorganization plan called for the formation of antitank companies by each regiment).[18]

Initially, the new antitank battalions were composed of .50 caliber machine guns, 37mm antitank weapons, and a limited number of experimental self-propelled 75mm guns mounted on halftracks. During the 1930s, the Army considered the .50-caliber an antitank weapon capable of stopping a light tank at 1,000 yards, which was a virtual impossibility even at far closer ranges. These units later discarded the .50-caliber and 37mm weapons and evolved into the Tank Destroyer Battalions, armed with heavy caliber guns mounted on a lightly armored tank chassis.

As envisioned by McNair, commanders would employ the antitank battalions primarily for defensive purposes in stemming mechanized attacks. A training memo issued by the War Department in September 1940 advised field units "to post a minimum of their antitank guns in frontline positions and to retain as many as possible in mobile reserve." Gable says that both Marshall and McNair eventually came out in favor of expanding the role of the mobile antitank battalions to go on the offensive when the situation dictated, "actually taking the fight to enemy armor." Activation of the new battalions by the War Department came on June 24, 1941.[19]

U.S. Army branch representatives did not universally share McNair's faith in the ability of the antitank forces to defeat armored operations. In fact, there was considerable skepticism from many of the Army's prominent military leaders, including Major Generals Chaffee and George A. Lynch, chief of the Infantry (appointed 1937), who "believed that armored forces could only be countered by other armored forces." During the upcoming maneuvers, commanders would put both the antitank units and the new armored forces to the test.[20]

10

The Carolina Maneuvers: October 2–December 3, 1941

Just before daylight on September 29, 1941, the troops of the 26th Yankee Division departed Camp Edwards by truck convoy and headed for the Carolinas. The division G-3 Operations and Planning Section established three bivouac areas along the 931-mile route, the first at Camp Smith at Peekskill, New York; the second at Hanover, Pennsylvania; and the last at Farmville, Virginia.[1]

The average speed of the long convoy was 25 miles per hour. During the motor march, the "Morale Wagon," a ½-ton Dodge panel truck with loudspeakers on the roof, would move up and down the column playing many of the popular tunes on the current Hit Parade. Between recordings, the truck broadcast the latest World Series score between the New York Yankees and their cross-town rivals, the Brooklyn Dodgers (the Yankees won the series in five games), as well as other news bulletins to keep the men abreast of what was happening around the country and the world.[2]

The truck was on hand on dark mornings after reveille, during the "confusion, swearing, and noise," to provide some mood music for the rising troops. The speakers would announce, "And now, gentlemen, Harry James plays, 'It's So Peaceful in the Country,' and the smooth strains of the record flowed over the entire area." As the long convoy traveled toward its destination, the "dare-devil motorcyclists" of the 26th Reconnaissance Troop "cut in and out of the fast [?] moving convoy maintaining order."[3]

"People along the way made certain we did not starve to death," wrote the historian for Company M, 104th Infantry. One fruit stand owner provided a bushel of apples for the troops of the company. Many kind and generous individuals handed out "gifts of newspapers, magazines, sandwiches, pastries, and even cigarettes." The convoy made a 10-minute rest stop "every hour or two" at convenient spots along the highway to give the troops a chance to get out for a stretch and to relieve themselves. At one of the halts by Company M in a Maryland town, the "well-wishing" owner of a nearby "dairy bar" declared an "open house" and began passing out free ice-cream cones and other treats.[4]

The convoy passed through successive temperature zones until it reached the sweltering heat of the Carolinas. When the units of the 26th Division rolled into McLeod, North Carolina, 55 miles southwest of Raleigh, on October 2, a huge tent city greeted them. The pyramidal tents, erected by an advance detail, would serve as their home base for the next two months. The 104th Infantry historian says, "A mile or two" separated each of the regimental combat teams.[5]

The division arrived in the extreme heat to find the place buzzing with swarms of "dive-

Members of Company H, 181st Infantry in first truck — "Benny Dymek driving, in rear Ray Catmen, Manny Costa, and John Regis" (Sulo O. Ruuska Collection).

10. The Carolina Maneuvers: October 2–December 3, 1941

Company H, 181st Infantry — "Left rear facing camera Lee Zuckerman. From right rear without helmets Al Charon, Arnold Washburn, in front of them Ray Catmen, Stanley Toczko. Middle front to rear Manny Costa, John Regis (with cigarette), Andy Oliva. I am in lower right and behind me Guy Cardillo and Dominick Cialone"— Sulo O. Ruuska. Unfortunately, the caption provided by Sulo is not very clear (Sulo O. Ruuska Collection).

bombing insects." One participant described the "insect inhabitants" of the region as "voracious." The 104th Infantry historian who provided the Introduction to the unit's history wrote, "For the first few days we were almost eaten alive." Exposed parts of the body soon became a mass of welts. McLeod was located in the heart of peach producing country in the central part of North Carolina between Greensboro and Fayetteville. The peach orchards, declared off limits to the troops, stretched endlessly over the relatively flat countryside, "a novel sight for men who thought peaches only grew in Georgia." The region was also at the center of the cotton farming area, which was nearing the end of the harvest season. "Many a cotton bud was sent back to the folks at home," the author wrote.[6]

The maneuvers took place in an area that extended over 6 million acres (9,375 square miles) in parts of North and South Carolina. The area extended from the Camden and Chester area in South Carolina north to Greensboro, North Carolina, a distance of about 130 miles, and from Charlotte, North Carolina on the northwest to Fayetteville on the east, about 113 miles. The War Department chose the Carolinas for a number of reasons: it had a rolling wooded terrain with numerous rivers, streams, swamps, and much open country; "good and poor roads"; and it was "away from sizable communities"; which planners considered ideal for maneuvers. The Kirkwood, "a fine old hotel" in Camden, South Carolina, served as the main headquarters for the GHQ staff and as a press relations center. C. Lincoln Christensen, who described the Kirkwood as "elegant," reported that the hotel "was filled with U.S. Army and visiting foreign military officers—many of whom were high-ranking—and with media representatives from around the globe."[7]

For the most part, the region was sparsely populated. Ellerbe, five miles away, the nearest town of any size to the base camp of the 104th Infantry, had a "population of 500, [the] majority of whom were Negroes." The next nearest town was Rockingham, about 15 miles distant. Most rural towns in this part of North and South Carolina were nothing more than a small cluster of homes, some painted, some not, a general store, and a church, usually located at a crossroads. "A striking characteristic of the country is the number of churches scattered about. One finds them everywhere," wrote the author of the 104th's history who provided the section on the types of scheduled maneuvers. He described the southern churches as "squat, old buildings," with a small cemetery located in the rear "or in the near vicinity."[8]

For the first few days, the regiments of the 26th occupied their time carrying out the usual camp duties and getting used to their new surroundings. While waiting for the maneuvers to commence, each of the regiments conducted small unit training and scheduled "conditioning hikes 12–16 miles long."[9]

The maneuvers, set to begin the second week, called for two shorter exercises of approximately five days duration each, culminating with a massive 19-day problem in two phases, the first, named "The Battle of the Pee Dee River," and the second, a shorter problem, called "The Battle for Camden" (South Carolina).

The Carolina war games, described by one company historian from the 104th as "the maneuver to end all maneuvers," began on October 6, 1941. GHQ divided participating forces into two groups: the First Army, designated the Blue forces, and the second, a reinforced IV Corps, the Red forces, representing the Blue and Red nations respectively. Red and Blue armbands identified opposing soldiers.[10]

Lt. General Hugh A. Drum, the First Army commander, commanded the Blue Army, a traditional infantry-oriented force composed of three corps (I, II, and VI), consisting of eight infantry divisions, one of which was the 26th, and six regimental-size antitank

Company H, 181st Infantry—Al Charon, Guy Cardillo, and Dominick Cialoni—identification by Guido Fratturelli (Sulo O. Ruuska Collection).

10. The Carolina Maneuvers: October 2–December 3, 1941　　75

181st Infantry encampment — McLeod, N.C. (Dorothy E. Dineen Collection — Massachusetts National Guard Military Museum and Archives, Worcester).

groups. During the first phase, the VI Corps Headquarters charged the 26th Division with securing and holding the high ground in the vicinity of the town of Candor, North Carolina.

The opposing Red Army, commanded by Maj. Gen. Oscar W. Griswold, was a highly mechanized armored force comprised of the IV Corps, which included the 43rd "Winged Victory" (after 1943) and the 31st "Dixie" Infantry Divisions, and the 4th Motorized Infantry "Ivy" (from IV) Division, and armored corps troops consisting of the newly formed 1st and 2nd Armored Divisions. The 43rd Division was composed of troops from Maine, New Hampshire, Connecticut, and Rhode Island, and the 31st of troops from Alabama, Florida, Louisiana, and Mississippi. Griswold's plan was to use the mobility and firepower of his two armored divisions and one motorized division to force the Blue army off balance at the very outset and to keep it off balance. Numerically, the Blue army had the advantage with 195,000 men to the IV Corps' 100,000 men.[11]

The Red Army had at its disposal a considerable number of U.S. Army Air Corps units from the 3rd Air Support Command using ground attack aircraft for support, which gave IV Corps air superiority.

Maj. Gen. Henry H. "Hap" Arnold, chief of the Air Corps, offered "600 combat aircraft, organized into 4 bombardment groups [2 medium and 2 light] and 4 fighter groups, plus additional noncombat aircraft." This included "2 medium bomber groups of twin engine B-25 and B-26 aircraft, 2 light bomber groups flying twin engine A-20 attack planes and single engine A-24 dive bombers, and 4 pursuit groups of single engine P-39, P-40, and P-43 aircraft as well as some twin engine P-38 interceptors." Gable noted that all of the aircraft types, "with the exception of the P-43 fighters, were modern enough to eventually see extensive service in World War II, and some were already in action with the Allies."[12]

General Griswold "directed his air commander, Col. Asa N. Duncan, to exploit the Red superiority in medium bombers, by destroying the Pee Dee bridges and keep them destroyed."

181st Infantry encampment — McLeod, N.C. (Sulo O. Ruuska Collection).

Blue forces had to be constantly on the alert for sudden air strikes. During the maneuvers, raids by Red bombers, flying in at low level to drop their flour sack bombs, resulted in heavy casualties and the loss of a considerable number of vehicles for the Blue forces. This distinct advantage, combined with the force's added mobility, Griswold felt, would offset the Red army's inferior numbers.[13]

The north-south Pee Dee River, which split the maneuvers area, served as "the international boundary line between Blue and Red nations." Both armies were given "offensive missions designed to produce a collision in the region between the Catawba[-Wateree] and Pee

Dee Rivers." Both rivers ran in a north-south direction, approximately 60 miles apart. Gen. McNair instructed Drum to cross the Pee Dee, "advance westward into Red territory, and prevent the Red army from crossing the Catawba River in force." McNair gave Griswold "the mission of crossing the Catawaba, marching east to the Pee Dee, and preventing a Blue invasion of the Red nation."[14]

It was the Blue general's intention "to neutralize Red armor with his six special antitank units and thus gain freedom for his eight infantry divisions to grapple with and grind down IV Corps' two." Command Headquarters used day and night attacks by the Red Army's mechanized units to familiarize opposing infantry units with methods of assault and other tactics used by a mechanized enemy.[15]

Antitank units performed better than expected, and played an integral part in the Blue army's successes during the first phase of the maneuvers. However, during the evaluation process that followed, the effectiveness of the antitank weapons came into question (see below).

The second phase, a shorter problem, designated as "The Battle for Camden" (South Carolina), presented an entirely new scenario. Instead of assigning offensive missions to both sides, GHQ ordered the smaller Red force to defend the town of Camden. This time, the international boundary was the east-west Monroe-Wadesville highway that separated the Blue force on the north from the Red on the south. In this exercise, General Headquarters divided air support squadrons equally. GHQ also attached the 502nd Parachute Battalion to Drum's command. The second phase was set to begin at 6:30 A.M. on November 25.[16]

Jim Tomasello — Company L, 181st Infantry, McLeod, N.C. (Dorothy E. Dineen Collection — Massachusetts National Guard Military Museum and Archives, Worcester).

* * *

All exercises took place under the watchful eye of designated umpires authorized to act as mediators. General Headquarters provided one umpire for each rifle company, approximately 36 per division. "These officers," Gable wrote, "would travel with the frontline units for the purpose of imposing the effects that would have resulted from real combat." Umpires evaluated offensive and defensive tactics and stratagems and ruled on the effectiveness of units in battle. During the various encounters, umpires declared men, as well as vehicles of all types, casualties and these were lost to service for a predetermined length of time, usually

Francis Kelly, Ed Bartula, Francis "Red" Fisher, James P. Bearsley, and Richard Goldberg — Company L, 181st Infantry, McLeod, N.C. (Dorothy E. Dineen Collection — Massachusetts National Guard Military Museum and Archives, Worcester).

six hours. On a number of occasions, umpires argued amongst themselves and had to rely on superior officers from GHQ to resolve major differences.[17]

During the maneuvers, GHQ wanted to impose as much realism as possible. The supply of blank ammunition, although "still below the Army's needs, had improved over the previous year." For the calendar year 1941, the adjutant general appropriated expenditures for 500,000 .50 caliber blanks, an equal number of 37mm antitank blanks, 45,000 75mm blanks, 4,000,000 .30-caliber blanks, 170,000 antitank rounds, and 10,000 practice land mines. "To make the sound of battle even more realistic, the Army authorized $15,000 for the construction of seven loudspeaker-equipped sound trucks to broadcast prerecorded battlefield noises."[18]

With regard to the demolition of bridges and the use of roadblocks, GHQ required that engineers "simulate such operations in detail.... In the case of roadblocks, real obstacles were to be constructed at roadside." When necessary to simulate the destruction of a bridge, "GHQ required the engineers to assemble the necessary materials and to place simulated charges on the span." Umpires were required to supervise all operations of this type and after determining that "a bridge had been properly destroyed," to post a sentry with "a signed declaration" stating the same as well as to mark the bridge with a flag. Units encountering such obstacles were required to take "appropriate repair measures" which, for example, "involved the actual construction of a new bridge beside the theoretically destroyed one."[19]

Gable included a tale involving the simulated demolition of a bridge, related by then Col. Dwight D. Eisenhower in his book, *At Ease: Stories I Tell to Friends*:

An umpire decided that a bridge had been destroyed by an enemy attack and flagged it accordingly. From then on, it was not to be used by men or vehicles. Shortly, a corporal brought his squad up to

10. The Carolina Maneuvers: October 2–December 3, 1941

the bridge, looked at the flag, and hesitated for a moment, then resolutely marched his men across it. The umpire yelled at him:

'Hey, don't you see that that bridge is destroyed?'

To which "the corporal answered, 'Of course I can see it's destroyed. Can't you see we're swimming?'"[20]

GHQ "discouraged taking prisoners, inasmuch as soldiers would receive no training while in prisoner of war (POW) stockades," wrote Gable. "Once a day, GHQ would arrange the transfer of prisoners, who would then be taken to their own army's replacement depot and processed as if they were combat replacements for their original units." This did not always happen as planned (see next paragraph). C. Lincoln Christensen, acting in the capacity of a War Department observer attached to the First Army during the maneuvers, wrote, "In these games, if you maneuvered your forces into an advantageous position without detection and sighted your enemy, you were considered to have captured him."[21]

Unknown soldiers with telescope (Sulo O. Ruuska Collection).

In some cases, one side or the other surprised and captured entire units and held the troops in the "Prisoner of War Camp" at Camden, South Carolina. "Prisoners were taken and were not returned to units, in some cases, for a week or more," wrote one historian for the 104th Infantry. Christensen related that at one point, the 2nd Reconnaissance Battalion of Patton's 2nd Armored Division captured Lt. General Hugh A. Drum, commander of the Blue Army, "while inspecting troops trying to cross the Pee Dee River." Drum, greatly embarrassed by the incident, "suffered the indignity of an hour's imprisonment."[22]

* * *

Christensen wrote that the Carolina Maneuvers "amply revealed how unprepared we were for the serious business of war." Christensen's mission, as an engineer with the U.S. Army Ordnance Department, "was to gather specific information for [his] superiors related to ordnance equipment effectiveness and reliability." Much of what he witnessed during the mock battles—the tactical blunders, the lack of experience on the part of the leadership, the severe shortage of weapons and equipment, and the deficiencies of armored vehicles and weapons—convinced him of "the nation's unpreparedness." Christensen described the Carolina Maneuvers as "amateurish war play."[23]

Christensen spoke of the substitution of "simulated" weapons for the real thing, mentioned in an earlier chapter, "Sticks in the hands of troops often served as rifles; stove pipes as mortars; wooden cannons were found on tanks, and trucks sometimes masqueraded as tanks." Occasionally, a soldier would jump out of the bushes, Christensen says, point a broomstick rifle at an opposing soldier, and shout "Bang! You're dead!" The *History of a Combat Regiment* (104th) also notes men standing guard with broomstick rifles. Christensen commented that "Jokes and wisecracks about our make-believe weapons circulated among the troops" (see earlier chapter).[24]

Everywhere Christensen went, despite his observer's badge, which supposedly allowed him to move about freely, he was "viewed with suspicion" and questioned numerous times "as a possible spy." However, in every instance, the written orders he carried on his person satisfied his interrogators and they allowed him to pass.

Christensen relates a humorous incident that happened during a ceremony held in honor of the governors of North and South Carolina at the Kirkwood hotel just prior to the start of the maneuvers. The Army prepared a 19-gun salute using a "motley collection of cannons—some of which ... dated back to the Civil War." The officer in charge gave the order to load and fire. The first cannon went off, producing "a veranda shaking roar." Each successive shot "was less impressive, and so on down the line." Christensen says, "The very last cannon released a feeble pop — about as loud as the sound of a tire blowout — which brought smiles and a few snickers from the less controlled onlookers."[25]

* * *

Wooden machine gun — Orlando Vitone, Company H, 181st Infantry (Sulo O. Ruuska Collection).

Over the course of the next several weeks, there were numerous skirmishes by infantry units of the 26th Division with enemy forces. The YD troops were constantly on the move. Forced foot marches of twelve to sixteen miles to engage the enemy were the norm. Units would attack and withdraw. The men dug an endless number of foxholes. In early October, temperatures exceeded 100 degrees. On October 4, 1941, the high was 111 degrees. The historian for Company D, 104th Infantry, a heavy weapons company, wrote, "Lugging the heavy guns for hours at a time, with the hot Carolina sun beating down, was a back breaking job." In between days of constant fighting, there were those of boring inaction.[26]

The troops of the 26th Division frequently crossed and re-crossed the "muddy" Pee Dee, referred to by the regimental historian as a "chocolate-colored body of water," over "highways, bridges, pontoon bridges," and "in assault boats, and by a great variety of other means of transportation." The Company B (104th) historian wrote, "I will remember the Pee Dee for we guarded it ... fought for it, and even had the questionable pleasure of drinking it."[27]

The author who provided the section "Looking Backwards" in the "History of the 104th," related that Stephen Collins Foster actually wrote his "immortal song"—"Way Down Upon the Swanee River"—about the Pee Dee River. The "title," he claims, "was later changed for reasons of harmony." He commented, "The neighborhood and the living conditions of the people in the vicinity showed us why Foster wrote as he did when he said, 'That's where my heart is yearning ever, that's where the old folks stay.'"[28]

The Carolina soil consists of red clay, used in making red bricks and ceramics, which one company historian noted, "sticks like glue to everything." Ever-present were the clouds of thick red dust, "the most hated enemy," that followed every vehicle as it traveled over narrow dirt back roads, choking the men and irritating their eyes. After a movement, "the entire personnel looked like weird statues," wrote 1st Lt. Owen W. Eames, the Protestant chaplain for the 104th Infantry. Each truck raised so much dust that the one following could not see the one ahead, causing numerous accidents and pile-ups.[29]

Airplanes of the opposing Red Army watched for dust clouds on the roads and dropped their flour sack bombs on the columns. Drivers soon learned why it was necessary to maintain march discipline and to carefully conceal vehicles when off the road.

Mass movement of 26th Infantry units generally took place at night to prevent detection. There were some wild rides in vehicles at night during blackout conditions traveling at breakneck speeds. The Company D (104th) historian described a blackout ride "as a sum total of a hair raising experience by the simple addition of 1 'cowboy' driver, zero visibility due to the dust, and 2 large drainage ditches on the edge of the narrow road." On November mornings, as temperatures began to drop, drivers often had the added disadvantage of peering through small openings in windshields thick with frost.[30]

Between problems, the units either stayed in

Above: Al Charron, Company H, 181 Infantry. *Below:* Sulo Ruuska (both photographs from Sulo O. Ruuska Collection).

Above and opposite: "Somewhere in Carolina — A Souvenir Picture — Army Maneuvers of 1941" (courtesy The Dietz Press, Richmond, Virginia).

the field or returned to the base camp. Groups of men went into town by truck to take a shower, see a movie, or take in whatever entertainment local nightspots and roadhouses had to offer. At night in the field, the men would build a nice warm bonfire, permitted when there was a lull in the maneuvers, sit around and relax, have a few beers, shoot the breeze and swap stories. Sometimes there would be "song fests" around the campfire, with "inspired solos," harmonizing by a trio or quartet, or group sing-alongs. "Amateur Night" was a regular feature of some of the companies.[31]

Division used the huge horse vans of the 101st Cavalry Regiment (New York National Guard), when available, to transport the troops and move them into position for conducting a surprise pre-dawn attack against an enemy force. The men had to ride in the back of the horse vans for as long as 12 to 14 hours at a time. A mixture of manure and urine soaked hay littered the floor of the carriers, due to neglect on the part of the cavalrymen to clean up after the last shipment of horses. The men swept the vans out as best they could, but the odor was ever-present. After a while, everyone got used to the smell.[32]

* * *

Kennett says that periodic contact with friends and family was absolutely essential to the GIs' morale during the maneuvers. The homesick guardsmen exchanged letters and postcards with friends and loved ones, but the quickest and most direct means was the telephone call. During the 1941 maneuvers, "the Army discovered that soldiers would often stop at a farmhouse, ask to use the telephone, and call their homes collect to say hello from the field, a practice the authorities condemned as 'unwarlike.'"[33]

One thing the troops could always rely on was the mess truck getting lost. Hungry and irritable, the men had to resort to a reserve supply of canned goods, crackers, and other food

Tanks — Carolinas (Sulo O. Ruuska Collection).

items, originally intended for snacking, while they lasted. Troops "would descend like locusts" upon the crossroads stores and roadside gas stations to stock up on soda, candy, and smokes, or whatever else that might be available, usually cleaning them out "to the bare walls." These forays to local grocery and convenience stores became "a daily military objective."[34]

"Throughout our stay in the South," wrote the historian for Company B (104th), "there was a noticeable lack of good drinking water and what little we had was either heavily chlorinated or a by-product of the Pee Dee." The water usually consisted of "3 parts chlorine to 1 of water" (an exaggeration?), when it was available. "Few drank it," said the D Company (104th) historian. If soda was not available, many resorted to drinking water from rivers, streams, and ponds.[35]

This may very well have been the cause of the high number of dysentery cases among the men, mentioned by illustrator Earl Mayan, a member of Company C, 84th Combat Engineer Battalion. Dysentery, Mayan wrote, is "a condition that knocks you out completely." It "MAKES YOU WISH YOU WERE DEAD; you really don't care about anything, no matter what it is." To combat the problem, Mayan said he tried, while in the field, to keep his mess-kit clean, "but it is very difficult under these conditions," he commented.[36]

When hot food was available in the field, the mess section usually provided GI cans (30-gallon corrugated garbage cans) to clean mess kits, two with hot water and soap and a third with clean hot water to rinse. Unfortunately, most of the time the water never got hot enough to kill the bacteria that caused the disease.

After days of hiking without sufficient water or regular meals, the men were hungry, thirsty, and thoroughly exhausted. Mayan wrote, "The stomach ... is insatiable. I'm always hungry, no doubt due to the enormous amount of energy used, daytime, as well as on night missions, which has been happening quite a bit lately."[37]

The winter season was fast approaching, and the troops had to contend with extreme temperature changes. During the day, men sweltered under the broiling Carolina sun. Hot days turned into cold nights, where temperatures often dropped well below the freezing mark. There were periods of continuous rain for days at a time, soaking troops to the skin. Bone chilling cold combined with rain made for very uncomfortable conditions both in camp and out in the field. Mayan described what it was like to his wife in a letter dated November 30, 1941:

> We are plagued by the constant rain, we function, if you could call it that, in a vast morass of Carolina "muck." Vehicles of many kinds, including tanks, slide off the roads, getting bogged down, unable to move. I don't believe I have been dry for months, even perhaps longer, as one loses track of time under conditions like this. My God, Jean, I would give anything, anything, to have a shower and dry clothes. Ah, just to snuggle up in a warm blanket, in a shelter with a roof over my head.

Because of the adverse weather conditions, sleep was nearly impossible at times. No sooner would the men drift off in slumber, when the non-coms would roust them for a night movement or operation. Many men slept fitfully, troubled by the stories of poisonous snakes and spiders that circulated.[38]

Earl Mayan had this to say about the maneuvers he described as "'mucking' around in the mud of Carolina" in an e-mail to the author dated December 14, 2002: the training was "dirty, tedious, also dangerous, to a lesser extent than combat, but a nasty, exhausting experience." To this he added, "I remember the mud, the ever-present red dust, everywhere, the accidents, the blue and red armies, the chiggers, the confusion, the antiquated equipment, the blackout, ah, and the great relief finally to get to a regular base for a shower and some decent food." On October 19, 1941, Mayan wrote to his wife:

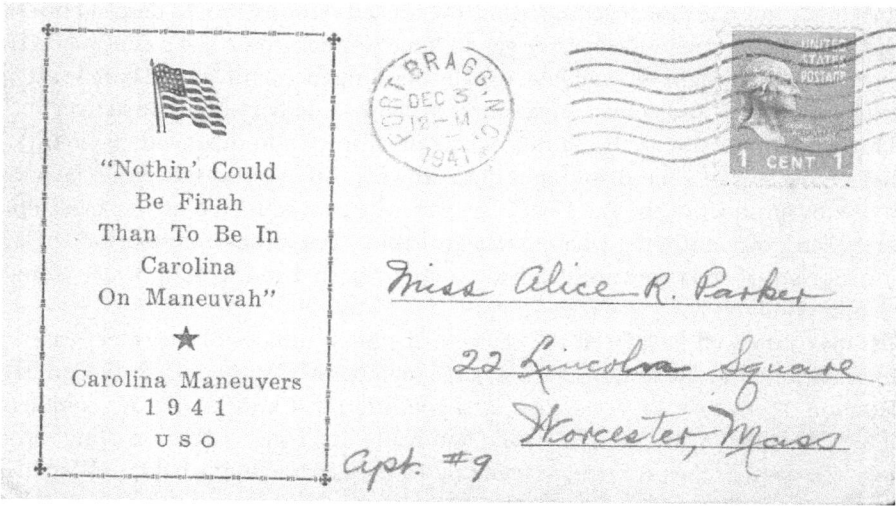

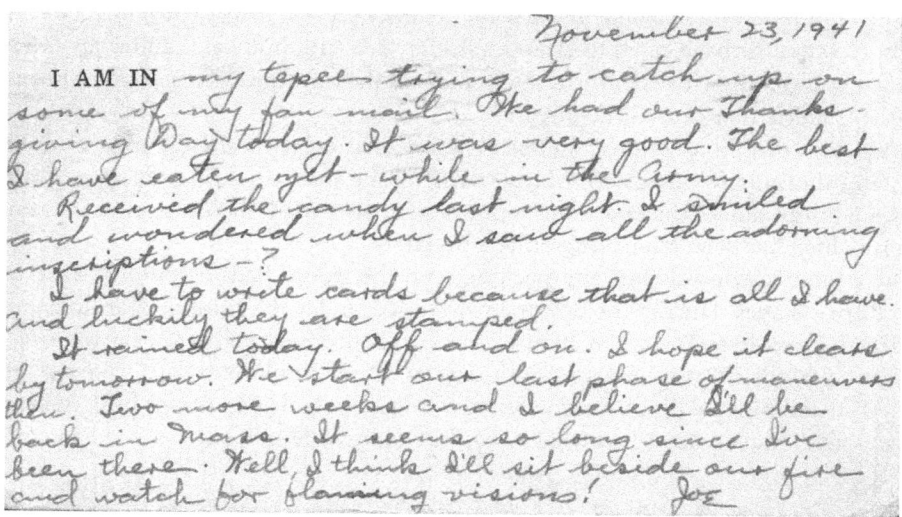

Postcard from Joe (not my father), on maneuvers in the Carolinas, to Miss Alice R. Parker of Worcester, Mass.

We have just returned [to the base camp] from the war games, dirty, fatigued, infected by chiggers, but happy to get back to where we can get cleaned up and enjoy a few of the amenities of life again.... We are all in bad shape after two long months in the field, blistered cracked lips, sores on our bodies from chigger infections, and feet infested with a fungus that tenaciously resists the bright purple medicine provided by the medics as a cure.

The "common things" Mayan enjoyed prior to the maneuvers, "the ordinary things we take for granted"—"a cold beer ... a movie," or "the luxury of a shower"—he said, "take on a critical importance, and small things ... take on magical qualities." While "out in this God-forsaken place" at night, "on the perimeter of the maneuver area, you are reminded of this fact again and again. The life you have known is reduced to a primitive level; there is nothing to anticipate; nothing to enjoy; and I wonder if anything is worth this kind of suffering...," he lamented.[39]

10. The Carolina Maneuvers: October 2–December 3, 1941   87

"Bob Gibson leaning on tank," Fort Devens Maneuvers (Sulo O. Ruuska Collection).

Mayan told his wife about one of the soldiers in his outfit, who claimed to have seen action in the Spanish Civil War (1936–1939), and said "what we were going through was far worse than 'real battle,' except you stood a very good chance of getting through it without getting shot." Despite all Mayan's grumbling and complaints, he actually expressed high praise for the military. In a letter dated November 18, 1941, near the close of the games, he wrote, "These maneuvers are as realistic as the army can make them, and, to my mind, they have succeeded admirably. It is as close to the actual experience on the battlefield as you can get with the exception of using 'DUMMY AMMUNITION.' These so-called BLANKS still explode ferociously, are dangerous, and can scare the hell out of you if they catch you unexpectedly."[40]

Units of the Red and Blue armies made surprise attacks in the dead of night. Riflemen and supporting machine gun units from the heavy weapons companies opened fire, "routing the 'enemy' from a sound sleep and putting them to flight." Sometimes, it would be the other way around. Most nights, units were lucky if they had to move only two or three times. The men were thankful if the non-coms allowed them to sleep as late as 3 or 4 A.M. When the night exercises ended, the men usually slept where they dropped. After a time, they learned to get by with just a few hours' shut-eye. During a lull in the action, or during brief 10-minute rest stops, men took catnaps. The lieutenant would no sooner say, "Take 10 when, it seemed, he would shout "On your feet."[41]

* * *

Generally, the men were free on weekends, and unless otherwise restricted to base or on duty, the companies issued passes. Headquarters arranged for convoys to transport the men to nearby cities and towns. Greensboro, Winston-Salem, Raleigh, Charlotte, and smaller towns like Carthage, Rockingham, Pinehurst, and Southern Pines were some of the places they visited. Many men had pleasant memories of the times on leave in North Carolina, the "friendly associations" and the "warm southern hospitality of their southern hosts ... that made their weekends so pleasant and happy." The visiting soldiers "were wined and dined and fussed over" by members of the community, rich and poor alike. None of the veterans will ever forget the delicious southern fried chicken; for most it was their first taste of this specialty.[42]

People would drive around with signs on the inside of the windshield that read, "Hello soldier, going my way?" With hotels filled, theater owners stayed open most nights to provide the GIs with a place to sleep. Citizens drove around "at the wee small hours of the morning to look for forlorn and weary soldiers with no place to sleep" and graciously invited them to stay overnight in their homes. "These people were total strangers to us, yet all did that little something to make us feel as if we were at home and not in some strange place," wrote one 104th historian. Another commented that the soldiers "made thousands of friends, whom we shall never forget."[43]

Some men attended college football games, dances, parties, or went out to dinner at a restaurant or as a guest of one of the many host families. One special occasion was a formal dance held at the Women's College in Greensboro on Saturday nights, attended by more than 300 beautiful southern ladies. Others went on sightseeing trips to points of interest, tobacco plants, stately old pre–Civil War southern plantation homes, and scores of other popular tourist sites.[44]

The USO had established clubs in the larger cities where troops took advantage of the hot showers, reading and writing rooms, and the many social functions and other activities that the organization sponsored. There was always something doing at the clubs—shows, dances, or just a quiet evening if preferred. Many went to the local YMCA during the hot weather to lounge around the pool.[45]

One of the "greatest benefits" of the maneuvers, one historian of the 104th emphasized, was that it brought together in Carolina "Yankee soldiers and boys from Dixie, alike in Khaki, bedding down together in the woods, being 'friendly enemies,' with a constantly growing emphasis upon the 'friendly' relationship." The men from both regions got along famously in a spirit of cooperation and mutual assistance making the maneuvers the unparalleled success that they were. The author closed with, "More and more did all of our soldiers from the North and the South grow to realize we were all one nation preparing to fight a common foe."[46]

* * *

Thanksgiving Day (November 27) found the troops of the 26th Division thoroughly worn out and exhausted. Later that morning, General Headquarters relieved the division to give the men a well-deserved rest. Everyone was looking forward to a nice holiday dinner when, two hours later, the order came down from GHQ to commence the second phase of the maneuvers. GHQ ordered the advance on the city of Monroe, North Carolina, in a night maneuver. From a distance away, the men could smell the aroma of the "perfumed cavalry vans" waiting to transport them to the jump off point. The holiday meal, eaten in the vans, consisted of a few "withered apples" and "dried up jam sandwiches," washed down with "nice tasty chlorine juice." The troops were bitterly disappointed.[47]

Units of the division closed on the city of Monroe under cover of darkness in a surprise movement, catching many units of the Red Army unaware. Blue units captured, or put out of action, a considerable number of gun emplacements, tanks and other armored vehicles, and took hundreds of prisoners. "There was street fighting on a large scale, machine guns chattered their messages of 'death,' rifle fire flashed from street corners and from behind hastily thrown up fortifications." The Blue forces managed to push the Red defenders to the outskirts on the far side of the urban area, "thereby capturing the city."[48]

The war games finally ended at 4:20 P.M. on November 28, when GHQ declared an armistice. A wild and jubilant celebration ensued with elated troops honking horns, yelling, and everyone "trying to fire more blanks than his buddy." All guns blazed away to the last cartridge. The Antitank Company historian for the 104th reported that units fired off more 37mm blanks than they had during the entire maneuvers.[49]

A dirty but happy bunch arrived back at the bivouac area that night to clean up and begin preparations for the return trip to Camp Edwards. On the Sunday following the Thanksgiving holiday, mess sections treated the men of the 26th to "a grand dinner" of roast turkey with all the fixings.[50]

11

Conclusions of the Carolina Maneuvers

The first phase of the Carolina maneuvers was clearly a decisive victory for General Drum's Blue forces. Antitank units of the Blue Army successfully neutralized the Red Army's armored forces, "exactly as Drum had planned." The two armored divisions of the Red Army "suffered the staggering total of 844 tanks ruled out," 82 more than called for by their combined tables of organization (TO&E). Gable noted that even though Griswold's Red forces "had suffered the most thorough maneuvers defeat to date," the general and his command "had not disgraced themselves." Faced with "overwhelming numerical odds, IV Corps had never been able to disengage its mobile forces for decisive blows without thinning its lines to the breaking point." As a result, attacks launched by armored units "were conducted in piecemeal fashion" and therefore lacked effectiveness.[1]

General McNair, who participated in the final critique, "suggested that Griswold could have used motorized infantry and reconnaissance elements to contain the Blue bridgeheads on the first day, leaving the armored division free for decisive maneuver."[2]

Even though the Blue commander was satisfied with "the thoroughness with which First Army antitank units neutralized ... the 1st Armored Division," he called into question the effectiveness of certain measures during the general critique held on November 30. Gable points out that many of the tanks ruled out of action by umpires "were destroyed by questionable means." Of the 844 Red tanks lost, 113 "fell victim to the useless .50-caliber antitank machine gun and another 47 to the highly unrealistic flour-bag grenade." Either the 37mm guns or the new 75mm half-track weapons, of which there were a limited number, had destroyed the rest. "GHQ observers also asserted that antitank units" were given far "too much credit for the armored force's difficulties."[3]

General McNair "did acknowledge that such tank losses may well have been unrealistically high." Overall, McNair expressed his satisfaction with the performance of the antitank units.[4]

The second phase of the games, the battle for Camden, which lasted four days, "ended without a clear tactical decision." It was, however, determined that IV Corps (Red Army) had essentially "fulfilled its assignment," which was the defense of Camden. "At the termination of the maneuvers," the final report stated, "Red still retained possession of the area necessary for the accomplishment of its assigned mission." Gable contends that during the second phase the "Red armor regained much of the prestige lost in the first maneuver."[5]

The "major import of the maneuver was to re-emphasize the crying need for more infantry within the armored division and better cooperation between infantry and armored divisions." GHQ observers repeatedly noted "that the paucity of infantry within the armored division cost the tankers dearly." In the final analysis, GHQ "was beginning to learn that the tank was not an irresistible offensive weapon and that a small army could not expect to overwhelm an alert, determined, numerically superior foe merely because the inferior foe possessed armored units."[6]

* * *

During C. Lincoln Christensen's assignment as an observer for the U.S. Army's Ordnance Department, he soon found himself "heavily involved in considering the suitability" of the M3A1 standard medium tank "for combat operations." The primary concern of War Department officials, "based on what had been learned from armored operations [conducted by the British?] in Europe," was that the M3A1 "would be unable to compete against tanks of some possible opponents." Of major concern, was the "efficiency of the engine—a Wright Aeronautical nine-cylinder Whirlwind air-cooled radial engine—a more powerful version of the type of engine that was in Spirit of St. Louis, the plane Charles Lindbergh had used on his transatlantic flight." Based on field observations, it did not take Christensen long to discover "that the engine was not delivering its rated power, resulting in sluggish performance." He concluded that the engine was "overheating" within "its confined area in the tank, which resulted in various mechanical problems."[7]

The "general commanding the Ordnance Department section that had produced the tank," Christensen's "boss," was summoned to attend "a critique session of the top brass of the War Department ... scheduled to take place in a large tent in a field near Camden." The general had ordered Christensen to write up "a brief report," which he says he did "under severe pressure," as well as to attend the meeting to provide "technical support." After discussing other issues, the panel took up the matter of the M3A1's reliability under simulated combat conditions during the maneuvers. The tank "soon came under fire for sluggish performance and poor mechanical reliability, as well as for certain combat design weaknesses—particularly its high silhouette and the limited traverse and low muzzle velocity of its 75mm gun."[8]

When called upon by the chairman of the committee to present his assessment of the tank's performance, Christensen's commanding officer "made a detailed and spirited defense of the M3A1, declaring in conclusion that it was better than the British heavy tank." At that point, an incensed "high ranking general at a command level in the maneuvers exploded, saying '[Expletive]! We're not going to fight the British!'"[9]

As a result of the outcome of the meeting, the Ordnance Department "soon produced a modification kit for the M3A1 that greatly improved performance and reliability." In the spring of 1942, Christensen became part of a team involved "in scheduling the modification of existing engine installations." The new model became the M3A5, "which had a lower silhouette, a fully rotating turret, and a higher muzzle-velocity cannon—called the General Grant by the British." Christensen reported that the improved model "was used very effectively by Bernard Montgomery in the desert fighting against Erwin Rommel and his somewhat better armed PzKw.IIIs and IVs, beginning at the battle of Gazala in June 1942."[10]

* * *

General Headquarters considered the many mistakes, failures, and blunders that occurred throughout the maneuvers due to confusion, carelessness, and sometimes ignorance, all part of the learning process. Units of the 26th Division frequently ran headlong into a concealed enemy tank position; encountered surprise tank attacks from the woods that annihilated entire companies; and were, on numerous occasions, caught "flat footed" by advancing enemy units and taken prisoner. From these mistakes, the officers and men learned the right and wrong way to do things, as well as how to prevent future mix-ups and problems from occurring. Through experience, they also learned the most effective measures and countermeasures to take during a specific tactical situation to minimize losses to men, equipment and materials. The knowledge gained in tactics was invaluable (see below).[11]

Christensen's assessment of U.S. Army forces during the Carolina Maneuvers, based upon his recollections and notes taken as an observer, was that the military was far from ready to go to war which, at the time, caused him a great deal of worry and concern. He did admit, that despite "the scarcity of real weapons" and the oftentimes unavoidable mistakes made by inexperienced leaders and troops, the "temper of the maneuver operations was generally serious." In the intervening years, his opinion of the military's preparedness in 1941 had changed little. What had changed, however, was his appreciation for the value the extensive war games had on future combat operations.[12]

Christensen writes, "In retrospect, I am stirred by the sharp contrast between the amateurish war play in the Carolina Maneuvers and the carrying out of Operation Torch"—the invasion of North Africa—a joint operation by British and American forces under the command of General Dwight D. Eisenhower beginning on November 8, 1942, just one short year later. "Although there were obvious difficulties with our first offensive operation and still much to be learned," noted Christensen, the "turnaround I had seen in our Army since my first experiences during the maneuvers was," in his qualified opinion, "profound."[13]

Christensen credited this remarkable improvement directly to "the professional planning and intensive training of our officers and men that began during the Carolina Maneuvers in the autumn of 1941." The pre-war mobilization program, he says, "certainly" seems "to have paid off in America's first assault against Nazi-controlled territory, and what was the stepping stone to Sicily, Italy and, finally, France and Germany." The war games, Christensen added, "served as an important testing ground for a variety of new equipment," and that "the obvious shortcomings of our forces during the maneuvers led to accelerated development of all the arms and services of the Army."[14]

The following is an assessment of the war games by an enlisted man writing for the 104th Infantry history:

> For approximately two months we were engaged in a great variety of military exercises and maneuvers. Each succeeding one seemed a little more trying and involved than the preceding one, and our state of training improved accordingly. Simulated battles were engaged in, and marches and exercises continued for a length of time which we could not have endured a few months before.... When we were first faced with tanks and scout cars in the Carolina Maneuvers ... we had "tank fever" for many days. The general impulse seemed to be to run away as soon as a tank or scout car appeared, which was just what the operators of such vehicles desired us to do. In a short time we learned that the only way to fight them was to use our weapons against them and we soon developed a very efficient technique in fighting those armored vehicles.

He said in conclusion, "Perhaps that improvement was one of the greatest values of the maneuvers to us."[15]

General Lesley J. McNair's "satisfaction" with the overall outcome of the Carolina Maneuvers, Gable wrote, "was evident in the confidential remarks that he sent to the commanding generals afterwards ... the maneuvers were well-planned and executed in most essentials and indicated intensive and intelligent collective effort toward achievement of training goals."

McNair also stated that while the U.S. Army had made "remarkable progress" during the maneuvers of the past year, there was still a need for further training.[16]

Major General Karl Truesdell, VI Corps commander (Blue army), in his final critique of the maneuvers, "singled out the 26th Division in comparison with regular Army units and unreservedly qualified the 'Yankees' as the best in his book." The History of the 26th remarked that the general's evaluation was "a fine compliment and a hard won achievement."[17]

12

Return to Camp Edwards: December 6, 1941

On December 3, after more than two months of strenuous training, the troops of the 26th Division began the four-day return trip to New England and home. Thousands of the Carolina natives came out to shout their farewells and wish the men "Godspeed." There were tears in the eyes of many of the young women that lined the streets of every city and town within a hundred miles of the cantonment.[1]

The division convoy "experienced rainy, cold weather all the way back." When the long line of vehicles finally reached the New England states, throngs of people lined the roadsides in Connecticut, Rhode Island, Massachusetts, and on Cape Cod, waving and cheering. Many signs of "Welcome YD" greeted the motorcade along the route.[2]

"It was a happy group on their return from the south," wrote one historian of the 104th, and a number of the "old timers," promised discharges following the maneuvers, were looking forward to "their expected return to civilian life." Upon arrival at Edwards on December 6, 1941, troops reopened the barracks, made bunks, and cleaned and stowed gear. After more than two months in the field, all were happy to once again be sleeping in a bed with a mattress and clean sheets, have running water, take showers with plenty of hot water, and eat regular meals in the mess hall. The troops discovered that during their absence, civilian work crews had completed many structures still under construction when they left, such as "the huge Service Club," and had also erected many new buildings including theaters and chapels, paved more roads, and made many additional improvements. That night the men "tumbled into bed to dream of furloughs and home."[3]

On Sunday, December 7, the men awoke and prepared to go on leave. A considerable number had already left the camp for home the previous evening. At 2:25 that afternoon, the almost unbelievable news that the Japanese had attacked Pearl Harbor came over the airwaves. Throughout the camp, men, "filled with tenseness," remained glued to every available radio listening to the latest news bulletins. Word of the "dastardly attack ... burned itself into the minds of all concerned," wrote one contributor to the history of the 104th Infantry. On December 8, President Roosevelt addressed the Congress, asking for a declaration of war against Japan.[4]

The men were shocked and surprised at first, but their attitude soon changed to one of "fierce indignation and anger." Throughout the camp sentiments were running high. Having trained for more than eight months, and in the best physical shape of their lives, the boys felt they were ready. Another historian of the 104th Regiment wrote:

> The morale of the command improved, if such a thing was possible, upon the declaration of war by the Congress on the 9 Dec. Everyone knew now just why they were in the army, and were thankful that they had the benefit of almost a year's training.

12. Return to Camp Edwards: December 6, 1941

Above: "Yankee Division soldiers, fresh from the Carolina Maneuvers rush to phones to call home — December 6, 1941." *Below:* Soldiers at Camp Edwards gather around the radio to listen for news about Pearl Harbor — December 7, 1941 (both photographs courtesy Massachusetts Army National Guard).

They "faced the future with a resolve that no nation, least of all Japan," could do what it did to the U.S. "and get away with it." Men "vowed" to make the Japanese "pay dearly for their act of treachery." "'Let us at the yellow b[astards],' was the cry."[5]

During the division's stay in the Carolinas, Congress passed legislation authorizing the discharge of all men 28 years of age and over on or before their date of induction. Discharges of the "old men" were to take place beginning on December 10, at the rate of 45 per day from each unit. The army based individual release dates on length of service. Needless to say, there was no longer any question of this being carried out as military officials immediately rescinded the order. "All thoughts of discharges

One of the thirteen chapels on the base. The chaplains for the various religious denominations shared in the use of the chapels (W.R. Thompson & Company Publications, Richmond, Virginia).

and furloughs passed out of the men's minds." From that day forward, they were in it "for the duration, plus six months."[6]

Taffe recalled that after church the men were sitting around the barracks, "killing time until the handful of regular Sunday afternoon family visitors showed up," when word came over the radio that the Japanese had bombed Pearl Harbor. He said that immediately following the broadcast someone shouted, "'Pearl Harbor? Where the hell is that?'

"'Hell, I don't know, but they just said the Japanese bombed Pearl Harbor.'

"Another voice chimed in, 'I think it's in Hawaii.'

"And such was the announcement that we finally had entered World War II." The majority of the men in the unit had been in the National Guard for several years before federalization and "we really considered ourselves to be seasoned soldiers," wrote Taffe. "We long ago had anticipated that sooner or later we would join the Allied forces facing the Nazi juggernaut in Western Europe, but most of us never even considered that the Japanese would be the reason." What he says was "perhaps the most frequently asked question in the next few hours," by far "more important to most of us than the war: 'Is this going to louse up our Christmas leave?'"[7]

On the night of December 7, the men sat in small groups in the barracks, the canteen, the infirmary, or in town, and talked about what the day meant to them, to their future and to the future of the country. Many waited in long lines at the PX to make telephone calls home. "The intensive maneuvers over the previous months, filled as they were with difficult and testing experiences, brought [the men] to a high peak of efficiency." Protestant chaplain 1st Lt. George E. Owens (104th) of Wilbraham wrote, "We were fighters, hardened by our experiences, ready to face whatever lay ahead with Fortitude and Courage."[8]

The historian for Company M (104th) wrote, "After war was declared we were doubtful of getting furloughs but to our surprise they came through so we began making plans for our first wartime Christmas. The Holidays that year were different than ever before but it was still swell to see the folks again." Division Headquarters devised a plan to issue general furloughs for the Christmas holidays on a staggered basis. Staff placed the men in two groups, lettered A and B. "Regardless of which group one was in, he spent Christmas and New Year's Day at home." Each company "retained a skeleton crew in camp over the holidays," rewarding these men "with extra time off after the first of the year."[9]

13

On Shore Patrol in New England and New York: December 1941 to May 1942

On Saturday, December 6, 1941, Captain John S. "Jack" Gerety, the commanding officer (CO) of Company F, 181st Infantry, and his men, had just returned to Camp Edwards from the Carolina Maneuvers after a three-day motor march. The troops reopened the barracks, made up the bunks, and spent the remainder of the day cleaning weapons and equipment. Following a brief inspection, Gerety dismissed the company. Most of the men, who had not been home in more than three months, received weekend passes or furloughs and wasted little time departing the camp. The only personnel left in the company area were Gerety, who was the officer in charge (OIC), two non-commissioned officers (NCOs), and a skeleton force of a dozen or so enlisted men. The captain was looking forward to sleeping in a bed with a mattress, clean sheets, and warm, dry blankets for the first time in several weeks.

The following morning, Gerety slept late. He arose, showered, shaved, and headed over to the company mess hall for something to eat. After finishing "a fine breakfast," the captain returned to the officers' barracks to relax and read the *Boston Sunday Globe*. He was lounging on his bunk about 2:30 in the afternoon when someone came in and shouted, "Turn the radio on." In a "strident voice," the announcer reported, "The Japanese have bombed Pearl Harbor, there are many casualties."[1]

Later that day, Division Headquarters placed Gerety in command of a special task force made up of parts of Company F and Company H (the men remaining at the camp), along with several attached units, and ordered the group to move out at six o'clock the following morning (Monday).

As directed, Gerety reported to Colonel Roy W. Smith, the regimental commander, and Lt. Colonel William L. McBride, commander of the 1st Battalion. Col. Smith ordered Gerety to turn the command of his company over to 1st Lt. Alfred E. Trubenback, the executive officer (XO), and handed him a sealed manila envelope containing his orders. Smith instructed Gerety to travel ten miles in the direction of New Bedford, Massachusetts, at which point he was to read the contents.

"It did not take long to make that ten miles," Gerety said, "and with sweaty hands I got into that envelope." Much to Gerety's astonishment, the only thing inside the envelope was a "Socony road map." Upon examination, he found the following handwritten statement at the bottom of the map:

> The United States is at war with Germany and Japan. It is presumed that enemy forces will attempt to land agents and to commit acts of sabotage within your area of responsibility. You will outpost and defend all critical areas, boundaries inclusive. Your base for all logistical support will be Fort

Rodman. Standard operating procedures will apply to all communications. Your headquarters will be Fort Rodman, New Bedford.

By Order of the Commanding General [Roger W.] Eckfeldt, Major General Commanding.

Thus, the special task force commanded by Capt. Gerety became part of the far-flung coastal defenses of New England, under the command of the New England Frontier Defense Sector, headquartered at Fort Adams in Newport, Rhode Island. Fort Adams, one of the largest seacoast fortifications in the United States, protected the entrance to Narragansett Bay. In a letter to Major Theodore "Simmy" Simmington, Ret., dated April 27, 1998, Gerety closed with, "And this is how I started the war."[2]

On the day of the attack, General Eckfeldt sent a second detachment to guard both ends of the three spans across the Cape Cod Canal — the Bourne, Sagamore, and Railroad Bridges — connecting the cape with the mainland. Military officials were concerned that the destruction of the bridges by German saboteurs would strand the 26th Infantry Division on the Cape. Such was the paranoia that existed in the days and weeks after December 7, 1941.

* * *

Immediately following the attack on Pearl Harbor, a War Department contingency plan for "a comprehensive defensive organization," previously drawn up for just such an emergency, "rapidly went into effect." Part of the defense plan recognized the need for additional personnel to protect vital military installations, safeguard industrial production plants vital to the war effort, and protect shipping facilities along the eastern seaboard, as well as to defend the coastal frontier against possible attack by an enemy invasion force. Under the guidelines of the plan, military planners designated certain select units of the military for immediate reassignment to reinforce existing coastal defenses. The plan involved the rapid deployment of fighter aircraft, antiaircraft batteries, and other combat units.[3]

The War Department issued emergency orders for these units to make all necessary preparations for the deployment of troops and equipment to specifically designated areas or sectors. Several regiments of the 26th Infantry Division, which had just returned to Camp Edwards from the Carolina maneuvers, were among those alerted.

During the early days of the war, the Navy and Coast Guard were without sufficient personnel to patrol the entire East Coast of the United States. On December 11, 1941, the 26th Division received orders to provide three "battalion combat teams" (4 companies each), one each from the 101st, 104th, and 181st Infantry Regiments, for coast patrol duty in New England. Division placed the three teams under the jurisdiction of the New England Sector of the Eastern Theater of Operations (part of the First Army), based at Fort Adams, Newport, Rhode Island. The sector commander reattached one battalion to each of the three sub-sectors — Portland, Maine; Boston, Massachusetts; and Newport, Rhode Island. The latter included the harbor defenses of New Bedford, Massachusetts, Narragansett Bay, and Long Island. Other First Army divisions provided units to assist in protecting the remainder of the coast south to Florida.[4]

The primary responsibility of division commanders, as outlined in the official War Department order, was to deploy the various infantry units on sentinel duty along every mile of unsecured coast within the assigned sector. The mission of sector forces "was to observe and patrol the coastline; to attack and destroy any enemy landing raids or attempts to land enemy agents; and to be prepared to operate in the rear areas of the Sector in protecting vital installations in support of Service Commands." The men on coast patrol were part of the country's second line of defense behind Coast Guard and naval patrol craft. "Readiness, alertness, and continuous observation was the mission of all units," reported the *History of the 26th Yankee Division*.[5]

* * *

Division assigned the 2nd Battalion, 181st Infantry, to the Newport Sub-sector; the 2nd Battalion, 104th Infantry, to the Boston Sub-sector; and the 2nd Battalion, 101st Infantry, to the Portland Sub-sector. The "History of the 181st Infantry [Regiment]," a paper on file at the Massachusetts National Guard Military Museum & Archives, Worcester, Massachusetts (see Appendix D), states the 2nd Battalion's area of responsibility extended from "Woods Hole, Mass. to Montauk Point, Long Island." Presented here is a partial list of duty stations for the regiments of the 26th Division based on available information contained in a limited number of sources, combined with that provided by a number of division veterans through correspondence and interviews.[6]

The 2nd Battalion, 181st Infantry, commanded by Lt. Col. John A. Amberg, left Camp Edwards on December 11, 1941, and proceeded to the Cranston Street Armory in Providence, Rhode Island, home of the state's National Guard unit.

Sulo O. Ruuska of Quincy, Massachusetts, a corporal with Company H, my father's company, wrote, "After we returned to Camp Edwards from the maneuvers in No. Carolina, I was lucky to go on furlough." He left for home on Saturday night. "While home we heard the news about Pearl. I finished my furlough and returned to Edwards nine days later." Ruuska described the situation at the camp:

> When I returned to camp there were but only a few of the company cooks and drivers there. No one could tell me where "H" Company had gone. The men in the next regimental area, the 182nd, wore helmets and field packs and even carried their rifles when they went to the mess hall. Their commander was ready for an invasion of the camp; made me feel safe.

Shortly thereafter, the War Department detached the 182nd Infantry from the division and shipped the unit to the Pacific Theater (see below). James V. "Pimple" Carnivale (H-181) said, "When the 182nd left for the Pacific, the men of Companies F and M had to turn their new [M-1] Garands over to the regiment. They were issued Enfield rifles" in their place (.30 caliber bolt action rifles from World War I).[7]

For the next few days, a number of men returning from leave or furlough continued to arrive back at the barracks. "One morning an officer from regiment came to the company area and told us to prepare to move out," Ruuska said. "They put us on a truck that took us to the Cranston Street National Guard Armory in Providence."[8]

Ruuska remembers that the unit stayed at the Cranston Street Armory "only for a short time, no more than a couple of weeks." Guido J. Fratturelli of Fitchburg, a mortar section sergeant and later sergeant (S/Sgt.) of the mortar platoon of Company H, said that from the armory, Battalion Headquarters dispersed various units to specific duty stations along the coast. Fratturelli was my father's sergeant while he was a member of the mortar platoon.[9]

The state of Rhode Island constructed the massive 140,000 square foot armory between 1903 and 1907. The yellow brick building with a granite base has an enormous drill shed that measured 170 feet by 235 feet (39,950 sq. feet), by 90 feet high was, at the time, the largest indoor facility in New England. By comparison, a football field, less end zones, is 45,000 square feet.

The Rhode Island National Guard paraded an entire brigade (two regiments) with bands and vehicles on the drill floor, and still had plenty of room to spare. It was so large that promoters booked traveling circuses, rodeos, and other major events inside the building. The armory, which is on the National Register of Historic Places, has been vacant since the National Guard moved to a new building in 1996.

Sulo Ruuska's recollections of the Cranston Street Armory "are not very pleasant." Ruuska, a member of the 2nd machine-gun platoon, says he "hated the place." "Inside the drill hall, there were mortars of the type you see in pictures of the siege of Vicksburg," remembered Ruuska. "They were the size of a fifty gallon oil drum but the bore fired a round about the size of a softball."[10]

"The latrines were especially bad," Ruuska wrote, "cold porcelain toilets with no provisions for seats." This must have proved quite a shock to a person's backside on those chilly December mornings in 1941. Like most latrine facilities in the Army, there were no stalls for privacy. The men had to do their duty in full view of other members of the company, which for many was very embarrassing. It took quite a while for some men to adjust to this situation; others just never felt comfortable doing so.[11]

Battalion restricted the troops to the building and surrounding grounds. The men were under strict orders not to cross the four main streets that formed the outer bounds of the property. One night, Ruuska and another squad member were on guard duty patrolling the perimeter of the armory grounds. In need of cigarettes, Ruuska spotted two young ladies walking on the opposite sidewalk. Waving two one dollar bills in the air, Sulo called out asking if they would go to a nearby store and pick him up a couple of packs. "Evidently, the two girls misunderstood my intent and got scared." He laughed and said, "Boy, did they run."[12]

Romeo C. "Ro" LeBlanc of Fitchburg, Massachusetts, was a sergeant with Company H, stationed at Fort Rodman. At this time, a heavy weapons company consisted of four platoons: two .30-caliber, one .50-caliber, and one mortar platoon. When the U.S. Army triangularized the 26th Division in February 1942 (see below), this configuration changed. According to LeBlanc, shortly after Company H arrived at the armory the CO split up the machine gun platoons and attached them one each to the rifle companies (E, F, and G).[13]

The mortar platoon, Fratturelli reported, went to Fort Rodman in New Bedford, Massachusetts. The primary assignment of the platoon was to patrol the area around Horseneck Beach in Westport Point, near the Massachusetts-Rhode Island line. LeBlanc says he remembers the Cranston Street Armory, but could not recall anything interesting that happened. He believes that Battalion sent one of the machine gun platoons to Fort Rodman and another to the town of Riverhead, New York, near the eastern end of Long Island, where the Peconic River enters Great Peconic Bay, while his platoon remained at the armory.[14]

Clifford P. Welcome of Orange, Massachusetts, a corporal with Company F, remembers that "shortly after Pearl Harbor" Division stationed his unit (3rd platoon) in the town of Southampton, Long Island, 30 miles west of Montauk Point. The company billeted in the town's fire station and patrolled the beaches to Amagansett, 24 miles east. Welcome remembers being there "for about a month." On June 13, 1942, a German U-boat landed four saboteurs on the beach at Amagansett setting off a nationwide search by the Federal Bureau of Investigation (see below). Staff Sergeant Stanley J. Zapustus of Orange was the leader of the platoon.[15]

John D. Turini of Clinton, a cook with Company G, 2nd Battalion, stationed at Fort Rodman, says that his outfit patrolled the beaches from Fall River to New Bedford.[16]

John J. Voellings of Company B, 181st Infantry (Worcester) says he "was stationed on the coast of Rhode Island near Quonochontaug and Weekapaug" (south of the Burlingame State Park) in the town of Westerly.[17]

Carl P. DeVasto, a member of Headquarters Company, 2nd Battalion, 101st Infantry,

"High upon a rock, along New England's shore, this ever watchful soldier looks through his field glasses to detect the enemy, Jan. 1, 1942" (U.S. Army Signal Corps photograph).

wrote that units of the regiment were on patrol in the Boston Sub-sector from January to June 1942. The command post for the 2nd Battalion was located in the fire station in Hull, Massachusetts. "The companies of the battalion were strung out along the coast from Hull south to Nantasket Beach." Later, he says, Battalion moved the CP "to the foot of the Blue Hills Reservation with the closest entrance off Route #28 in Milton, Massachusetts."[18]

In a letter written September 18, 2001, Paul T. Metcalf, a member of Company G, 101st Infantry, said "The night of Pearl Harbor I remember walking up and down the Bourne Bridge over the Cape Cod Canal carrying a BAR over my shoulder."[19]

Regiment stationed Company G at Rocky Point, located at the southern end of Plymouth Bay, Massachusetts. The 2nd Battalion's area of responsibility extended from Plymouth to the Cape Cod Canal. The company stayed at "a large estate with separate servant's quarters where we billeted." From Metcalf's quarters, he walked down a path from the estate to the duty station, described as a "small building, not much bigger than a phone booth, with room for two men." The outpost, located on the point, afforded "views up and down the shore and straight out over the ocean." Inside the building, "there was a shelf upon which was a map of the area with quadrants and a swivel pointer with which one could locate [plot the position of] a vessel or plane." A telephone connected the outpost with headquarters "to report a suspicious ship or aircraft."[20]

Metcalf recalled an incident that occurred one afternoon at the outpost. A soldier on duty spotted what appeared to be a German submarine on the surface and made a frantic call to notify his superiors. Headquarters called the officer in charge (OIC) at air control, who dispatched a U.S. Army Air Corps reconnaissance aircraft to investigate. "The submarine turned out to be a tugboat towing a barge. Both vessels were close to the waterline and were hard to make out," wrote Metcalf. "From that day on, the GI became known as 'Submarine _____,' last name omitted to save him embarrassment if he should be with us today."[21]

"Somewhere along New England's shore this alert Coast Artillery soldier is on the lookout for the enemy, January 1, 1942" (U.S. Army Signal Corps photograph).

Orders originally called for the 26th Division to assign three battalion combat teams to Coast Patrol. Division Headquarters soon discovered there was insufficient personnel to cover such a vast area and added at least one additional unit, the 3rd Battalion, 101st Infantry, to assist. Regiment stationed the battalion in Saco (pronounced Soco), Maine, with headquarters at the High Shoe Factory, 18 Park Street (see chapter 18, Saco, Maine).

For some reason, the enlisted members of the battalion did not occupy space inside the factory building at this time. Francis H. "Frank" McInnis, with Company M, says the battalion "was bivouacked in a nearby field where the men lived out of pup tents." Apparently, there was not enough space in the factory building to house the entire battalion. According to McInnis, the company guarded the major beaches in the Saco area, and that the other companies of the 101st Infantry covered the coast from the area south of Saco to Hull, Massachusetts.[22]

The official history of the 104th Infantry Regiment (*History of a Combat Regiment 1939–1945*), reported that in January the "2nd Battalion, commanded by Lt. Col. William McGarry, left for patrol work along the coast of Maine." Further on, the history states, "From January until March, the 104th guarded the vital New England coastline." Division assigned the 104th to the Portland Sub-sector and units covered the northern part of Maine just north of the 101st Infantry's area of responsibility, possibly Portland to the Canadian border (?). Edward J. Griffin, a member of Company L, 101st Infantry wrote in his wartime *Diary* under the date March 1941, "101st Infantry relieves 104th Infantry on Coast Patrol (Mass. Border to Maine), [104th] C.P. at Portsmouth, N.H. Quarters in Morley Button Factory."[23]

* * *

The army transferred Colonel Roy W. Smith, commander of the 181st Infantry Regiment, to the 114th C.A.S.U. (Combat Assigned Service Unit) on December 31, 1941, and Colonel James P. Powers, the executive officer and a veteran of the unit for many years, assumed command. On February 3, 1942, the 26th Division was streamlined and re-designated from a square to a triangular division, similar to the configuration used by the German Army. The Yankee Division, "one of the few remaining square divisions in Federal Service," consisted of two brigades, each with two regiments. At this time, the War Department reduced all existing square divisions to three regiments and used the detached units to form new divisions or assigned personnel as needed to bring existing units up to strength. In this case, the 26th Division lost the 182nd Infantry leaving the 101st, the 104th, and the 181st.[24]

What happened to the 182nd Infantry is an unusual and interesting story. One day after Pearl Harbor, on December 8, 1941, the 26th Division received urgent orders from Washington to provide "one reinforced [regimental] combat team, plus some additional troops," for a special top-secret assignment. The War Department selected the 182nd Infantry Regiment along with seven other units (see *The History of the 26th Yankee Division*, p. 145) to be detached from duty with the 26th and reassigned to Combat Task Force 6814, destined to be shipped out to the South Pacific. The War Department selected Brig. Gen. William I. Rose, commander of the 51st Infantry Brigade, 26th Division, to command the combat team.[25]

During the first week in January, units of the 26th Division selected for reassignment boarded "special trains" for the "secret departure" that would take them to the Brooklyn Navy Yard, New York, Port of Embarkation (POE), where seven troop transports were waiting to carry the force to its destination. Task Force 6814 sailed for Australia on January 23, 1942, arriving in Melbourne on May 6, after a voyage of 33 days. The 26th Division historian wrote, "The destination beyond the Brooklyn port was closely guarded and the embarkation from an Atlantic port, gave rise to many conjectures as to what point in Europe the task force was headed." After reaching the open ocean, the convoy headed southward along the East Coast. The guessing game continued unabated until the transports entered the Panama Canal.[26]

On March 7, the secret task force embarked once again, this time for the island of New Caledonia in Melanesia, a French colony since 1854, situated approximately 850 miles northeast of Brisbane. Military officials believed the Japanese planned to invade New Caledonia and several other major islands in the South Pacific. As it turned out, the move was indeed an integral part of the overall plan by the Japanese War Ministry to isolate Australia and establish bases of operations to attack shipping lanes and military installations. The U.S. dispatched the task force to occupy and hold the island in an attempt to halt the southward expansion of the Japanese as well as to prevent the more serious threat of a full-scale invasion of Australia from developing. Defense planners intended to establish adequate defenses, build airfields and port facilities, and stockpile munitions, equipment, and supplies "in widely dispersed supply dumps," to support "the inevitable offensive" by the Allies. Japan cancelled its planned invasion of New Caledonia on July 11, 1942.[27]

The task force arrived in New Caledonia on March 12, where Major General Alexander M. Patch, Jr., took formal command as the unit's first commanding general. In April and May 1942, Patch's staff "reshuffled ... certain combat elements ... to give some semblance of a division formation." The reorganization resulted in the formation of the Americal Division, so named on May 27, 1942 — "a division without a number — basing its designation 'Americal'" on "Americans in New Caledonia." John D. Cronin (Capt.), author of *Under the Southern*

Cross, the official history of the Americal, wrote that when General Patch could not come up with a suitable name for the division, he decided "that an opportunity to name the organization should be given to the men who were to serve in it." He credits the name to an enlisted man in the 26th Signal Company, Pfc. David Fonesca, of Roxbury, Massachusetts. The Americal was one of only two divisions in the history of the U.S. Army that did not have a numerical designation, the other being the Philippines Division.[28]

The "famous" Americal Division, "reportedly the first combat task force to leave the country in World War II," completed four years of combat duty in the Pacific Theater of Operations and served with distinction in the Guadalcanal, Northern Solomons, Leyte, and Southern Philippines campaigns.[29]

* * *

On February 8, 1942, the War Department placed all U.S. Army units ordered to provide security for the East Coast under the jurisdiction of the Eastern Defense Command (EDC). The EDC was under the command of Lieut. General Hugh A. Drum, First Army chairman, Inter-American Defense Board, whose headquarters was located at Governors Island, in New York Harbor. At the outset of World War II, the continental United States was divided into four major defense commands—Western, Central, Southern, and Eastern. The primary responsibility of military commanders within each sector was "the large-scale protection of the home front against enemy attack from without, and protection against sabotage, espionage, and subversion from within."[30]

The Eastern Defense Command's area of responsibility extended "2,500 miles through sixteen states from Maine to Florida, together with the bases of Bermuda and Newfoundland," designated as the Eastern Military Area.[31]

Executive Order 9066, establishing the authority of the EDC, came directly from the desk of President Roosevelt in February 1942. The directive authorized the commanding general to "assume military control over civilian activities within the Eastern Military Area." Under one of the provisions of the order, "any and all persons deemed dangerous to national security may be excluded [from the area] by the military commander having jurisdiction, and with respect to which the right of any person to enter, remain in or leave the area is made subject to whatever restrictions may be imposed by military authority." Also included in the order was a provision authorizing the commander to call upon "the Federal Bureau of Investigation, State Governors, and Civilian Defense Agencies" to render assistance. The president stated in the proclamation, "A successful prosecution of the war, requires every possible protection against espionage and sabotage."[32]

Within hours of the Japanese attack, U.S. Army Air Corps fighter aircraft, antiaircraft batteries, and other combat units converged on the East Coast to join regular units already in place. Interceptor squadrons of the First Fighter Command, operating out of dispersed fields, provided general air defense for the entire Atlantic seaboard. Coast Artillery defenses, using fixed guns as well as mobile units, began a 24-hour, seven day a week alert schedule. Antiaircraft batteries set up battle stations in parks, atop office buildings, and on piers at key locations along the coast.[33]

The plan included a provision authorizing the use of civilian volunteers as aircraft spotters to staff air defense operations centers, and to process incoming reports under the direction of regular Army officers. "These indispensable workers scan the skies day and night for enemy aircraft," wrote Drum. Personnel assigned to these secret nerve centers coordinated the air defense of the East Coast. The civilian volunteer force eventually numbered more than 350,000.[34]

Shortly after the units of the 181st Infantry arrived at their duty stations, Division ordered all troops to remove the YD patch worn on their left shoulder and replace it with the patch of the 1st Coast Artillery (CA) District (New England), a subdivision of the Coast Artillery Corps (CAC). The Coast Artillery patch is an olive drab square, approximately two and one half inches on a side, with a red artillery shell over a yellow circle (see front cover). Clifford Welcome says that a few weeks after they made the change to the new patch, the men received an additional order to sew the YD patch back on, this time on the right shoulder.[35]

The Coast Artillery, "a distinct branch of the U.S. Army," consisted of a series of fixed artillery fortifications in harbor forts, mobile ground artillery units, searchlight battalions, and antiaircraft artillery units. Historian Shelby Stanton says, "The largest portion of Coast Artillery available was antiaircraft in nature." The "stated mission" of the CA "was to protect fleet bases, defeat naval and air attacks against cities and harbors." During this period, all other units of the 26th Division remained in training at Camp Edwards.[36]

14

Living Accommodations for Men on Coast Patrol Duty

When the units of the 26th Division arrived on location for Coast Patrol duty, G-3 (Planning and Operations) initially billeted the soldiers patrolling the beaches in temporary living quarters, which the government rented from the owners. These included summer beach houses, garages, barns, public buildings, or any available unoccupied space the troops could readily convert to livable quarters. Some of the temporary accommodations were very luxurious.[1]

On March 4, 1942, an unsigned article titled "Sentries Watch Our Shores: Outposts Move from Porches and Beach Houses to Their Own Huts," appeared in the *Falmouth Enterprise*. The story described several of the temporary quarters housing the troops and provided the reader with an idea of what living conditions were like during the first several months the units were on patrol duty. In the latter part of February, the engineers began the construction of small, one-room buildings along the shore (see below).[2]

One of the borrowed quarters on Cape Cod was "a spacious and impressive oceanfront summer home with as beautiful a water outlook as any spot on the Cape." The front door exited just to the left of the driveway on the street side. Attached to the waterfront side of the house was an L-shaped sun porch only 50 yards from the edge of a bluff "facing a glorious" wide sweeping view of Cape Cod Bay "which must be the pride of the owners," the reporter wrote. On a bright day, the sun streamed through the glass to help warm up the whole room and gave it a nice cozy feeling. On stormy days, however, the house, built for summer occupancy only, was very drafty.[3]

The soldiers had turned the sun porch, with its beautiful panoramic view, into a "cozy" living area for several of the occupants. Army cots lined both inside walls. On the wall opposite the door leading into the house was a kitchen table with a portable hot plate, on which there was always a simmering pot of freshly brewed coffee, its robust aroma filling the room. Around the corner of the porch on the opposite end of the L, separated by a small partition, some of the daytime sleepers were able to find privacy from the daily goings on around them. A couple of the men stood at a picture window pointing out to the *Enterprise* reporter the extent of the "beat" they had to cover on their rounds.[4]

Discarded wooden packing crates were stacked and used as cupboards filled with cans and rations of food. Some of the cases supported boards used as shelving for an array of tableware — varying from army mess kits and cups to an assortment of miscellaneous pieces of china, most donated to the men by friendly neighbors. A telephone stood on a small table near the entrance, where a member of the squad was on continuous duty. The boys took "pride in their housekeeping" and the quarters always looked neat and clean.[5]

In another borrowed beach house, the men lived in two comfortably furnished rooms with complete kitchen facilities and built-in cabinets. A half wall and a screen partition separated the rooms from the main part of the house. The reporter opened one of the kitchen cabinets to find it well stocked with supplies, including a large jar of sugar, a rationed item during the war, which the civilian population had a very difficult time obtaining in large quantities. "How much do they let you fellas have?" he wanted to know. "Let's just say, we don't have to worry," one of the occupants replied with a sheepish grin. The reporter asked how lunch was that day, to which one of the boys replied, "We had a swell feed. French fried potatoes and ham, and oh boy what a swell cake." All that was left of the large cake, donated by a neighbor, were a few crumbs.[6]

Army supply vehicles delivered groceries and fresh foods on a regular basis, without the "necessity of planning or ordering." A stock of canned goods as well as a "leg of lamb or a ham" was part of the regular delivery of supplies. A baker's truck and milk truck with fresh daily goods made regularly scheduled rounds of the scattered outposts.[7]

When the neighbors discovered that a group of boys in uniform had moved into the area, donations of homemade brownies and cookies, or a batch of delicious fudge "[found] their way into the larder." A USO worker visited the men on a regular basis to drop off books, magazines, writing paper, and pens and pencils. Other gifts, which included more permanent items, such as items of furniture, rugs, cooking utensils, lamps, and portable kerosene heaters, were always welcome.[8]

The designated cooks usually used their "own ingenuity in concocting meals from the supplies provided." One day it might be spaghetti and meatballs with salad and fresh bread; on another day, it might be a baked ham dinner. For dessert, there were delicious layer cakes, with thick vanilla or chocolate icing, or brownies, home baked or donated as a gift. For lunch, it would often be hot soup and sandwiches or leftover meatloaf, for example. French fried potatoes were regular fare. Some of the cooks were men who had past experience, or had made a particularly good meal and their mates coaxed them into taking on the job full time. As an added incentive, the duty roster excluded volunteers from regular beach patrols.[9]

Many of the cooks took advantage of every opportunity to find new and pleasant ways of preparing the food. To these men, cooking was not just a task—it was a pleasure. Many of the men considered food preparation to be a "fine art." One of the men complained to the *Falmouth Enterprise* reporter that the cooking was too good: "I've gained twelve pounds on Jake's cooking," he remarked jokingly.[10]

Visitors from other outposts or neighbors were always welcome. The men were "eager to exchange magazines and books," most they had read and re-read many times over, for new or different ones. The most popular were magazines such as *Mechanics Illustrated* or *Popular Mechanics* containing semi-technical articles about aviation and weapons developments or recent advances in engineering. Some of the men liked to discuss popular novels like *The Web and the Rock* and *Of Time and the River* by Thomas Wolfe, or *For Whom the Bell Tolls* by Ernest Hemingway. Mystery stories were a favorite genre of many of the young men. In most outposts, there was a plentiful supply of recent issues of movie and glamour magazines scattered about.[11]

The troops very nicely fixed up some of the less luxurious quarters, like barns and garages, into very comfortable living places. In a big old barn near enough to the ocean to hear the pounding surf, one might find the off-duty patrolmen sitting about the makeshift living area relaxing. To pass the time, the men sat around chatting, writing letters, or playing checkers.[12]

In one area off to the side was a small table with a portable Victrola and a stack of 78-

rpm records. Some of the boys might be listening to the latest pop records—Frank Sinatra, Bing Crosby, or one of the other big name crooners of the day—or it might possibly be an old sentimental standard. The music, played softly so as not to disturb others, filled the room with its sweet sound. If no one happened to be asleep, it might be the lively music of Benny Goodman or Kay Kaiser, with just a tad more volume. Sometimes the radio would be broadcasting the latest news, or a favorite radio show such as Fibber McGee and Molly or Jack Benny.[13]

Army cots filled half the floor space, with at least two always occupied with men trying to catch up on their sleep. The boys coming off their regular beach patrol or other assignment would simply flop down without bothering to undress, cover themselves with an olive-drab blanket, and drop off in slumber. A couple of others might be getting their gear ready to go on duty.[14]

The boys plastered the rough wood walls of the barn with many pictures and magazine covers. Most were pin-ups of beautiful girls or famous celebrities in brightly colored clothing, with an emphasis on the lightly-clad form and shapely leg. Most popular with the men were the sultry paintings of pretty young girls that appeared each month in *Esquire Magazine*. So sexy were the ladies portrayed in the drawings that, in 1944, the Postmaster General banned them from the mails, thus invoking the ire of GIs around the world. One veteran made the comment, "Those pictures gave us guys a good idea of what we were fighting for." In a corner given over to personal possessions, one could find framed photographs of a girlfriend, wife, or other loved one.[15]

* * *

Outpost life included many unusual pastimes. Some of the boys spent idle time writing poetry. One young man, interviewed for the *Falmouth Enterprise*, was an aspiring songwriter. He volunteered to sing his latest creation, and did so with gusto while beating time with a pencil on his notepad that contained page after page of scribbled lines. The songster apologized for his voice stating, "it would sound a lot better ... if he could really sing good."[16]

His choice of songs, to demonstrate his writing ability, was a ditty containing verses and a chorus about what the Americans would do to the enemy when they got "over there." He peppered the verses with "side cracks" aimed "at Hitler and the Japs." An admiring buddy commented that his friend "makes up the music, too." Picking up a framed picture of a curly-haired lass, his girl back home, he informed the reporter, "She writes out all the music for me. I just send her the tune and she fills it all in."[17]

At another outpost, the reporter for the *Enterprise* "persuaded" an art student "to show him his portfolio of drawings." One of the men in his squad urged him to show the picture he had just finished painting. The large leather case contained "highly colored watercolors of a variety of blondes, brunettes and red-heads." These were just as popular with his squadmates as the magazine covers and commercial pin-ups that adorned the walls.[18]

The artist's portfolio also included a number of "pencil sketches, mostly incomplete," depicting life in the Army. The collection included several illustrations of soldiers in various training or action poses with full battle gear carrying an assortment of weapons. Others portrayed an array of military vehicles and tanks speeding down a road or pushing across an open field churning up a trail of dust. There were a number of portraits of the fellows in his outfit, one, the "hard-bitten distinctive face" of an officer under a Class A uniform cap.[19]

The young man's mother had sent along his watercolors, pastels, and other artist's supplies so that he could keep his skills intact. Before the Army drafted the talented youth, he attended art school and had done a little professional freelance work. He was planning a career in advertising when the war was over. Rarely did his mates see him without either pencil or brush in hand during his off-duty hours.[20]

* * *

Approximately three months after the troops arrived on shore patrol, attached engineer battalions began the construction of a number of new one-room buildings approximately 15 X 15 feet, "from which foot patrols would operate." The "huts" or "hutments," as they were called, were "made of pre-fabricated walls with set-in windows," and roofs (see photograph on p. 144). Division wanted the men to move into the new quarters "well in advance" of the arrival of summer vacationers to the seashore. The engineers spaced out the pre-fab buildings along the coast, approximately two miles apart, in inconspicuous, out of the way spots where visitors to the beaches were "not likely to notice them." The *Enterprise* reporter assured his readers that "they have not, by any stretch of the imagination, 'taken over' the Cape's beaches," which, upon hearing the news of their construction, many Cape Codders feared. "It's rather reassuring to dwellers in our towns" that the men of the division "are there — these boys, on the alert 24 hours a day for anything that may approach our coast by sea or air, are our first line of defense on shore."[21]

These structures were very primitive, nothing more than tarpaper shacks without running water or toilet facilities. When asked where the men would go to relieve themselves, one Yankee Division veteran quipped, "the nearest bush." Actually, the engineers built "two-hole" outhouses that they positioned a short distance away. John D. Turini (G-181 and Hq. Co., 2nd Bn.-181) of Clinton wrote that the quarters had electricity to power the lights, "an electric plate" to brew coffee, and a small refrigerator. A telephone connected each of the huts to battalion headquarters.[22]

Each hut could accommodate six to eight men. In the middle of the room stood a coal fired pot bellied stove. The thin-walled buildings, just exterior boards with studs exposed on the inside, were difficult to keep warm, especially when the temperature plummeted as it so often did in New England during winter months. During extreme weather, the men had to feed the stove continuously. Supply trucks delivered bags of coal every day.

In one corner was a small kitchen area with a "military stove" for cooking. These portable units used bottled gas, similar to today's Coleman camping stoves. When furnished with as many bunks, together with a few other essential pieces of furniture, plus equipment and supplies, it made for very cramped living quarters for the occupants.

Colonel Walter E. Whitney, Ret., a member of Company L, 181st Infantry, stationed in Ipswich, says that Supply also dropped off two five-gallon cans filled with water each day for cooking, drinking, and washing. During the winter, a sign posted on the inside of the door said, "BE SURE TO GET YOUR WATER IN BEFORE 5:00 PM ON ACCOUNT OF FREEZING," wrote the *Falmouth Enterprise* reporter. These were similar in appearance to the olive-drab gasoline cans with the word "WATER" stenciled in black on the outside. Turini pointed out that the gas cans had screw on caps while the water cans had a "large snap tight cover," which "were a lot easier to handle."[23]

Battalion Headquarters designated two non-coms as outpost sergeants. Lt. Colonel Rinaldo M. Delsignore, Ret., then a sergeant with Company A, 1st Battalion, 181st Infantry, alternated the duty with Sgt. Clarence H. Quillia, one week on outpost and one week at Fort Rodman. The two NCOs were responsible for "the discipline and proper behavior of the outpost personnel." Delsignore made sure the men shaved regularly and maintained a reasonably neat military appearance. Getting the men to shave was a major problem, he said. Most did so only when absolutely necessary or when given a direct order. Sergeants Delsignore and Quillia were also responsible for the distribution of rations to all outposts.[24]

Delsignore said he had to make sure the men did not get in trouble with the local girls, who were always coming around the outposts to visit the handsome young soldiers and keep them company. On a number of occasions, he unexpectedly arrived at one of the huts to find one or more beautiful young lasses lounging about with the men. The ladies would drop by the outposts to cook, clean, or do other chores. Most of the time though, it was just to keep the soldier boys from being lonely. It seems the girls were just trying to do their part for the war effort. "There were a lot of stories," Delsignore says; "many of course were 'tall tales.'" His final remark on the subject reveals he sometimes wondered if there had not been some truth to the widespread rumors: "Then again, who knows what went on when we weren't around?"[25]

The soldiers stationed in the outposts "were treated very well" by the people living nearby. "They would occasionally allow them to use the bathrooms in their homes to shower and clean up," wrote Delsignore. Normally, the men had to take sponge baths. Some of the men would make periodic trips to local USO clubhouses to shower or bathe, but they could only go occasionally because of the distance and the fact that their off-duty time was so short. Getting clothes cleaned was also a problem while on outpost duty. At times, the shelters must have taken on the smell of a locker room. Many of the men slept in their uniforms and as a result were apt to look disheveled and unkempt.[26]

According to Delsignore, many of the men never wanted to come off outpost duty. "Back at the barracks the men were required to perform close order drill every day, which they hated." To avoid this, and other unpleasant garrison duties, he said, some of the men would volunteer to remain on beach patrol at one of the outposts on a continual basis. One guy was on duty so long that he began to smell pretty bad, much to the dismay of his hutmates. He did not want to leave. Delsignore had to eventually remove the man from the outpost and return him to the barracks.[27]

The *Falmouth Enterprise* reporter noted that one young man, who had just returned from the USO Club, looked clean and fresh after a hot shower and a shave. He had stopped by the local barbershop for a badly needed haircut and was dressed in a freshly pressed uniform and clean shiny boots. In "a couple of days," he would "probably look just like the others," the reporter commented.[28]

* * *

On February 1, 1942, approximately six weeks after the companies of the 2nd Battalion, 181st Infantry, arrived at their duty stations, Division ordered the unit to return to Camp Edwards for "three months of combat problems," presumably in preparation for an overseas assignment. The "History of the 181st Infantry" states that at this time the 2nd Battalion, 104th Infantry, relieved the unit and assumed its overall responsibilities. The 104th regimental history reported that the infantry's remained on shore patrol from "January until March." Clifford Welcome says that Coast Guard personnel replaced the men of the 3rd platoon, Company F, 181st Infantry, on Long Island.[29]

At the end of March, division ordered the 104th to return to Camp Edwards for "three months of advanced training." At this time, the 101st relieved the 104th and continued the beach patrols until early May, when 1st Army Headquarters ordered the 181st Infantry to return to coast patrol duty and take over the unit's duties (see below).[30]

* * *

At this time (February 1941), the War Department authorized the 26th Division to bring its numbers up to "full war strength." Only figures for the 181st Infantry are available for comparison. Full strength for a regiment at that time was 123 officers and 3,325 enlisted men. In accordance with the order, the regiment increased the number of EMs by 824, from 2,436 to 3,260. The incoming replacements received their basic training at Camp Wheeler, Georgia. Between February and December, there were some losses, a result of numerous transfers. During this period, Officers Candidate School (OCS) selected a significant number of applicants to fill the Army's growing need for qualified leaders.[31]

Based on this information, total strength for the division (three regiments) would have been approximately 10,745. This figure includes the Division staff of 15 officers, 44 men of Headquarters Detachment, and the approximately 340 men that comprised the Special Troops section, which included Headquarters Detachment Special Troops, Military Police Company, Signal Company, Tank Company, 101st Ordnance Company, and the Medical Department Detachment.

15

Return to Coast Patrol Duty, May 1942: German Spies and Saboteurs Land on American Shores

On April 10, 1942, East Coast newspapers carried a press release issued by General Sherman Miles, commanding officer of the First Corps Area, calling for the assistance of citizens in the event German submarines attempted to land enemy agents along the Atlantic coast. The statement read in part:

> An attempt may be made to land enemy agents from Axis submarines operating off our shores. Such agents would carefully avoid attracting attention, but may betray themselves through their unfamiliarity with the locality.
> If you see a strange face in an unlikely spot and have sound reason to believe the person is acting suspiciously, notify your local police at once.

The alert issued by Miles is an indication that the military was aware, or strongly suspected, that the Germans had already landed agents on the shores of the United States. Miles warned the people to let "good judgment and commonsense govern [their] actions in this matter" and that they "should be careful not to start a spy-scare or witch-hunt."[1]

Approximately one month after the alert by Gen. Miles, in early May 1942, the Eastern Defense Command recalled the 26th Infantry Division to coast patrol duty to assist the Navy and Coast Guard. The War Department expanded the division's area of responsibility along the entire eastern seaboard from Maine to Florida, with the exception of key areas, which the EDC assigned to the Navy or Coast Guard. Units of the 101st Infantry (3rd Battalion and 101st Field Artillery Battalion) had remained on patrol in the Boston Sub-sector since January (see below). Shortly after receiving the order, Division Headquarters moved its command post to Fort A.P. Hill, Fredericksburg, Virginia.[2]

Provided here is a list of the areas assigned to the military by the EDC: the 181st Infantry was responsible for securing the coast from the Canadian border south to the Connecticut, Rhode Island line; the U.S. Navy patrolled the Connecticut coast, from Quonset Point, Rhode Island, west to the naval base at New London; Coast Guard personnel patrolled the Washington, D.C., area as well as all areas around naval bases; and the 104th Infantry covered the remainder of the East Coast from North Carolina southward to Key West, Florida, a distance of more than 1,000 miles.[3]

At this time, division relocated the 181st Infantry Command Post from Boston to Camp Framingham, Massachusetts. Regiment assigned the battalions as follows: the 1st Battalion to the Newport Sub-sector, with headquarters at Camp Burlingame, Westerly, Rhode Island (minus Company C, attached to the 2nd Battalion); the 2nd Battalion to the Portland Sub-

Company L, 181st Infantry outpost at Coolidge Estate, Coolidge Point, Manchester, Massachusetts (the caption says Magnolia, Massachusetts, which is part of Gloucester, Massachusetts). Jim Dineen, Johnny Soubble, and Bob Welch. Notice telescope at right (Dorothy E. Dineen Collection — Massachusetts National Guard Military Museum and Archives, Worcester).

sector, with headquarters in Saco, Maine; and the 3rd Battalion to the Boston Sub-sector, with headquarters at South Hingham, Massachusetts. For a list of stations assigned to the individual units of the 181st Infantry, see Appendix C.[4]

On May 11, 1942, division attached the following support units to the 181st Infantry: the 211th Field Artillery Battalion; two companies of the 22nd Quartermaster Regiment "Trucks (Colored) attached for transportation"; one company of the 132nd Combat Engineers; and a detachment of the 114th Medical Battalion. Together, they comprised the 181st Infantry Regimental Combat Team (RCT 181). According to the 26th Division history, the combat team "was the basic foundation for providing a highly mobile, self sufficient, shock producing and well balanced strike force." This pattern of organization, made standard throughout the division, created a number of "highly flexible" combat ready units, "which could be adjusted by adding or detaching supporting troops to the Infantry Regiments as the situation required."[5]

* * *

Rosaire J. "Ross" Rajotte, a native of Northbridge, Massachusetts, joined the National Guard at age 19 on November 3, 1939, and received an assignment to Company D, 1st Battalion, 181st Infantry, a heavy weapons company. Before entering the guard, he enrolled in the Civilian Conservation Corps (CCC) at age 17 in July 1937 (government officials referred to corps workers as enrollees). Ross wrote, "When I left home, my mother said, 'Son, make sure you go to church and always obey those over you.'" His enlistment in the CCC began with a 30 day training period at a Citizen's Military Training Camp (C.M.T.C.) at Fort Devens, in Ayer, Massachusetts. The CCC sent him to Pittsfield, Massachusetts, from September 1937 to September 1939, where he "worked on a crew doing forestry work and fighting forest fires." Rajotte worked six days a week with Sundays off. After the devastating 1938 hurricane, he "moved from Pittsfield to Warwick, Rhode Island, for a time to clear fallen pines."[6]

Ross was a member of D Company's 1st machine gun platoon. In May 1942, the company moved from Camp Edwards to Camp Burlingame in Westerly, Rhode Island. The units stationed at the camp included "part of Headquarters Company [1st Battalion]; Company B; [211th] Field Artillery [Battalion], Battery 1; and 22nd Quartermaster Colored Soldiers." The CO of Company H attached Rajotte's platoon to Company B, a rifle company. He wrote:

> We patrolled from Westerly to the Point Judith, Narragansett Police Station. Every two miles we had an outpost, 2 huts, one to sleep — one [for] operations, outdoor latrines. Two man patrols with dog. First shift from 6 P.M. to midnight, 2nd shift midnight to 6 A.M. If a lot of fog, we had day patrols. Based at Coast Guard Station [Westerly?] 4 of us on rotation. Acted as Coast Guardsmen on watch under Coast Guard Officers.

Rajotte says, "We learned what a Coast Guardsman's life was like." When he first arrived, Ross asked a Coast Guardsman, "Where's the latrine? The man said to me, 'What's a latrine?' I said 'a toilet,' they called it the 'head.' We called [the patrols] 'guard duty,' they called it 'on watch.' 'Leave' they called 'Liberty.' Ross said, "During our off hours we would fish for striped bass."[7]

Rajotte remembers an incident involving some of the black truck drivers from the quartermaster company attached to the 1st Battalion in Westerly, Rhode Island. One day, some of the men in his company were off-duty and decided to kill time by playing a game of volleyball. A group of the quartermaster drivers was hanging around nearby watching the competition. One of the men came over and challenged Rajotte and the others to a game; they readily

Comp. L, 181st Inf.— Mess Hall, Ipswich, Massachusetts (Dorothy E. Dineen Collection — Massachusetts National Guard Military Museum and Archives, Worcester).

Jim Dineen's barrack, Ipswich, Massachusetts. Jim looking out the door with Lucy Arent and Dorothy Dineen standing to right (Dorothy E. Dineen Collection — Massachusetts National Guard Military Museum and Archives, Worcester).

accepted. The men from the quartermaster corps "were excellent athletes and gave our guys a good game.... It was a spirited rivalry and the men got along fine," he said, "when a white officer from D Company, a captain, approached [the group] and demanded to know what was going on." He "gave the men Hell for playing with negroes" and "told us to break up the game."[8]

* * *

Paul J. Turini (G-181) said in an interview, "When we arrived for duty at Horseneck Beach that May, there was no place to stay while out on patrol." The platoon leader, 2nd Lt. Russell W. Vinton ordered Turini to break the lock on a nearby vacant summer cottage and the men moved in and set up quarters. Other than the damage to the lock, he said they were very respectful of the property and kept it neat and clean. Then one day, the owner and his family showed up. A neighbor had called him to say the soldiers were occupying the house. "The owner was bitching and moaning," Turini said. "Lt. Vinton told him, 'Would you rather have us or the Germans in your house?'"[9]

* * *

Two quite celebrated incidents involving the landing of enemy agents on American shores occurred in June 1942. One of the landings took place on Saturday, June 13, 1942, near the tiny coastal hamlet of Amagansett on the southern shore of Long Island, about one hundred and five miles east of New York City. It was widely publicized in the media at the time and became known as the "Amagansett Incident" or "Amagansett Affair." The second incident took place at Ponte Vedra Beach, Florida, twenty-five miles southeast of Jacksonville, a few days later (June 17). Two of Admiral Karl Doenitz's U-boats transported eight highly trained Nazi agents across the Atlantic, four of whom landed at each point.

The Abwehr II, the intelligence arm of the German High Command, was fully aware "that the long coastline of the U.S. could not be easily defended." The Germans were convinced that "America's defenses were paltry" and devised an elaborate plan designed "to take advantage of the unprepared and apparently naïve new enemy." The beach patrols "were the second line of defense of the U.S. coastline, behind the paltry handful of patrol craft," wrote historian Edwin P. Hoyt. "Small wonder the Germans were contemptuous of American defenses," he commented. In 1939, the German High Command, under direct orders from Adolf Hitler, implemented a top-secret program to recruit and train a group of specialists for the destruction of industrial plants and other vital installations in America.[10]

The Abwehr carefully picked the candidates considered for sabotage training after a thorough investigation of their background. All of the trainees chosen to participate in the program were born in Germany, had spent a good portion of their lives in the United States, and had become well acquainted with American customs. Recruiters placed "a high value ... on individuals who had belonged to the German-American Bund [Friends of the New Germany] or similar organization." One of the criteria for selection was that they spoke fluent English, without the slightest trace of an accent. Before the outbreak of the war these men, for one reason or another, returned to their native land where, because of their ties to America, Abwehr officials recruited them for the sinister mission. The inducement was "that they would be fulfilling their duty to their country," plus the "promise of good positions in Germany and other rewards" if their mission was successful.[11]

Thoroughly trained by the Abwehr "in the most modern methods of destruction," the team of agents carried with them more than $175,000 in U.S. currency to use for expenses in carrying out their work, along with enough demolition materials to carry on a two-year campaign of sabotage against vital war industries. Training took place at Quentz Lake, a facility designed and built by the Abwehr. Described as "a seminary of sabotage," the school was located about 40 miles west of Berlin near Brandenburg. Teachers at the facility were experts in their particular fields: explosives, chemicals, electricity, and allied arts useful in destruction.[12]

Once in the country, the leaders at the school instructed the agents to settle quietly in some of the major U.S. cities and develop contacts with Nazis and other known sympathizers. After the team had set up a base of operations, its mission was to engage in acts of sabotage against a number of specific targets. The saboteurs were to place "particular emphasis ... on interrupting production at aluminum and magnesium plants" (used in the production of military aircraft) as well as to disrupt the rail network necessary for the transportation of war materials. German leaders realized the importance of interfering with the production of aluminum and magnesium by the "light metal industries," as "it would have a serious effect on the number of military aircraft produced by the United States," which would in turn "have a definite effect on the outcome of the war."[13]

The Abwehr designated the combined Amagansett-Ponte Vedra mission Operation Pastorius, after Franz Daniel Pastorius, the leader of the first community of German immigrants in America. The group, consisting of thirteen Mennonite and Quaker families, founded Germantown, Pennsylvania, in 1683.

The landing of *U-202* at Amagansett, which took place shortly after midnight on the morning of Saturday, June 13, occurred three miles west of Easthampton on the sparsely populated east end of Long Island. Sand dunes along this part of the beach extended "for several hundred yards to the beach road," running roughly parallel to the coastline. An occasional summer cottage and fisherman's shack dotted the roadway. A twenty-one-year-old Coast Guardsman, Seaman 2nd Class John Cullen, had just left the East Amagansett Coast Guard

Comp. L, 181st Inf.— Inside of Recreation Hall, Ipswich, Massachusetts (Dorothy E. Dineen Collection — Massachusetts National Guard Archives & Museum, Worcester).

Life Saving Station about twenty minutes before, and was patrolling the beach alone and unarmed. Cullen carried with him only a flashlight and flare gun. It was a pitch-black moonless night with a thick swirling fog drifting in and out off the choppy water. Visibility was limited to only fifteen to twenty feet.[14]

As the "sand pounder" walked along the well-worn path through the dunes covered here and there with a "few scraggly bushes and beach plants," he heard muffled voices a short distance down the beach and approached to investigate. In the distance, he could make out the ghostlike silhouettes of three men "faintly visible through the fog." When Cullen moved closer, he saw one man dressed in a civilian suit and tie on shore, and two others in bathing suits laboring around an inflatable rubber raft near the waterline.[15]

The man in the suit was Georg Johann Dasch, the leader of the four-man team of saboteurs. The men in swimming trunks, sailors from the submarine who had paddled the raft ashore, were standing in the surf up to their knees and appeared to be unloading something from the boat. Three other men, Dasch's accomplices, had taken some of the equipment and supplies to higher ground for burial among the dunes and were out of sight.[16]

Dasch just happened to glance over his shoulder and noticed "a light moving slowly down the beach." He said, "My heart nearly stopped beating." Without a word, he left the sailors and dashed off in the direction of the light beam to intercept whoever it was. The order to kill anyone who interfered with the landing party was uppermost in his mind. The two German sailors attending the rubber raft were armed with light machine guns. If by chance the landing party happened to encounter anyone upon reaching the beach, the crewmembers were under "strict instructions" from the U-boat commander to overpower them and bring the body or bodies back to the boat. When they were back at sea, the captain was going to "feed them to the fish."[17]

Dasch had already made up his mind that once he arrived back in the United States he would go directly to the FBI in Washington and turn state's evidence. The last thing he wanted to see happen was for an innocent American to get killed. "Coming upon the light," he wrote, "I found myself confronted by a boy in an American sailor's uniform." Dasch ordered him to put the light out. "You don't know what danger you're walking into," he whispered to him. "Are you Coast Guard?" Dasch asked. "Yes, who are you?" replied Cullen. He then introduced himself to the young man as George Davis and asked the patrolman what his name was. "He answered something that sounded like John Cullen or Collins," Dasch recalled.[18]

Cullen inquired if he was a fisherman, and was he in some kind of trouble. Dasch answered, "No, we're not fishermen, and I can't tell you what this is all about." Cullen said, "Hey, what is this anyway?" and started toward the other men. Dasch grabbed his arm and pulled him back. "Look here boy," he said, "I can't tell you what's going on just now. This is only a matter for Washington." Cullen still did not seem to understand the danger he was in, and again headed toward the men near the boat. Dasch pleaded with him again, "You have a mother don't you, boy? Well if you ever want to see her again, please do exactly what I tell you." Dasch said to Cullen, "You have undoubtedly given your oath to do your duty, and you are performing your duty by doing exactly what I tell you." He then pulled his hat back and said, "I want you to shine your light in my face so that you'll recognize me when I have you called in Washington."[19]

At that point, Ernest Peter Burger, one of the saboteurs who had returned to the raft with the others came out of the shadows and said something to Dasch in a foreign language that Cullen thought was German, but was not sure. With this, Dasch got very angry and growled, "Shut up you damn fool." He told his companion that everything was all right and ordered him to get back to the boat and wait with the others. Dasch said sternly, "I'll handle this myself." Cullen, recalling the incident years later, said that when the other man spoke in German, it "jarred" him, and made him "suspicious."[20]

Unsure of what to do next, Cullen asked the man to return with him to the Coast Guard station and wait for daylight. In his desperation to get rid of the guardsman before any danger befell him, Dasch reached into his pants pocket and pulled out a large wad of bills. Cullen thought at first he was going for a gun. He offered the seaman a bribe of $150, if he would forget what he had seen. The young man refused at first. Dasch immediately raised the offer to $300. Realizing at this point that he was in grave danger, and knowing he did not stand a chance against four men, Cullen agreed to accept the money. It had also occurred to him that without the money as evidence, no one would ever believe his story.[21]

A very fearful Cullen backed up slowly for several steps, then turned and walked swiftly away not knowing if at any moment he was going to be gunned down from behind. When Cullen was sure he was out of sight, he ran as fast as he could back to the station. He recalled later, "I made it in record time." Dasch went back to the others and assured them everything was all right.[22]

After Cullen left, Dasch ordered the two sailors back to the submarine, and instructed them to report to the captain that the landing was successful. The saboteurs hurriedly buried several waterproof oaken boxes containing hundreds of pounds of TNT and numerous incendiary devices along with some discarded clothing in the sand among the dunes.

When Cullen arrived back at the station, he immediately reported the incident to Boatswain's Mate 2nd Class Carl Ross Jenette, the acting duty officer in charge, who "listened to his story with understandable credulity." Cullen turned the money over to his superior. Jenette counted the bills and found the German agent had short-changed Cullen by $40.[23]

Jenette put a telephone call through to the Headquarters District Supervisor at the Napeague Station (on the ocean side of Long Island, approximately 10 miles southwest by west of Montauk Point Light) and spoke with Chief Boatswain's Mate 2nd Class Warren Barnes, the officer on duty. Barnes telephoned Coast Guard Headquarters in New York City and reported the incident to the duty officer who swore him to secrecy. The duty officer relayed the information up the chain of command, which eventually reached the desk of Rear Admiral Adolphus Anderson, commander of the Third Naval District. Jenette then alerted the men at the station, armed them with .30 caliber rifles and, with Cullen leading the way, headed down the path toward the beach area.[24]

After the U-boat made its drop-off, it ran aground in the shallow water about 150 feet from shore. In an attempt to free the vessel, the captain ran the engines up to full speed and discharged a large quantity of fuel oil from its tanks to lighten the ship. Visibility had increased somewhat by the time Jenette and his men reached the landing site. They heard the whine of the diesel engines and spotted the faint image of the submarine's superstructure offshore. Cullen remembered, "She had a blinker light. We ducked behind a dune, not wanting to get shelled." The tide began to shift and the commander finally managed to free the craft from the sandbar. The U-boat moved slowly off to the east gathering speed as it went. After the submarine departed, Jenette and his men combed the area for any sign of the landing party. After a lengthy search turned up nothing, Jenette decided to return to the station. As the detail was about to leave, a unit from the Army's 113th Infantry Detachment, part of the area's Sector Mobile Force, arrived at the scene.[25]

The "History of the EDC" explained that the 113th "had not been alerted through normal channels," but by radio operator on-duty at the nearby Amagansett Naval Radio Station, who heard the sound of the U-boat's throbbing engines and smelled a strong odor of diesel fuel. At first, the radioman called the Coast Guard Station. "The Coast Guardsman who picked up the phone," said, "I'm sorry. We can't discuss enemy activity.... He hung up." Coast Guard Headquarters had ordered all personnel not to discuss the matter (see above). Next, the radioman contacted the Third Naval District command post at Riverhead, Long Island. The officer in charge (OIC) informed him that they had no information to give and did not take the report seriously. Finally, the radioman contacted the 113th Infantry Detachment, "and after some difficulty" managed to convince the officer on duty that "something was up."[26]

The command post of the 113th, consisting of 100 officers and men, was located five miles down the beach to the east. The OIC dispatched 20 men and an officer to the site of the landing, arriving at about 2 A.M. He then telephoned the Federal Bureau of Investigation Headquarters on 42nd Street in Manhattan to report the incident. The New York office immediately alerted field agents. When the Army unit arrived at the landing site, it met and joined with the Coast Guard detail. The officer conferred with Boatswain's Mate Jenette, who apprised him of the situation.[27]

The "History of the EDC" reports that the "information given [to the Coast Guard District Headquarters] was apparently not very forceful or urgent or at least was not treated as such" and it was 2 A.M. before notice of the incident reached the OIC at the Navy's Eastern Sea Frontier Headquarters in New York. This apparently "was not the only intelligence that was mishandled," he added. The previous evening, a Navy radio direction finder had established a fix, "presumably on the same submarine." The U-boat commander had sent out a radio transmission to his base at Lorient, France, "from a point not 30 miles from the Amagansett radio station at 8:53 P.M. on the night of the landings." Hoyt related that the "transmission had been noted and reported to Washington, where red tape delayed it for two and a half hours before it was forwarded back to the New York area for action."[28]

At first light, a second detail from the Coast Guard Station arrived and made a more thorough search of the area around the landing point. One of the men discovered an empty package of German made cigarettes half buried in the sand. A short distance away, searchers found a wet bathing suit (left out in the open by Ernest Burger — see below). The search team followed signs of dragging in the sand until they came to the end of the furrows. Coast Guardsmen dug up four large boxes loaded with metal tins packed with explosives, along with a duffle bag containing four German Marine fatigue uniforms, worn by the saboteurs when they came ashore. The uniforms would "ensure" that if captured they would be treated as prisoners of war "rather than being shot as spies." The Coast Guardsmen delivered the wooden boxes and other items to Coast Guard Headquarters in New York. The cases were later examined and found to contain a number of ingenious sabotage devices: brick sized blocks of high explosives, bombs disguised as "lumps of coal," a wide array of fuses and detonating caps, and incendiary devices disguised as innocent looking "pen and pencil sets."[29]

Around 6 A.M., units from other commands in the area began arriving at the scene of the landing. Several high-ranking officers from the Third Naval District Headquarters in Manhattan, as well as personnel from Navy, Coast Guard, and Army Intelligence showed up at various times during the day. At 10 P.M. that evening, agents from the FBI arrived on the scene "in force" and launched their own investigation. Shortly thereafter, the agent in charge announced to all present that the bureau was assuming jurisdiction over the investigation, which did not sit well with the officers in charge of the teams from the various military branches. The chief Navy intelligence officer protested vehemently. He put a call through by radio to Admiral Anderson, who asked to speak with the lead investigator for the FBI team. The FBI agent complained to the commander that Navy personnel "were getting in the way" of the investigation, and that he believed the Coast Guardsmen "were actually withholding evidence." Hoyt says, "The latter charge was true."[30]

After burying the waterproof boxes and disposing of their uniforms, the four saboteurs cautiously moved inland through the dunes and made their way to the Amagansett Railroad station in time to catch the 6:30 A.M. commuter train for Jamaica, in the borough of Queens just east of New York City. Upon arriving in the city, Dasch gave each of the men $700 spending money. They shopped for new clothes and accessories at several local haberdasheries, and changed in the men's room of a nearby restaurant. The men easily assimilated into the neighborhood, which had a sizeable German immigrant population. The agents split into pairs, agreeing to meet later in the day at a cafeteria in New York City. Dasch and Ernest Burger remained together and registered at the Governor Clinton Hotel opposite Pennsylvania Station in mid-town Manhattan, one of the city's finest.[31]

Dasch and Burger discussed the group's plans in their New York City hotel room and confessed they had reservations. Both men admitted to each other that they signed on to the mission only as a means of returning to America. Burger informed Dasch that he left incriminating items on the beach in the hope that someone would discover them soon after the landings and report it to the authorities.[32]

Thirty nine year old Georg Dasch, a German national, was born in Germany in 1903. He came to America as a stowaway in 1922, settled down and married an American citizen. He worked as a waiter in some of New York's finest restaurants and served in the U.S. Army Air Corps. Disgruntled because he could find work only as a lowly waiter, Dasch decided to return to his homeland in 1939.[33]

Ernest Peter Burger had worked as a machinist in Detroit and Milwaukee and had been a member of the Michigan National Guard. He became a naturalized citizen in 1933. Burger returned to Germany and worked for the Nazi Party in Munich and later Berlin. In early 1940, party officials sent Burger to Poland to investigate "reports of abuses of authority and profiteering by a number of high Nazi officials." The governing Nazis in Poland "learned his purpose," and "framed" him for "violating party rules." His accusers had him arrested and charged him with being disloyal to the party. Burger "spent seventeen months in the basement prison at Gestapo Headquarters in Berlin," where "Nazi bullies" reportedly beat and tortured him. Gestapo agents "grilled" his wife "so mercilessly" that she suffered a miscarriage. Following Burger's release from prison, "his standing in the party was partially restored," and because of his background the Abwehr recruited him to attend the Quentz Lake training facility. Burger was so bitter about the Gestapo's mistreatment of his wife and his own wrongful imprisonment and torture by party officials that "he had vowed to betray Hitler (whom he had known personally) at the first opportunity."[34]

Dasch's plan was to go straight to the top and see FBI director J. Edgar Hoover in Washington, D.C. On Sunday evening, the day after the landing, he telephoned the FBI's New York office from a public phone booth, while Burger waited outside on the street, to make his intentions known, but the agent on duty dismissed him as a "crackpot." On Thursday the 18th, Dasch traveled to the capital by train where he surrendered to FBI agents and betrayed his comrades. He revealed the whereabouts of the other members of the group and the details of the sabotage operation. Dasch told authorities he had planned to turn himself in long before he left Germany. Swanberg wrote, "Dasch felt that by exposing the plot he would become an American hero celebrated in headlines and honored by the President."[35]

The landing by U-584 at Ponte Vedra Beach, Florida, on June 17 went "totally unobserved by any Americans." The party, led by Edward John Kerling, buried four heavy wooden cases containing explosives and other sabotage materials near an abandoned house about 200 feet east of U.S. Highway A1A. They walked north along the shore to Jacksonville Beach, "and dashed into the surf as if they were young men on vacation." The four saboteurs put their clothes on over their swim trunks and walked to the main highway where they boarded a bus to Jacksonville, without arousing even the slightest suspicion of the driver or any of the passengers. When they reached Jacksonville, the team paired off, staying at separate hotels in the city. The next day, two of the men went to New York City, while the other two traveled to Chicago as planned.[36]

The landings set off one of the biggest manhunts in FBI history. As a result of the information provided by Dasch, all eight would-be Nazi saboteurs were in federal custody by July 27, 1942, only two weeks after they arrived.

President Roosevelt "was determined that a speedy example be made of the eight in order to discourage further conspiracies." He was "of the opinion that the two saboteurs who were American citizens [Dasch and Burger] were guilty of high treason, and that the other six were in the category of spies, and that all deserved the death penalty." At the time, the president was unaware of Dasch's involvement. Roosevelt was against a public trial, which would result in "too many sensitive details ending up in the public records" and might not insure a verdict of guilty, since the men committed no acts of sabotage. After consulting with the attorney general and the secretary of war, he decided to try the accused as "enemy soldiers" before a closed military tribunal, with seven prominent generals of the army acting as judges.[37]

The court appointed Army Colonel Kenneth C. Royall, a noted civilian attorney, and Col. Cassius M. McDowell, a 40 year veteran of the Regular Army, described as attorneys of "superlative skill," as defense council for the accused. The lead prosecutor was Attorney General Francis B. Biddle, assisted by Maj. Gen. Myron C. Cramer. The trial, which began on July 8, 1942, lasted 20 days. Royall appealed to the U.S. Supreme Court for a writ of habeas corpus, challenging the legality of the president's decision. The justices convened on July 29, 1942, the court's first special session since 1920, and after two days of deliberation denied Royall's motion "upholding the jurisdiction and authority of the military tribunal."[38]

On August 3, the tribunal reached its verdict. In a unanimous decision, the justices found all eight defendants guilty of the charges and recommended the death penalty. The court, however, submitted a request that the president commute Dasch and Burger's sentence to 30 years and life in prison respectively. After five days of review, Roosevelt affirmed the decision. On August 8, 1942, the six condemned men, their faces masked, were executed by electrocution in the District of Columbia jail. Corrections officials buried the six saboteurs in the district's "Potter's field at Blue Plains"; the headstones "consisted of unpainted boards bearing only the numbers from 276 to 281."[39]

J. Edgar Hoover and the FBI received all the credit in the media for capturing the eight saboteurs and foiling Operation Pastorius. Had it not been for the voluntary surrender of Georg Johann Dasch, kept secret by Mr. Hoover, the agency might never have discovered the whereabouts of the agents. The FBI director even kept the pertinent details regarding the extent of Dasch's involvement in the apprehension of the remaining seven saboteurs from the president. The public never knew the complete story until many years after the war. Hoover's course of action in this matter was a calculated move to enhance the bureau's image.

Federal agents informed Dasch that he would be imprisoned "for a few months" and then eventually "receive a presidential pardon." Dasch and Burger spent five years and eight months in the Federal Penitentiary in Atlanta. In April 1948, the Department of Justice, with President Truman's approval, commuted their sentences to deportation.[40]

* * *

The two landings demonstrated to government and military officials, "quite forcefully," that the "patrols then operating" were not adequate to guard the East Coast of the U.S. Following an official government inquiry, investigators determined that the military had badly mishandled intelligence regarding the two incidents, and "that the systems of liaison and dissemination of intelligence" in place at the time between the various branches of the service "were not effectively understood or applied." Officials ordered that immediate steps be taken to correct "both of these shortcomings."[41]

One of the subsequent outcomes of the affair was the decision by the War Department to bolster the country's home defenses by committing more men to the patrol and surveillance of America's coastline. Government officials also urged that the military consider using sentry dogs to aid in beach patrols. The U.S. Army took immediate steps to have canines and handlers delivered to the units of the 26th Division as soon as the Quartermaster Corps could make the necessary arrangements (see Chapter 21, Patrol-Scout Dogs).[42]

The landings also had a profound influence on the fate of the 26th Division, resulting in a delay in receiving an assignment to a combat theater of operations. Original plans called for the eventual takeover of all coast patrol duties by Navy and Coast Guard personnel, which would have freed up the division for reassignment overseas. The two incidents were definitely a contributing factor in the War Department's decision to continue the 26th Division on patrol duty for an indefinite period.

* * *

A diary written by Edward J. Griffin, a T/Sergeant with Company L, 101st Infantry, while recuperating from wounds received in France in 1944, indicates that shortly after the enemy landings took place, the 26th Division detached Company L, and sent the unit to Long Island. At the time, the company was on shore patrol duty in the Boston Sub-sector. Griffin's entry dated "June '42" reads:

> Emergency mission (German saboteurs landed on Long Island June 16 [sic]) 3rd Bn. (101st) on Special duty from Div. arrive at Camp Mills adjacent to Marshall Field provides protection for the airdrome and also resumed Coast Patrol duty from outposts along the No. and So. Shore. Co. L had sector on No. shore from Kings Point to Lloyds Neck, on So. the 15 mi[le] strip known as Jones Beach.

In a letter dated July 6, 2000, Griffin wrote, "I will always remember our first night on Long Island. Our Captain had us pitch our squad tents in a cabbage patch, sure enough it poured all night and we woke up to find water up to the top of our cots. Thankfully, we moved to higher ground and dried out."[43]

In July 1942, the company moved its base of operations to the town of Bethpage, Long Island, near the Grumman and Republic aircraft plants. Griffin says that they had four days duty on the beach and twenty-four hours off. New York City was only a "1 hour ride" away. This was, he wrote, "the best 'deal' we ever got in the Army." Griffin's October 1942 entry reads: "All good things must come to an end, Bn. rejoins Regt. at Ft. Geo. G. Meade between Baltimore and Washington, D.C."[44]

16

U-Boat Sightings and Encounters by the Men of the 181st Infantry

There have been a number of unconfirmed reports related to me by veterans of the 181st Infantry whom I interviewed, and from other sources, which indicate that many other landings may have taken place on remote beaches and other points along the coast of New England during this period.

One incident, as reported by Capt. Theodore Simmington, Jr., of Company K, 181st Infantry, stationed at Plymouth, Massachusetts, took place on Cape Cod (date unknown). Company K patrolled the beaches from Nantasket to East Dennis, with the exception of the Cape Cod Canal area, which was the responsibility of the Coast Artillery and the Coast Guard. "We had a scare one night about 10:30 P.M.," Simmington wrote, "when we got a call from the Coast Guard that their men shot a[t a?] couple of men coming ashore in a rubber boat in Truro."[1]

Simmington, the officer of the day (OD), was on duty at Company K headquarters. He ordered his men to gather their weapons and equipment and fall out on the double. Men and gear were loaded onto three trucks that sped off toward Truro over the main roads with their blackout lights on. The captain led the procession in his jeep equipped with a .30-caliber machine gun mounted on a pedestal in the back. The detail's assignment was "to cut off the Cape so the enemy couldn't move toward the bridges."[2]

Michael Stubinski (K-181) was a member of the 26th Division who, like my father, eventually ended up with the 36th Division in Italy as a replacement. Knowing Mike was a member of Company K, I sent him a copy of this manuscript chapter for review and he wrote back to tell me he was Captain Simmington's driver on the night in question. Stubinski wrote, "I had a Hell of a time getting to the canal without lights. The Captain was worried, but we made it without incident." I put Stubinski in touch with Simmington and the two men corresponded.[3]

The following morning, a detail from Battalion Headquarters in South Hingham relieved Simmington's unit. Word filtered down later from higher up that the FBI caught two men in the trunk of a car going over one of the bridges to the mainland. "You know how rumors fly under those circumstances," Simmington said, "so we never knew what the real story was."[4]

Romeo LeBlanc (H-181) remembers two incidents involving suspected German agents. On one occasion, a company patrol picked up three suspicious looking individuals and delivered them to Military Police Headquarters in Saco, Maine, for interrogation. When the men failed to satisfactorily explain their presence in the area, the MPs handed the suspects over to FBI agents. LeBlanc also recalls a second incident where a patrol took two men into custody. "One of the men apprehended was carrying a suitcase full of money," he said. His final comment was, "We never did find out what happened to them."[5]

Joel W. Eastman, a history professor at the University of Southern Maine, reported in his paper "Casco Bay During World War II" that in May 1942, "the State Director of Civilian Defense announced that German spies and agents had been landed on the Maine coast." This was the same month that General Miles issued his statement warning the public of attempts by German submarines to land enemy agents.[6]

Marc P. Fecteau, the son of the late Phillip Fecteau, a member of the 3rd Platoon, 26th Mechanized Cavalry Reconnaissance Troop, attached to the 181st Infantry, says his father once told him that his unit picked up two German speaking men coming from the area of the beaches. Stationed at Ellsworth, Maine, the 26th Recon Troop took over the old Ellsworth Hotel on School Street, which also served as its headquarters. The unit's area of responsibility included all the seaport towns between Ellsworth and Machias (see Chapter 23, The Rockland Sector). Fecteau and the other members of the patrol questioned the suspected agents and then turned them over to superiors. "Headquarters never informed him if those captives were actually spies," the son said.[7]

Talmadge "Ted" Allen of Company A, 132nd Combat Engineers (attached to the 181st Infantry), stationed at the Saco Armory, says that in 1943 "some other members" of his company "captured six German spies who had come ashore near Ocean Park [located between Saco and Old Orchard Beach] in a rubber raft." The Germans "had their submarines all over the place. They were looking for good places to land, Old Orchard Beach was a good place for them to come in, I guess."[8]

While stationed in Weekapaug, Rhode Island, during the summer of 1942, John J. Voellings (B-181) says that he "observed an object on the horizon that resembled a sub." In a later interview, Voellings says he "spotted the sub using a telescope." He "radioed this information" to headquarters "and was told to disregard." "Shortly thereafter," he heard that "the object was destroyed." Years later, while visiting the area where his company had been stationed during the war, Voellings "learned from some of the local scuba divers that there was a sunken German sub in the waters off Block Island that they explore." In 1996, Voellings contacted his congressman, Peter Blute, and asked him to check into the matter.[9]

One of Congressman Blute's aides wrote to National Personnel Records Center (NPRC) in St. Louis and they in turn contacted the Navy Department. It seems the Navy referred the matter to the National Archives and Records Center (NARA) at College Park, Maryland. On February 21, 1997, Voellings received a letter from Barry L. Zerby (no title) of the Textual Archives Services Division, stating that his agency needed more information, including "the date of the sinking, the name of the U-Boat, and the name of the ship or unit which sank the U-Boat." This reply seems very unusual, since this is the very information Voellings was seeking. The letter did include a copy of a "fishing chart of the area that is between Block Island and Montauk Light on the eastern tip of Long Island" indicating a sunken U-boat in area 43880. Zerby added a postscript: "A few months ago, the Germans complained about the looting of the sub by scuba divers."[10]

The evidence presented here, and in the Rockland chapter, detailing encounters with suspected subversive Nazi agents by the men of the 181st Infantry, is a strong indication that there were many other incursions along the East Coast of the U.S. It appears also that most of the incidents were hushed up before they reached the press. Was there a deliberate effort by J. Edgar Hoover and the FBI to prevent the public from knowing the extent of the problem? The number of enemy operatives that may have successfully entered the country by submarine or other means is subject to conjecture.

17

Problems and Developments

As reported in the "History of the Eastern Defense Command," the observation and patrol of such a long stretch of the coast presented the military with a number of logistical problems and other difficulties, "not only of terrain and weather conditions but the personnel problem of patrolling so long a line with so few men." To offset the manpower shortage problem, Regiment scheduled fewer patrols during the daylight hours. If during the day fog, haze, or heavy rain limited visibility, sector commanders added additional patrols. Generally, patrols covered every part of the shoreline "at least once every two hours."[1]

"At its maximum in the New England Sector, the combined Army-Coast Guard patrol system permitted a density of approximately one two-man patrol for every mile and a half of beachfront." Motor patrols supported the foot patrols wherever the situation demanded and reconnoitered isolated areas of the coast daily for evidence of landings.[2]

Beginning in the fall of 1942, having increased its numbers to full war strength, the Coast Guard began to assume responsibility for more and more of the coastline defense. In September 1942, the War Department authorized the use of horses for beach patrol by the Coast Guard. The Army's Remount Service provided the horses as well as required riding gear. As far as is known, the Coast Guard used no horse patrols in New England. The Coast Guard "conducted patrols with at least two mounted riders" equipped with radios. Riders "were usually armed with rifles and sidearms." Patrolmen on horseback allowed the patrols to cover more ground in a shorter time. Dennis L. Noble says, "In some cases, dogs and horses patrolled together."[3]

In many areas of the East Coast there were major problems involving features of the terrain—promontories and rocky headlands, large rivers, inlets, vast stretches of wetland areas, as well as other obstacles and hindrances. In some parts of the south, patrolmen had to beware of alligators, blood sucking insects and leeches, as well as venomous spiders and snakes.[4]

Due to the ruggedness and contours of the rocky Maine coast, "some stretches ... were entirely impractical for foot patrols." Two man patrols covered these areas in jeeps and other vehicles, usually ½-ton weapons carriers. The motorized patrols covered the out-of-the-way roads along the coast as well as all side roads leading to some of the more isolated small beaches that might serve as possible landing sites for enemy agents.[5]

The 104th Infantry, which had "to patrol the coast from North Carolina to Key West, a line more than a thousand miles long," experienced a severe manpower shortage. The history of the 104th states, "Such an enormous distance required constant motor patrols between key points along the shore." Wherever "large rivers and inlets made motor reconnaissance impossible, the regiment maintained its own naval unit," with the "flagship" of the fleet—a 75-foot cruiser—"stationed at Brunswick, Georgia." A number of smaller auxiliary craft, docked at various points along the coast, supplemented the sea-going patrols. The vessels comprising the flotilla were on loan from private owners. The 104th also had help from civilian pleasure boaters who reported any suspicious vessels by radio.[6]

* * *

On June 1, 1942, the 101st Infantry, which had remained on coast patrol duty in the Boston Sub-sector since January, received orders to return to Camp Edwards, leaving behind its 3rd Battalion and B Battery of the 101st Field Artillery Battalion. One month later, on July 1, the 101st Infantry departed Camp Edwards and moved to A.P. Hill Military Reservation for "intensive small unit training." The regiment relocated once again on October 10, 1942, to Fort George G. Meade, Maryland. The 3rd Battalion, 101st Infantry, remained on coast patrol in Massachusetts until October 12, 1942, when division ordered the unit to rejoin the rest of the regiment at Fort A.P. Hill. The regiment's next move was to Fort Jackson, South Carolina, on January 1943, to undergo a reorganization.[7]

In January 1943, the Eastern Defense Command removed the 104th Infantry from shore patrol duty and ordered the regiment to reassemble at Camp Blanding, Florida, where it also reorganized.

The 26th Division history states that at this time (January 1943) "it was decided to separate the 181st Infantry from the Division and leave it on Coast Patrol in the New Jersey [sic — a mistake for New England] area." This left the triangular division with only two regiments.[8]

The first step in rebuilding the 26th Infantry Division was to establish a third regiment. The Army accomplished this by taking one-third of the personnel from the 101st Infantry and the 104th Infantry to form the nucleus of the new regiment and then adding replacements to bring all units up to full combat strength. Division designated the third regiment as the 328th Infantry. From January to April, the 328th underwent basic training and small unit exercises at Fort Jackson, South Carolina. In May 1943, the entire 26th Division reassembled at Camp Gordon, Georgia, where it remained until July 1943. Over the next 11 months, the division moved several more times to undergo additional training exercises and combat maneuvers.[9]

There was much speculation and controversy as to why the War Department continued to keep the 26th Division in the United States. Walter Winchell, the *New York Herald Tribune* correspondent, questioned why the 26th had not been committed to overseas duty and laid the blame for the delay on "political interference." Winchell's on-air comments and opinions during several broadcasts of his national radio show as to why the Army continued to retain the division in the U.S. gave rise to speculation that the unit might be "an inferior organization."[10]

His remarks "attracted high-level attention" to the YD's "predicament," and "probably did much good" in resolving "the unsettled fate of the division." Finally, on August 24, 1944, units of the 26th Yankee Division boarded several troop ships tied up at the New York City waterfront. Later that day the convoy got under way, bound for France and the war.[11]

18

Saco, Maine — Headquarters, 2nd Battalion, 181st Infantry: May 1942 to November 1943

In mid–May 1942, a convoy of trucks and assorted vehicles transporting the troops and equipment of the 2nd Battalion, 181st Infantry, departed Camp Edwards and headed north for what turned out to be an extended tour of coast patrol duty in the Pine Tree State.

The commanding officer, Lt. Col. John A. Amberg, established his headquarters in the High Shoe Company factory building at 18 Park Street in the city of Saco, Maine. Saco, located approximately 4 miles inland from the mouth of the Saco River, is situated on the east side of the watercourse across from the city of Biddeford. The "twin cities" of Saco-Biddeford are 4.1 miles from Old Orchard Beach (OOB), a popular summer resort area, and 17 miles south of the city of Portland.

When the 2nd Battalion arrived in the Saco-Biddeford area in May 1942, the two sister cities had a combined population of 28,421— Biddeford with 19,790 and Saco 8,631 (1940 census records). As the Saco River passes through the Saco and Biddeford urbanized area, the watercourse drops 42 feet in 500 yards. In 1942, there were many factories and mill buildings adjacent to the river, originally attracted by the power potential provided by the swift rushing waters. There were the Pepperell and Bates Manufacturing companies and Saco-Lowell Shops, three of the city's largest, and many smaller factories. Some of the many goods produced by the city's major industries included sheets, pillowcases, textile machinery, and footwear.[1]

As the war progressed, the two municipalities began to bustle with activity. Many of the local manufacturing companies and textile mills in the Saco-Biddeford area received numerous government contract awards to produce much-needed textile and other goods for the war effort. Workers at the Saco-Lowell company produced "antiaircraft gun controls and vital machine parts." Many new jobs opened up and defense workers descended upon the twin cities from other parts of Maine and the eastern Canadian provinces. In the early 1940s, the population of Saco alone increased by a rate of more than 20 percent.[2]

The following information from an article published in the *Old Orchard Beach Times* in 1983, provides some perspective as to the region's unprecedented growth. In 1942, wrote staff reporter Michael Hughes, OOB experienced "the greatest leap in year-round population the town had ever known," when the population more than doubled "from 2,257 to approximately 4,500." "Town schools were immediately overwhelmed by the population surge." The town's

Sears & Roebuck Shoe Factory about 1910. Notice water tower — torn down some time after World War II.

superintendent of schools reported that enrollment "was up between 250 to 300 percent." "Acute overcrowding led to double sessions," with "classes held in the corridors." Staff and space shortages forced town officials "to petition the Federal Government for relief funding." Later that year, the town received "a Lanham Grant of $6,621 to hire additional teachers and for other needs." In 1943, the government awarded the town a "second endowment of $17,272" for the construction of a new school.[3]

Talmadge "Ted" Allen, a member of A Company, of the attached 132nd Combat Engineer Battalion, stationed at the State National Guard Armory on Franklin Street, met his wife, Frances, a Canadian citizen, "while walking down the street" in Old Orchard Beach. At the time, she was working at one of the textile factories in Saco making silk parachutes. Allen was originally from southern Georgia. Allen's outfit, "made up primarily of southern troops," received their training at Fort Benning, Georgia. After the war, Allen and his wife settled in Ocean Park, a small oceanfront community between Saco and OOB. Many of the men stationed in Maine married local women during this period.[4]

Upon arrival in Saco, several units of the 2nd Battalion, 181st Infantry, moved into the five-story High Shoe Factory building. Division leased part of the building from the owner for a command post and living quarters. The 181st took over parts of the first and second floors as well as the entire third floor of the factory. There was not enough room in the factory building, so the remaining troops bivouacked in tents on the grounds of the nearby Saco Armory until the engineers constructed several new barracks buildings. In the areas occupied by the battalion, much of the machinery was still in place. The company continued to operate in the remaining areas producing footwear.

Sears, Roebuck & Company constructed the High Shoe Factory building in 1915. The company used the building as a manufacturing plant for a number of its products and as a ware-

18. Saco, Maine—2nd Bn, 181st: May 1942 to November 1943

High Shoe factory building, Headquarters 2nd Battalion, 181st Infantry — Saco, Maine — 2001.

house. Many of the company's 400 workers built houses in the newly developed Nye, Spring, and Park Street neighborhood adjacent to the factory. Toward the close of World War I, Sears moved its operations to Springvale, Maine.[5]

One shoe company after another had occupied some portion of the plant almost continuously since that time until 2004. The first was Saco Shoe Company, making nationally known Soc-O-Mocs, then came Trail-Moc, Saco-Moc, Saxe-Glassman, followed by the High Shoe Company, whose owners purchased the building in 1935, and the last, Lunder Shoe Company. Lunder moved its operation to the Biddeford Industrial Park in 2004. After Lunder relocated, a Portland developer "converted the old mill into 34 condominiums ... which retain much of the building's industrial feel." Named the Park Street Lofts, the development company marketed the units "as live-work space for artists" and the first owners began moving in February 2005.[6]

Many of the veterans housed in the shoe factory remember it as being very cold and drafty during the winter months. John D. Turini (T/7) of Clinton, Massachusetts, a cook with Company G and later Headquarters Company, 2nd Battalion, wrote, "The windows were all old and those that could be opened leaked like a sieve." On numerous occasions, the boiler went out and took several days to repair. Eventually, the army replaced the heating system at the government's expense. Francis D. Donovan, a corporal with Charlie Battery, of the attached 211th Field Artillery (105mm howitzers), wrote, "We spent a few days now and then in 1942 and 1943 in rather uncomfortable conditions." The artillerymen occupied part of the second floor of the building. Other than the problems with the boiler, the living quarters in the shoe

Above: Rear of shoe factory building — 2001. Boston & Maine Railroad tracks run behind building. *Below:* 181st Infantry on parade in Biddeford, Maine — date unknown. Hotel Thacher is at left (Talmadge Allen Collection — Dyer Library).

factory were "quite decent," he remembered. Sulo O. Ruuska, a corporal with Company H, commented that he "didn't particularly like the smell of old leather that lingered there."[7]

Turini says that the floors were made of "thick maple planking commonly used in factories." "What scared us the most was that the floors ... were soaked with oil and the building was a real fire trap."[8]

"The latrines on each floor were all done over" with "new showers installed along with new sinks so there was plenty of room in the latrine areas for everyone," Turini wrote. Individual stalls enclosed the toilets, which lined one wall. "It was nice to use a toilet that had a little privacy," he commented.[9]

The Boston & Maine Railroad tracks ran directly behind the factory building. Trains on the "Portland-Biddeford high-speed freight route" made frequent trips both day and night. The steam locomotives pulling an endless line of boxcars "made a lot of noise, shaking the entire building as they chugged past. The men eventually got used to it," Donovan said. On a quiet night, the soldiers could hear the long, lonesome whistle of an approaching train many miles down the track.[10]

* * *

According to a "Station List — 181st Infantry Combat Team" dated "July 19, 1942," provided by former 1st Lt. Theodore "Simmy" Simmington, Jr. (K-181), the 181st Infantry deployed the companies and attached units of the 2nd Battalion as follows:

Battalion Headquarters Company, High Shoe Company, Saco, Maine.
"E" Company, Morley Button Factory, Portsmouth, New Hampshire.
"F" Company, High Pine (Wells), Maine.
"G" Company, Town Hall-Fire Station, Old Orchard Beach (OOB), Maine.
"H" Company (less one platoon), High Shoe Company, Saco, Maine.
"A" Company, 132nd Combat Engineers, Saco, Maine.
"C" Battery, 211th Field Artillery, High Shoe Company, Saco, Maine.
1st Platoon, "A" Company, 22nd Quartermasters, Saco, Maine.

From north to south, each company of the 2nd Battalion had its area of responsibility. Company G, commanded by Capt. Russell W. Vinton, patrolled the coast from Higgins Beach in Scarborough on the north to Camp Ellis on the southern end.[11]

John D. Turini of Company G wrote:

> The section of Maine we were assigned was almost too good to believe, as it was all of "Old Orchard Beach" from Camp Ellis, then on up the beach to Bay View. Next was Ocean Park, then Old Orchard to Pine Point at the northern end, a distance of 7 miles, then up to Prouts Neck where Higgins Beach was.... In order to get to Higgins Beach, we had to go back to Route 1 as there was no way to cross on account of an inlet to Pine Point Harbor. The natives called this "The Creek."

Turini closed, "As always with the good, there is always something that is not so good. Our base camp was the old Hi[gh] Shoe factory in Saco, Maine."[12]

Paul J. Turini (G-181), the younger brother of John, confirmed that the headquarters for Company G was located at the High Shoe factory building in Saco while troops on beach patrol stayed at the Old Orchard Beach Town Hall-Fire Station, contrary to what the station list states (it is possible the location was changed at a later date).[13]

Company H, my father's company, stationed at the shoe factory, covered the coast south of G Company's assigned sector from Camp Ellis south to Kennebunkport. The commanding officer was 1st Lt. Bernard C. "B.C." O'Connor.

Above: Old Orchard Beach Town Hall, Headquarters for Company G, 181st Infantry — 2001. *Below:* Joe Rahilly, Jr., in MP uniform (Dorothy M. Orrizzi Collection).

Company F stayed in what (Cpl.) Clifford P. Welcome of Orange, Massachusetts, describes as a "large apartment house or a large dormitory, with between 25 and 30 rooms. Possibly, it had formerly been a boarding school," he surmised. The building was located in High Pine, part of Wells, about halfway between Wells Beach and the town of Sanford. The current owner has converted the structure into an apartment complex. There was a firing range set up behind the building. "We fired 60mm mortars, machine guns, and the M-1 Garand. The sharpshooters in the company fired the .30 caliber Model [19]03 Springfield rifle," Welcome said. "Each platoon had one man who qualified as sharpshooter. They were accurate at 300 plus yards." Capt. John F. Assalta of Worcester was the company commander. Company F patrolled from Kennebunkport to York Harbor.[14]

Company E, with headquarters in the Morley Button Factory in Portsmouth, New Hampshire, patrolled from York Harbor south to the Massachusetts–New Hampshire line. Capt. John F. Lane was the commanding officer.

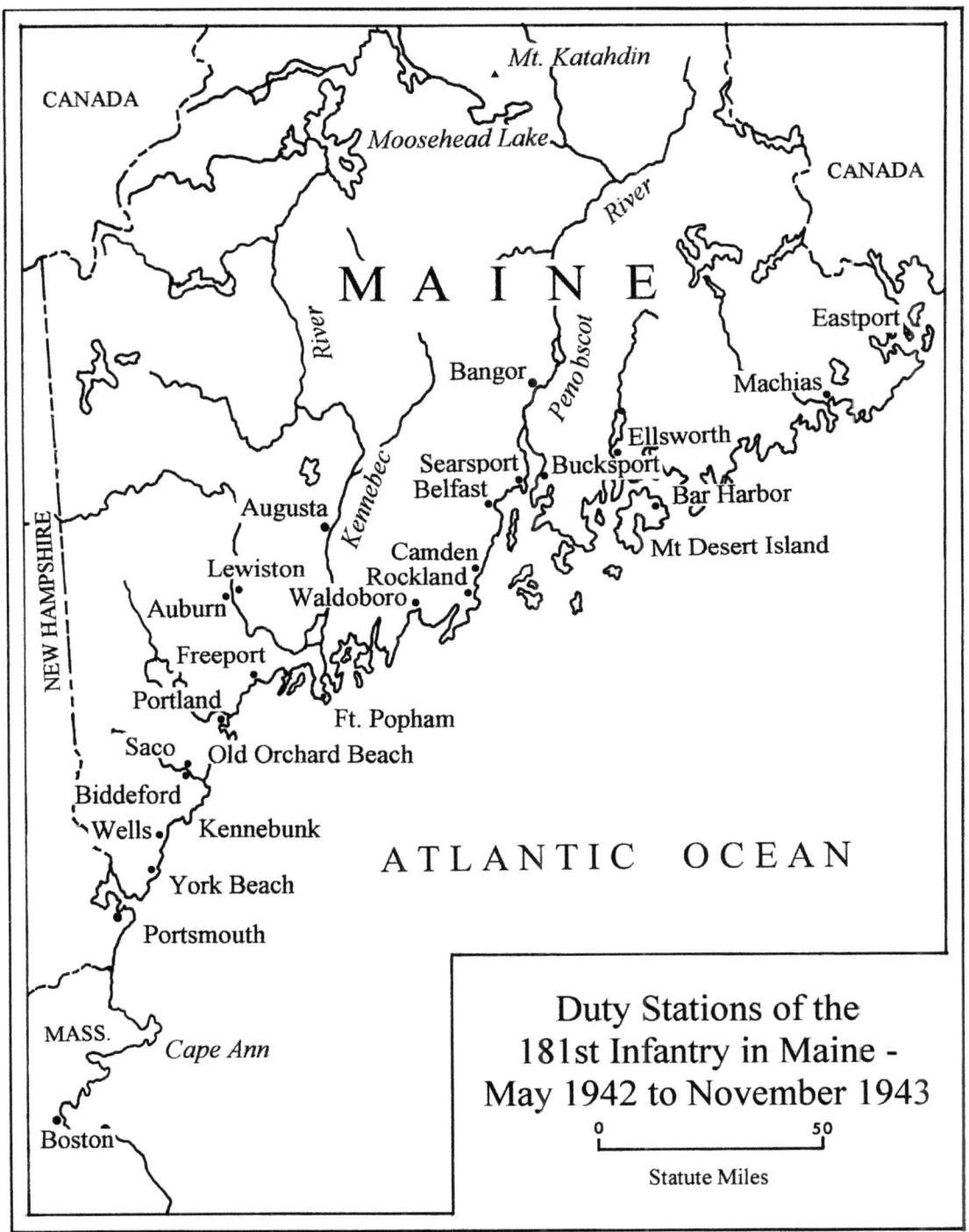

Map of Duty Stations.

Company H Mess Hall in front of High Shoe Company Building—"front row, Joe Kennedy, Robert Murphy, James Oliver, Louis Chamberlain, and Orlando Orrizzi; middle (behind Oliver) George Greenough; back row, Henry Machnik, John Neal, Niilo Krock, Wally Fini, Paul 'Whitey' Garganigo"— identification by Guido J. Fratturelli (Dorothy M. Orrizzi Collection).

A part of the 2nd Battalion with several attached units established its headquarters at Searsport, Maine. This unit, referred to as the Rockland Sector, was responsible for the coast from Freeport on the south to Machias near the Canadian border. 1st Lieut. Salvi J. Laquidara was the commanding officer (see Chapter 23, The Rockland Sector).[15]

* * *

One of the first duties of Company A, 132nd Combat Engineers, stationed at the Saco National Guard Armory, was to build a number of temporary buildings needed by the 2nd Battalion, 181st Infantry. Initially, the engineers constructed one building adjacent to the shoe factory, which the battalion used as a mess hall (above), and eight additional buildings next to the Maine State National Guard Armory, on Franklin Street. The state constructed the armory in 1941 as part of the military buildup prior to World War II. Two days after Pearl Harbor, historian Roy P. Fairfield says, the contractor "handed over" the keys to the facility to the state. Battalion used three of the new barracks to house troops, 54 men in each; one as a headquarters building; a bachelor's officers quarters (BOQ); a day room and recreation hall; a motor pool garage for the maintenance of vehicles; and a "bath house."[16]

John D. Turini says the engineers built several additional structures at a later date: one, a headquarters building for the 2nd Battalion, a second mess hall next to the factory on Park Street, and a barracks for the cooks and kitchen help.[17]

The structures, made of plywood and covered on the outside with tarpaper, were crude but solidly built. A photograph of the interior of one of the barracks, taken by Ted Allen, shows a row of bunks down both sides of the building with individual barracks bags tied to the bottom rail (see next page). Uniforms hang neatly from poles that extended out from the

18. Saco, Maine—2nd Bn, 181st: May 1942 to November 1943

Top: Talmadge "Ted" Allen in front of barracks adjacent to Armory, Saco, Maine. *Below:* Inside of barracks, Saco, Maine (both photographs from Talmadge Allen Collection — Dyer Library).

walls to a board suspended from the ceiling rafters. The outside area around the barracks, as can be seen in exterior shots taken by Allen, was a quagmire of mud, which frequently occurred during the spring thaw ("mud season"), or wet weather. There were wooden walkways, called "duck boards" or "duckboard walks," three (2 × 6 or 8 in.) planks wide on the "company streets" and between buildings.[18]

According to Talmadge Allen, the State Armory played an important role in the military operations at Saco. The 2nd Battalion used the main part of the facility for "storage and lock down of ordnance," which included machine guns, mortars, and other weapons and equipment. Allen said he and the other members of his company "pulled guard duty at the armory" and "also patrolled the beaches along Kinney Shores [Saco] and Old Orchard Beach." The motor pool, located on the left side of the building, provided jeeps, trucks, and other vehicles, with mechanics on regular duty for repairs and routine maintenance. Trucks shuttled back and forth between the armory and the factory carrying needed materials and supplies. The armory also supplied the other companies of the 2nd Battalion at other nearby locations. The Army transferred Allen's unit to Camp Bridgton, Auburn, Maine, in September 1943. The 132nd shipped out to the Pacific Theater on March 27, 1944, and saw action in Guam and the Philippines with the 77th Division.[19]

Orlando Orrizzi. Notice duckboard walks (Dorothy M. Orrizzi Collection).

* * *

At the 2001 reunion of Company H, 181st Infantry, in Shrewsbury, Massachusetts, (Sergeant) James V. "Pimple" Carnivale of Fitchburg related a humorous story about an incident that took place shortly after the unit arrived in Saco. On Sunday mornings, all the Catholics in the outfit would assemble outside the shoe factory and march smartly as a unit to Mass at the local Catholic Church.[20]

On one particular Sunday, the group arrived late. The priest, a bit annoyed, stopped the services long enough to allow the soldiers to file into the pews. Once the soldiers had taken their seats, the clergyman stared sternly at the group for a few seconds and in a loud booming voice pronounced, "Before I resume, I would just like to remind everyone here," then he paused for effect, "that the Japs were not late for Pearl Harbor." Needless to say, this was the last time the men of the 2nd Battalion were late for church.[21]

19

Duties and Assignments of the Units on Coast Patrol

The rifle companies of the 2nd Battalion (E, F, and G), 181st Infantry, carried out shore patrol duty along the beaches from the outposts to a fixed point, usually "about two to three miles" distant, and then they would return. Generally, shifts were two hours on and four hours off. John J. Voellings of Worcester, a member of Company B, 181st Infantry, mentioned that the "times were changed on a regular basis so the patrols wouldn't become predictable." U.S. Army foot patrol procedures required the men to travel in pairs. If the patrolmen detained any suspicious individuals, this allowed one man to cover the suspect or suspects while the other checked their identification papers and, if need be, frisked them for concealed weapons.[1]

Later, Battalion equipped the beach patrols with a portable radio backpack, which enabled the men to keep in constant contact with the command post. Occasionally the men on duty would run into a second patrol coming from the opposite direction and would stop to chat and exchange the latest "latrine rumors."[2]

Troops alternated on outpost duty, one week on and one week back at the barracks. The equipment of a U.S. Army soldier on patrol usually consisted of his individual weapon, a rifle or sidearm, a web belt with ammo pouches, a bayonet, and canteen. If there was a threat of wet weather, the men carried a raincoat or poncho. During the winter months, the men were heavily bundled against the cold weather (see below). During the earliest days of patrol duty, Coast Guardsmen usually walked alone carrying only a flashlight and a "flare pistol" (flare gun). The Coast Guard later armed the patrolmen with rifles or side arms.

The company armorer issued each man on duty one full clip of live ammunition. Clifford Welcome (F-181) said, "During the early days of the war everyone was on edge — we challenged everyone." There were rumors going around that the East Coast of the United States was about to be invaded. It was "pretty dark in the winter, but your eyes soon adjusted. Still, you could not see someone until they were almost on top of you." To ensure the safety of the public, military officials warned people through the media to stay off the beaches at night. Rosaire J. "Ross" Rajotte of Company A, 181st Infantry, said, "A lot of guys were trigger-happy. I'm surprised no one was shot and killed," he commented. If anyone resisted, the men had orders "to shoot to kill." There was "a standing order, to 'shoot first and ask questions later.'"[3]

Most of the men did not load the rifle, but carried the clips in their coat pockets. At the end of the patrol, the soldiers "turned the clip over to their relief." Paul J. Turini (G-181) related a story about one of the guys in his platoon who was on patrol one day at Old Orchard Beach. He ran into a man walking his dog and asked him to hold his rifle while he went across the street to get a cup of coffee to go. The civilian was a bit apprehensive at first. "Don't worry," the soldier assured him, "it's not loaded."[4]

"Despite stern warnings to stay off the beaches during hours of darkness," Turini said, "many times at night during the nice weather, we would come across couples making love on the beach. The lovers were very embarrassed." When asked his reaction, he answered, "We just kept walking. A lot of the guys got a big kick out of it, though."[5]

Duty officers made their rounds in jeeps to check on the men walking their beat. At night, they operated with ultra-violet lights. Welcome said, "The men on patrol could hear the noisy jeeps approaching from a great distance away, which kept them on their toes." Many of the officers were Regular Army (RA), including a number of West Point graduates, and were very tough on the soldiers under their command. Consequently, he said, "they were not very well liked or respected by the enlisted men." Eleanor Bishop noted that jeeps used to facilitate the beach patrols "were able to expedite their task by the use of special 900-by-13 sand tires."[6]

* * *

In some remote areas, the soldiers patrolled in jeeps or ½-ton trucks. Romeo LeBlanc (H-181) says that one day he and another man were on patrol in a jeep when they spotted two men in a "black sedan with a radio finder attached to the roof." They followed the suspicious vehicle for a while from a distance, then pulled aside the sedan and motioned for the driver to pull over. LeBlanc pulled up behind, got out and cautiously approached the automobile. Meanwhile, his partner manned the .30-caliber machine gun mounted on the back and aimed the weapon at the vehicle. LeBlanc politely asked the men to produce some identification and questioned their business in the area. The driver explained that they worked for a government agency (Romeo says he does not recall the name) and that they were checking for short-wave radios that might contact a submarine off shore.[7]

LeBlanc again asked the men to show their IDs. The man at the wheel told him to call his CO and began questioning his authority to stop them. He pulled out his .45, stuck it in the man's face and said in a loud voice, "I'M THE AUTHORITY HERE, NOW SHOW ME SOME IDENTIFICATION." LeBlanc said his partner was getting very edgy, nervously moving the gun back and forth ready to fire the weapon if a problem developed. Romeo said he was afraid his partner "might accidentally pull the trigger and open up on the vehicle."[8]

The driver and passenger "pulled out their wallets with ID cards and gold badges" and handed them over to him. LeBlanc then went back to the jeep and radioed headquarters to report the incident. A few minutes later, the officer on duty (OD) radioed back and said it was OK and to allow the men to proceed. When LeBlanc got back to headquarters, the lieutenant complimented him on a job well done. Romeo said he later received a commendation for his actions.[9]

* * *

Originally, the heavy weapons companies (D, H, and M) of the division consisted of a headquarters section, two .30-caliber machine gun platoons, a .50-caliber platoon, and one 81mm mortar platoon. In early 1942, the army converted the .50-caliber machine gun platoons into battalion antitank platoons. Lt. Col. Antonio J. "Tony" Tata (Ret.), Massachusetts National Guard, of Leominster, Massachusetts, was a member of Company H. He wrote that Division later removed the antitank platoons from the heavy weapons companies and attached them to Battalion Headquarters Company. The antitank platoons retained the machine guns until sometime in the fall of 1942, when the units received four 37mm antitank guns, one per squad. Tata reported that the crews attended a special gunnery school at Ellsworth, Maine, to train in the use of the new weapons (see Appendix E, no. 7). Romeo LeBlanc was the sergeant of the Antitank Platoon, until July 1943, when he left for OCS. Battalion then promoted Tata to the position.[10]

In addition to the 37mm antitank weapons, the platoon received jeeps and ½-ton trucks (Dodge open-cab pickup 4 × 4 weapons carriers). Crews towed the antitank guns behind jeeps, while support personnel followed in trucks. Gun crews manned permanent emplacements located up and down the coast at strategic vantage points. One of the emplacements, Tata says, was located in Old Orchard Beach to the left of the main pier on the front lawn of a house facing the water. Gunners sharpened their skills by firing at floating targets towed behind Coast Guard vessels. LeBlanc commented with a laugh, "I'm glad *I* wasn't riding in one of those boats."[11]

The duty schedule for heavy weapons companies differed somewhat from the infantry companies, whose primary function was to conduct regular beach patrols. Members of the (.30-caliber) machine gun squads were required to man permanent gun positions along the shore. Sulo Ruuska was part of a detail involved in the digging of emplacements when the outfit first arrived in Maine. "One day," he wrote, "[2nd] Lieut. [James T.] Lofgren [of Worcester] and I went out with about eight to ten men to plot and dig positions for the machine guns. These were, at the time, he explained, "so called 'heavy' machine guns, water-cooled." We made big holes in the beautiful lawns of seaside mansions."[12]

37mm Antitank gun—George Greenough, Joe Kennedy(?), Harvey Chappelle, and Orlando Vitone, Comp. H (Dorothy M. Orrizzi Collection).

The detail constructed the emplacements by digging a pit about a foot and a half deep, approximately nine feet by nine feet square. Crews lined the edges of the pits with six railroad ties (eight feet six inches long), two stacked in front and two on each side at slight angles outward toward the back. The men reinforced the front edge of the emplacement with sand bags. "All the homeowners were very cooperative" and "gladly gave us their permission," Ruuska said. Everyone was eager and willing to do his part for the war effort. Usually, the men of the heavy weapons platoon were on duty for six hours and had six hours off.[13]

On occasion, Battalion would assign the men of the heavy weapons company to beach patrol duty, especially during foggy or hazy weather when there was a need for additional patrols. Another duty was to man telescopes mounted on tripods, which were set up at various vantage points along the coast. The duty soldiers used the telescopes to determine the direction, or compass bearing, of an enemy submarine at specific time intervals, and radioed this information to headquarters.

Romeo LeBlanc says that at Old Orchard Beach there was a telescope station set up at the end of the pier at the southeast corner on the second floor walkway above the dance pavilion. The crew occupied a small room furnished with a desk and a telephone for the officer in charge (OIC). "We were equipped with binoculars which we used to scan the horizon." If one of the men spotted a suspicious vessel, the person manning the telescope would take a closer look. "On dance nights, the guys would take turns dancing while others observed," he said.[14]

Clifford Welcome (F-181), who was a member of a rifle platoon, says that the men in his unit occasionally pulled duty at one of the many searchlight stations positioned at key locations along the coast. The portable lights, he said, "were about 4½ to 5 feet in diameter" (60 inches) and "were powered by an electric generator." These were M1941 Sperry or General Electric 800 million candlepower searchlights that produced an effective beam width of 5 feet visible from 28 to 35 miles. The carbon arc high-intensity searchlights, with a 60-inch parabolic mirror, had the ability to illuminate a ship six to eight miles out to sea. The men on duty turned the searchlights on only when they suspected something might be out on the water.[15]

Overall, shore patrol for the men of the 181st Infantry was relatively easy duty compared to time spent during the alternate week at the barracks. Life in the outpost quarters was considerably different from the routine of camp, marked by rigid discipline. When their two-hour stretch of duty was over and sleep caught up, the men could spend their free time however they wished. There were no drills, no inspections, no guard duty, and no bugle calls to obey. Back at the barracks, the troops were not idle. The men had to pull guard duty, K.P., clean equipment, attend training sessions and classes on a wide variety of military subjects, and, on an almost daily basis, participate in close-order drill, which they hated. The units in garrison were "on alert" at all times in the event of an emergency.

* * *

"Two infantrymen of the Beach Patrol determine the exact position of an unidentified vessel off shore — May 1942" (U.S. Army Signal Corps photograph).

The "mission of the 211th Field Artillery [105mm howitzers] in Maine," wrote Francis D. Donovan, with Charlie Battery, "was to establish gun positions along the coast, from South Portland to near Kittery. We had three survey crews, and I was in the one led by a Lt. Schiavone. He was from New York, and a Civil Engineer." Donovan wrote, "When the 211th was assigned to the Eastern Defense Command, Headquarters and Headquarters Battery and Service Battery went to Fort

19. Duties of the Units on Coast Patrol

At various strategical points along the coast, giant searchlights stand ready to throw their millions of candle-power beams far out to the sea. These lights help to prevent the undetected approach of the enemy to our shores" (U.S. Army Signal Corps photograph).

Dawes, Mass. [located on Deer Island in Boston Harbor], 'A' Battery went to [the] Burlingame State Forest, RI, 'B' Battery went to Hamilton, Mass., and 'C' Battery went to Saco."[6]

* * *

According to Talmadge Allen, the men of the 132nd Combat Engineer Battalion stayed in one of the barracks buildings next to the Saco Armory on Franklin Street. In addition to the construction of barracks and outpost huts, the engineers repaired bridges and culverts "throughout northern New England" for which, Allen says, "he and the roughly 100 other members of his company were primarily responsible."[17]

Another job of the 132nd was to "stake out" barbed wire entanglements at sensitive locations for miles along the beaches. Engineers constructed the framework for the grid by pounding special looped rods, called "steel pickets, 6 feet in length," deep into the sand at "four pace intervals" (ten feet). Once inserted in the sand, these rods extended in height approximately 18 inches above ground level to form a square or rectangular pattern. The rods enabled "wiring parties" to stretch out the tightly coiled spools of wire and hold it taut to form an "apron." The loops, located near the top end of the rod, prevented the wire from slipping down.

The entanglements began above the high-tide line, extending approximately 50 feet higher up on the beach. Men of the engineer battalion laid out sections of wire for varying distances, sometimes 50, 75, or 100 feet in length, with a break or lane about ten feet wide between each section. Machine gun emplacements protected the open lanes. The men of the 132nd also dug and sandbagged foxholes on the high ground overlooking the beaches for the men on guard duty.

* * *

At the September 11, 2001, reunion of Company H, 181st Infantry, in Shrewsbury, Massachusetts, Romeo LeBlanc related a story that took place while the unit was stationed in Saco. "One night" (March 25, 1943), he said, "everyone in the barracks woke up to the noise of several loud explosions." Battalion headquarters alerted all units. Officers notified the troops to prepare to move out as soon as possible. "Word spread throughout the barracks that an airplane had crash-landed on the beach in the nearby resort town of Old Orchard Beach. We thought it was a German plane," Romeo added. "The company entrucked and headed down the highway toward the beach area at a high rate of speed."[18]

The aircraft turned out to be a Royal Canadian Air Force (RCAF) Lockheed B-34 Ventura medium bomber with a crew of four, the pilot and three crewmen, based at "RAF Station, Pennfield Ridge, New Brunswick." The Canadians used the bomber primarily for anti-submarine patrol.

It seems the bomber had lost its way and was about to run out of fuel. The pilot "decided to try" a "belly landing" on the beach, putting the plane down "in the soft sand about 400 feet west of Goose Fare Brook, in the Kinney Shores section of Old Orchard Beach" (Kinney Shores is actually part of Saco). The *Biddeford Daily Journal* reported that the crash "damaged the underside of the plane and the propeller[s?].... Whether or not the landing gear stuck was not disclosed." Fortunately, no one was injured.[19]

The B-34, powered by two Pratt & Whitney radial engines with 2,000 horsepower each, carried a bomb load of 3,000 pounds.

Clifford P. Welcome, Company F, 181st Infantry, in front of outpost hut. Photograph taken by Everett Belloli in 1942 (courtesy Clifford Welcome).

The pilot jettisoned his bombs over the ocean and made the emergency crash landing. The article reported that the "landing was within 50 feet of the bulkhead [?]." LeBlanc recalls it being "a bright moonlit night," which was most fortunate for the pilot and crew. Had it been dark or foggy, the incident might have resulted in an unfortunate ending for all aboard. Jillian Carle Jakeman, a resident of Ocean Park, wrote, "The bomber story was told to my husband by another person from Old Orchard Beach, who died several years ago." The man said he "could see the bomber from the end of one of the streets in Ocean Park."[20]

According to the *Journal* article, "Within a few minutes after the crash, a detachment of U.S. Coastguardsmen from Biddeford Pool Station were at the scene." Guardsmen kept "spectators ... at a distance from the plane." The pilot and three crew members were walking about the craft checking the damage. A short while later, the *Journal* reported, "Army men and trucks from nearby barracks" had arrived and "were at work towing the plane out of the sands to where repairs could be made." Romeo, whose duty station was located at the end of the pier at Old Orchard Beach, claims, "The airplane remained on the beach for several days." Finally, he says, a large truck with a flatbed trailer, followed by a large crane, arrived at the site accompanied by a work crew from the air base. The men removed the wings, hoisted the dismantled craft onto the trailer, and carted it away.[21]

The wing commander, "S/ N.W. Timmerman," sent a letter to the 2nd Battalion commander, Lt. Col. John A. Amberg, conveying his appreciation and thanks to the officers, NCOs, and men of the unit "for the assistance and cooperation" accorded crewmembers. The closing statement reads, "The crew of the aircraft concerned have spoken very highly of the reception and treatment which they received, and I can assure you this has created an excellent impression of our Allies in the minds of our men, and instances such as this serve still more to strengthen relations existing between our two nations."[22]

* * *

One of the men in Clifford Welcome's squad was a good friend from his hometown of Athol, Massachusetts, who shall remain nameless. The young man, whom he described as "a wild sort of guy," "was always fooling around with Molotov cocktails." His buddy would take a glass bottle, fill it with gasoline, and stuff a rag in the neck. Apparently, he took great delight in igniting the crude but effective bombs, letting them fly and watching as they exploded in a huge ball of flames.[23]

Late one night while on beach patrol, the friend took two of his homemade devices, lit the saturated cloth, and hurled them high up against one of the seaside cliffs near York Harbor. They exploded with a tremendous roar and set the night sky aglow for some distance around. Concerned homeowners flooded switchboards at the local police station and 2nd Battalion Headquarters in Saco with telephone calls inquiring as to what all the commotion was about. "Some," Welcome said with a laugh, "feared that the Germans were invading the East Coast of the United States."[24]

* * *

Romeo LeBlanc (H-181) remembers a humorous incident that occurred one night near Camp Ellis, north of Saco. A young man and woman in an automobile pulled up to the edge of a steep seaside bluff. The driver, his mind on other matters, had forgotten to turn off the headlights. Two patrolmen from Company H walking up the beach spotted the lights shining out over the water. One of the duties of the men on coast patrol included enforcing the "dim out." Unable to climb to the top of the steep embankment, they shouted for the occupants to shut off the headlamps. By this time, the amorous couple was busy in the back seat, completely oblivious to the warnings. Together the two men raised their rifles, took careful aim, and shot the headlights out. Needless to say, the lovers were scared out of their wits. A very nervous driver cautiously emerged from the vehicle to learn the reason for the shooting.[25]

* * *

The men walked the lonely beaches, headlands, and rocky promontories, all points that provided a view of the surrounding seashore. Weather conditions along the Maine coast during the winter months were extremely harsh, especially in the northern region of the state. Inevitably, whenever I interviewed any of the veterans of the 2nd Battalion the first thing they would mention was the severity of the Maine winters. Comments ranged from, "It was damn cold," to the unprintable. The men had to patrol in all kinds of weather. They walked through rain, snow, ice, and sleet, bucking the cold, blustery, on-shore winds. Even though the men were heavily bundled against the elements, they could not keep out the bone chilling cold that cut through their clothing like a knife. On many a winter's night, a two-hour shift would seem to last an eternity.

Maine's cold weather was an experience that many, especially those from more moderate climate areas of the U.S., did not appreciate. Talmadge Allen (B-132), "born and raised in southern Georgia," arrived in Saco, Maine "in late August of 1942." Allen says, "I wasn't prepared for New England's weather." Although it was still summer, "I almost froze to death," he said with a chuckle. "At night, it got down to 50 or 60 degrees. You have to remember I was from a place where it was usually 110 in the shade." The nights were "'so cold, that I wrapped myself in my blanket and slept under my mattress,' Allen recalled, speaking of southern Maine's late summer climate."[26]

The typical garb worn by the beach patrolmen to keep warm during the winter included a wool undershirt, at least two pairs of wool socks, a wool shirt and trousers, a wool knit sweater (multiple), a field jacket or wool overcoat, a wool cap under the helmet, gloves, a scarf, boots, and galoshes. Most of the men refused to wear the galoshes because they were too heavy.

The Army eventually issued the troops on patrol new and improved clothing and gear recently develop by the Quartermaster Corps for "severe cold conditions." One of the first items received by units of the 26th Division in Maine was a reversible ski parka overcoat, field tested and evaluated by special ski and snowshoe patrols at Pine Camp (later Camp Drum), New York, during the winter of 1940–41. The long-skirted, hooded jacket formed the wind-proof outer shell, which came equipped with a "separable" pile liner (without sleeves) made of alpaca or mohair or both. "Inner garments layered under the windbreaker outer shell ... retained warm air while still promoting ventilation, which allowed perspiration to evaporate," wrote historian Shelby L. Stanton.[27]

The first parkas "combined the pile with the outer shell." Later versions came with a liner, which the wearer could add or remove depending on the temperature. "The final two part composition design gave better coverage to a wider range of climatic conditions and proved much easier to clean and maintain," Stanton wrote. The field jackets had "a detachable hood ... to give the soldier overall head and neck protection from the elements."[28]

The field parkas were reversible, olive drab on one side for normal wear and white on the other for snow conditions. Clifford Welcome (F-181) reported, "they were very good against the wind" and "very warm." He said, "I kept the parka after I left coast patrol and had it for

Left: Sulo Ruuska "wearing reversible parka [olive drab side], shoe pacs, lined trousers and gloves — excellent gear." *Right:* Sulo Ruuska, parka worn on reverse (white) side (both photographs from Sulo O. Ruuska Collection).

many years." Sulo Ruuska says he took his jacket overseas and it served him well during the European winters. During patrol, the men were required to wear their helmets under the hood, but most often, they just wore the helmet liner. Local Red Cross chapters provided thick knitted mittens as well as scarves to cover the neck and face, Welcome said.[29]

The Quartermaster Corps also provided some of the units in Maine with boots that had "moccasin style rubber bottoms" and 16-inch leather uppers. This special "shoe pac," specifically developed for cold weather duty, had a waterproof seem between the leather and rubber. Developers designed the boots "to accommodate two pairs of wool socks and one pair of felt insoles." During the European campaign the shoe pac "received high praise" from the troops, who "regarded" the improved footwear "as indispensable in combating trench foot despite wet-mud conditions."[30]

Stanton mentions two major problems with the new style boots. One, he says, was that their "frequent misuse as a marching boot caused severe foot problems." He explained, that "during winter marching the feet perspired excessively and then became painfully cold when soldiers stopped to rest." Second, there was "a tendency for the stitching to pull apart where the rubber foot was connected to the leather upper," causing the boots to leak. Later improved versions had a "more waterproof seam between the leather and rubber."[31]

The Army also issued YD troops "lined trousers" and "trigger-finger" mitten shells, "constructed of tough wind-resistant 9-ounce sateen" ["a glossy cloth made of cotton in imitation of satin"], with knitted wool inserts. These were leather-palmed with "enlarged gauntlets," cuffs that extended up the forearm about four inches, "secured with wrist straps." Stanton says, the "flexible finger design permitted the soldier to fire his weapon without exposing his hand to frigid conditions." The Armored Board Winter Detachment tested the prototype at Pine Camp, New York.[32]

Reminiscing about his days on patrol duty in Rhode Island, Lt. Col. Rinaldo M. Delsignore, Ret., then a sergeant with Company A, 181st Infantry, wrote that the salt-laden wind, combined with sub-freezing temperatures, caused the skin on the men's weather beaten faces to crack and peel. Open, oozing sores that refused to heal would develop. Some of the local women knitted special wool hoods with eye-slits, which protected the men during particularly nasty weather. The knitted fabric was such that the wearer could breathe right through it without any difficulty. These proved to do the trick and the problem was solved.[33]

During the summer and autumn months, the days and nights along the Maine coast were beautiful, which made beach patrol duty a pleasure. The men of the 181st Infantry casually strolled along the water's edge chatting about the latest news from home or the course of the war.

The cool, refreshing on-shore breezes during the day brought relief from the hot summer sun. Panoramic views of the Maine coast are stunning in their abrupt variety—steep, rocky ledges, sand and pebble beaches, bays, coves, inlets, and hundreds of offshore islands. Quiet little fishing villages—with a variety of commercial and pleasure boats sitting in the harbor, and picturesque lighthouses—complement the natural beauty of the seashore. The scenery of the rugged coastline offers a contrast between cloud-filled blue skies, the deep blue sea stretching to the horizon, and a carpet of evergreen trees extending deep inland to the hills of the interior. Lobstermen sat offshore in boats tending their traps as seabirds squawked noisily overhead.

The views on moonlit nights were absolutely breathtaking. Millions of stars sparkled in the clear night sky and light from the moon glistened like sparkling diamonds off the choppy water. Only the sound of waves lapping the shore broke the quiet solitude.

Men walking their beat often stopped to pick up seashells left behind on the sand by the outgoing tide or to explore a tide pool. It was not uncommon for the patrolmen to come across an array of flotsam and jetsam that had washed up on the rocky shore—oil-soaked life jackets or preservers, "some with bullet holes" or "burn marks"; "pillows and naval-issue mattresses"; pieces of broken lifeboats and ship's wreckage; and other debris—all evidence of disasters at sea. Now and then, patrolmen reported finding a body or other human remains, a grim reality of the war taking place just off the U.S. coast. "At one location on the East Coast," wrote Noble, "the traditional message-in-a-bottle was retrieved." Bishop says, that on this occasion "a bottle with a red cap" containing "a poignant message" washed ashore. "It read, 'Come out and rescue us on Faulkner's Island [there is a Faulkner's Island with a lighthouse off the coast of Connecticut in Long Island Sound]. All boats have been sunk by German sub. Signed 'Capt. White.'"[34]

For many, these would be quiet, reflective times to reminisce about the past or to contemplate the uncertain future, a time to think about family and friends or that special sweetheart back home. Many, especially the married men, had serious concerns about how their families were going to cope without them if the war continued to drag on indefinitely, or if they would eventually end up in a combat unit overseas. On days like these, some of the soldiers thought that shore patrol might not be a bad way to finish out the war.

20

Social and Recreational Activities

According to Francis D. Donovan of the 211th Field Artillery (FA), the city of Biddeford was the "principal center of social activity." The "main attraction" in town was "a couple of bars" in the downtown business district. A USO (United Service Organizations, Inc.) Club, located on the second floor of the Thacher Block at 177 Main Street, across from the City Hall, was also very popular.[1]

An article in the *Biddeford Daily Journal* dated February 5, 1944, states that the "popularity of the USO Lounge can be gained from the attendance figures which show that 24,540 servicemen" visited the meeting place the previous year (1943). "Among the facilities provided are: writing material, shaving material, shoe shining material, repair work supplies, reading materials, pool tables, ping pong tables, cards, dart games, [and] dancing." The lounge at the club had "a juke box, piano, and easy chairs." Staff members organized a regular program of dances, parties, and other social activities throughout the week. A group of young ladies acting as "hostesses" was "on duty during the evening" assisting regular staff members.[2]

The USO, founded on February 4, 1941, sponsored "nearly 3,000 clubs and services ... in this country and overseas in the western hemisphere." This number included "more than a thousand 'hometown USO's' conducted by local communities in affiliation with the national organization." The "goal" of the organization since its inception has been "to provide armed forces personnel with 'a home away from home'; a place where a soldier could spend time outside of a strictly military atmosphere." According to the *Biddeford Journal* article, "clubhouses" were the "heart of the USO," but "other services" included "USO Camp Shows, mobile service units, station lounges, USO Travelers Aid Centers, [and] aid to troops on maneuvers."[3]

"When our wives visited, we usually booked rooms at the Hotel Thacher [located in the Thacher block] in Biddeford for them to stay on weekends," Donovan wrote. Most of the wives made the trip by train, as gas rationing severely limited auto travel. Donovan says the 211th FA established gun positions along the coast from South Portland to Kittery, Maine.[4]

Many of the GIs would go to the local bars and clubs where they could get a good meal, something different from bland tasting Army chow. At the Cascade Lodge and Cabins, a popular restaurant on Route 1 in Saco, you could get a "Lobster Dinner Special" that included a broiled chicken lobster, French fried potatoes, hot rolls, dessert, and coffee, for only $1.25. For an additional 25 cents, you could get an order of steamed clams (1942 menu). The restaurant is still in operation. Some of the men liked to dance or enjoy the entertainment provided by a local band. Others preferred to go to the local movie house to catch the latest flick.[5]

* * *

Some of the men on shore patrol made deals with the local lobstermen to swap butter, coffee, sugar, and other hard-to-get items, which they finagled from the cooks, for gasoline. Lobster boatmen had an excess of this scarce commodity because the government considered commercial fishermen part of the country's food producing industry. The government's Office of Price Administration (OPA) issued boat owners a daily allotment of gasoline. Often, they did not use all that they received. Some days it would be too stormy to take their boats out, but owners received the regular fuel ration without interruption. The soldiers would fill five-gallon GI cans with as much gasoline as they were able to obtain in trade. This enabled many to travel back to their hometowns in Massachusetts while on weekend pass.[6]

Cook John Turini said he received more gasoline than was needed for the field ranges used to prepare hot meals for the men on patrol. He and his buddies used the extra gas to get home whenever he had a weekend pass. For many of the men, "finding gas was a big problem." One of Turini's friends in the company had a Model A Ford. They filled three five-gallon gas cans and carried them in the trunk. This got them back to his hometown of Clinton, but finding enough gas to make it back to Maine often presented a problem. "We had to beg gas stamps from our friends or get a few gallons on the black market."[7]

Occasionally, the townspeople in and around Saco invited the YD soldiers into their homes for a nice Sunday dinner followed by an afternoon of socializing. The families would go to great lengths to prepare special dishes for the visiting servicemen. Many of the veterans commented the people were "very nice and made us feel right at home." A group of local women from Saco formed a Service Men's Mothers Club in the fall of 1942, and the members took care of the soldiers' many needs as if they were their own sons.[8]

On Saturday nights, local residents held dances in the town halls of many nearby communities. Paul Turini (G-181) remembers the dances on the third floor of the town hall-fire station at Old Orchard Beach every Friday night during the winter. "If you were in uniform, you got in free," he said. Clifford Welcome (F-181), stationed in High Pine, attended the Saturday night dances at the town hall in the nearby town of Sanford with buddies from his outfit. "The townspeople did a lot for the servicemen," Welcome says. "Many of the families would invite us into their homes for dinner. If we had a pass, we usually had to be back by 11 or 12 P.M. Only officers could stay out overnight. The company provided trucks and drivers to take us into town or to some other location. A non-com was assigned to each truck."[9]

"Many of the people in the town were French speaking Canadians who worked at the Sanford Mills, which produced Sanforized cloth" (a process used to pre-shrink fabric), Welcome said. "At Sanford, there was a U.S. Naval air base [an auxiliary landing field in support of the U.S. Naval Air Station at Brunswick, Maine] where U.S. Navy instructors trained British Navy and Marine pilots to fly F4U [Vought] Corsairs." Welcome noted that the gull-winged fighter planes were "two seaters," apparently a special training model. The trainees "were not officers," they were "flight sergeants" of the British Naval Command Fleet Air Arm.[10]

The main pier at OOB, lined with games and curio booths, extended some 1,000 feet out over the water. There was a large, two-story casino and ballroom near the end of the pier called the Casino Dance Hall. The ballroom on the first floor featured all the nationally known big bands of the era — Guy Lombardo, Rudy Valle, Benny Goodman, Artie Shaw, Harry James, and Duke Ellington, as well as many well-known singers such as Peggy Lee, Frank Sinatra, Johnny Mercer, and the Andrews Sisters, and other musical acts. "If you were in uniform, you did not have to pay to get in," John D. Turini wrote. Beyond the hall, at the very end of the pier, was an open-air movie theater.[11]

A fire on July 19, 1969, severely damaged the structure. Over the next several years, a series of storms ebbed away at what remained of the pier. Finally, the great blizzard of February 1978 destroyed the rest. The town built the present pier, which opened in June 1980.

John Turini says that there was a Company G outpost station at the end of the pier and one on each side on the shore, with men on duty 24 hours a day. From the end of the pier, the men could see up and down the coast and out over the water for miles. The company dug machine gun emplacements from one end of the beach to the other. During the tourist season, two men would be manning the gun positions with bathers spread out on blankets and children playing in the sand all around them. With the hot sun beating down, they would be sweating profusely in their fatigues. To cool off, many of the men removed their shirts and shoes, against regulations.[12]

* * *

"One night, the Casino [Dance Hall] featured Wayne King's band. King was noted for playing the waltz and they were very good," John Turini wrote. "It just so happened, the old fashioned waltz was my best dance." There was a group of pretty young girls standing nearby. One happened to catch his eye and the young sergeant went over and asked her to dance. She accepted. "Well," he said, "we got on the dance floor and I don't think I ever danced so good." The girl said her name was Arlet, and she lived at Pine Point, just north of OOB. The couple danced to several more numbers. Suddenly, the music stopped, and the announcer said, "'I'm sorry folks, but there will be a short delay as we are having a blackout.'"[13]

Arlet told Turini that she wanted to go back up to the deck on the second floor where her friends were, so they headed up the stairs. Turini described what happened next: "As we went up the stairs, which were pitch black, one of us missed a step, and we fell into each other's arms. What happened after that, I cannot tell you. But what I tell everyone 'I do my best work in the dark.'" When the lights came back on, Arlet located her friends. The girls said it was getting late and they had better hurry if they were going to catch the last bus to Pine Point, which left at 10 P.M. "I tried walking them to the bus, but they would have no part of it. So there I was left in the dark with not too much hope of ever seeing them again."[14]

A few days later, Turini was passing through Pine Point with one of the kitchen trucks on his way to make a food delivery to the troops on outpost and decided to stop. He thought to himself, "There can't be too many Arlets around." Turini pulled up at the general store in the center of town, went in, and asked the woman at the counter if she knew a girl named Arlet. She answered, "No." She hesitated, then she said, "I'm sorry, but the best I can do for you is a young lady by the name of Arletta. She used to live in Pine Point, but now lives up the road toward Route 1 in Blue Point." She gave Turini the girl's address and directions on how to get to her house.[15]

A few minutes later, John pulled up in front of the house and there was Arletta outside cutting clams. "I stayed for a while and told her a little about myself, and she opened up a little and gave me a little of her life." John began stopping by every day while making his food deliveries. "After a while," he says, "it was only a matter of time when this became routine and one thing led to another and we were married."[16]

When the Army inactivated the 181st Infantry in November 1943, Turini became a member of the 90th Infantry Division. After John left Maine, Arletta and her two sisters moved to Clinton to be near John's parents. "The 90th hit the beach on D-Day where John took a little shrapnel in the leg." When he returned from the war, the young couple settled in the Still River section of Harvard, Massachusetts, where they raised two daughters. Arletta

Skillings Turini passed away October 27, 2000. The couple had been married 57 years. John joined her almost two years later, at age 82, on October 9, 2002.[17]

* * *

Guido Fratturelli remembers the 181st Regimental Band coming to Saco to entertain the troops during the summer of 1943. The "17 piece band" traveled to Maine from the headquarters of the 181st Infantry at Camp Framingham, Massachusetts, to play for the battalion. The setting for the gala affair was "a dance hall overlooking the Saco River." Fratturelli said, "The band was excellent, playing all the latest numbers. Everyone had a wonderful time." Some of the soldiers' wives and many young women from the area attended. As mentioned earlier, my Uncle "Mitt" Palumbo was a member of the band and my father was likely in attendance.[18]

* * *

During a nor'easter, or other large storm, many lobster traps and buoys washed up along the rocky shoreline. The lobstermen asked the men walking patrol if they would pull the wooden traps out of the water and stack them on higher ground, above the high water mark. This prevented the violent wave action from battering them along the rocky coastline and saved the owners much time and money due to lost or damaged gear, for which they were more than grateful. For providing this valuable service, they allowed the soldiers to keep any lobsters found in the traps. The patrolmen brought the lobsters back to the outpost and placed them in a 55-gallon drum filled with seawater. Within the next few days, they would celebrate their good fortune with a big lobster feed. To supplement the feast, some of the off-duty men would borrow a jeep or truck from the motor pool and go down to the beach to dig clams for steamers.[19]

On occasion, the mess hall staff would treat the men to a nice roast duck dinner. "Some of the boys," Clifford Welcome said, "got pretty proficient with the M-1s shooting ducks." The "cooks would wrap them in steam towels, which made for easy plucking." Next, "they would slow boil the birds in water to get most of the oil out, then fill them with homemade bread stuffing and oven-roast them." The birds were glazed with a loganberry sauce and served with baked potato, butternut squash, and warm rolls. "Sometimes," Welcome said, "they would cut the ducks up, dip the pieces in a flour batter, and deep-fry them like chicken."[20]

Rosaire J. "Ross" Rajotte (A-181) of Northbridge, Massachusetts, who was a member of Company A, 1st Battalion, stationed at Point Judith, Rhode Island, tells of the men at his outpost having an occasional meal of "roast pheasant, with all the trimmings." They sure were "good eating," Rajotte remembered. Many connoisseurs consider pheasant meat to be a delicacy. It seems there was a local Fish and Game Club a short distance from the unit's headquarters. The club's property bordered the ocean, and from time to time the members freshly stocked the adjacent fields with the popular game bird for hunting purposes. The men walking patrol would keep an eye out for the birds. If the men spotted a pheasant feeding on the ground, BANG. Rarely did they miss.[21]

Once, a frightened neighbor heard the rifle fire close by and was not very happy. She complained to Army officials that the soldiers were "shooting their guns" near her home and she wanted it stopped. Battalion headquarters notified the company commander and ordered him to conduct a full investigation. The platoon leader called Rajotte and his partner on the carpet to explain why they had been discharging their weapons so close to a private residence.

The quick thinking Rajotte told the lieutenant that they were only test firing their M-1s. The officer seemed to have bought the story, as he did not chew the two men out or punish them as expected, Rajotte said. The lieutenant was probably happy that Rajotte provided him with a logical answer he could pass on to the CO.[22]

The boys on coast patrol also enjoyed an occasional meal of fresh venison. Deer were plentiful in Maine and many of the men went hunting during their off-duty time. It mattered little whether it was hunting season or not as no one had a license. On occasion, while on night motor patrol, the man riding shotgun would "jack a deer caught in the headlights of the vehicle." Edward J. Adams, a member of the 26th Mechanized Cavalry Reconnaissance Troop in Ellsworth, wrote, "We had some of our guys on patrol reported to the CO by the forest rangers for using the wild-life as target practice. We had venison on the menu a few times," he said, "until the CO, Capt. [Arthur S.] Marcoullier [of Westfield, Mass.], finally put his foot down."[23]

21

Patrol-Scout Dogs

In the latter part of 1942, the War Department transferred specialized sentry dogs and their handlers to the 26th Division for use on beach patrol. The military "recognized that the use of dogs, with their keen sense of smell and their ability to be trained for guard duty would help enhance the patrols." Patrol dogs "showed great alertness and were formidable as attackers—a 50- to 75-pound snarling dog could be more frightening than a man with a pistol." Eleanor C. Bishop wrote, "Because of the keen sense of the animals, they were indispensable in detection and capture of would-be hostile persons, particularly in the dark of the night." The 181st Infantry alone employed 150 of the patrol dogs.[1]

Army and Coast Guard personnel usually conducted the dog patrols at night. Patrols consisted of a dog and one handler covering a distance of "about one mile." Trainers determined that "a dog worked better with but one master to give him orders," noted Clayton G. Going in his book *Dogs at War*. "Where canine patrols were in effect, the two man foot patrols were replaced, thus reducing personnel requirements," wrote Dennis L. Noble.[2]

According to Major Kevin M. Born of the U.S. Army Quartermaster Museum, Fort Lee, Virginia, the U.S. Army's K-9 Corps dog training program began on March 13, 1942. Shortly after the attack on Pearl Harbor, a newly formed citizen group calling itself Dogs for Defense sent out a call for dog owners across the country to lend or donate quality animals to the Quartermaster Corps for training. In March 1942, the War Department "appointed Dogs for Defense the official procurement agency for war dogs." By this time, the organization, with its national headquarters at 22 East Sixtieth Street, New York City, "had lined up 402 dog clubs throughout the nation that were willing to provide dogs, and a number of obedience trainers ready to give their services."[3]

Dogs for Defense obtained "recruits from every state in the union [forty-eight at the time], and the Territory of Hawaii." They came "from rich homes and poor, from the nation's best kennels, from the city and the country." The national headquarters received thousands of letters from people wanting to donate their pets. A boy from Morgan Hill, California, wrote:

> I am eight years old and live on a farm. I have a large Australian Shepherd Dog about two and one-half years old that is a very good hunter and I think he would be good hunting Japs. He sure likes to kill skunks.
> I go hunting with him almost every weekend. In the last three weeks he has caught 1 coon, 1 rabbit, 1 fox, 3 opossums, 3 skunks, and 1 bird. I am not big enough to hunt with a gun and sometimes we have to get some of the neighbors to come and shoot the coon and the foxes. If you need a real good dog, I will loan you mine until the war is over.
>
> Bobby Britton

Many of Hollywood's biggest stars donated their dogs. The list included "Greer Garson's Poodle, Cliquot; Mary Pickford's German Shepherd, Silver; Bruce Cabot's Boxer, Fritz; Rudy

Vallee's Doberman Pincer, King"; and Ezio Pinza's "two Dalmatians, Boris and Figaro." Pinza sent along several albums of his operatic recordings with the instructions: "If they get lonesome, play one of these records for them."[4]

Dogs for Defense eventually enrolled "as many as 1,500 dogs a month not only for the Army, but for the Coast Guard and Marines." The expense of processing the dogs, veterinarian examinations, and shipping to induction centers— was "borne by Dogs for Defense." "In all," Major Born says, "a little over 19,000 dogs were procured between 1942 and 1945." Many of the dogs "went into action against the enemy" in war zones "throughout the world." "Time and again," Going wrote, "they have proven their worth in saving human life."[5]

When the program started, Dogs for Defense personnel, working with qualified civilian volunteers, trained the dogs for the military. As requirements increased, the Army transferred reception and training responsibilities to the Quartermaster Remount Branch of the Army, commanded by Colonel E.M. Daniels. This branch had years of experience procuring and training horses and mules for use in combat. The civilian Dogs for Defense agency continued with its highly successful campaign to solicit the donation of dogs for the program.[6]

"In the fall of 1942, the Quartermaster Corps expanded the program to procure and train dogs for the Navy [and Marines] and Coast Guard." "Later," Born says, "these branches procured and trained

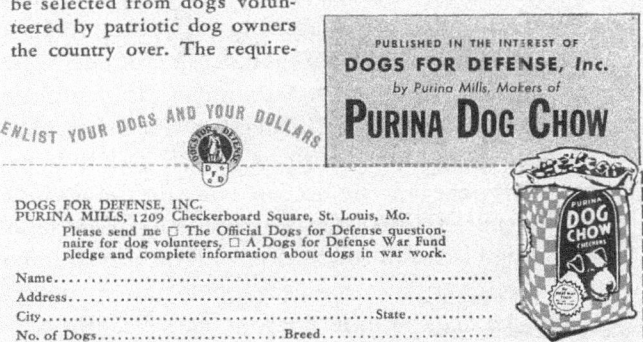

Purina Dog Chow advertisement — Appeal to the public for dogs by Dogs for Defense, Inc. (*Field & Stream Magazine*, December 1942).

their own dogs." Eleanor C. Bishop reported that one month after the Nazi landings, the 1st Naval District, headquartered in Boston, established dog training facilities "at Dennis, Massachusetts, on Cape Cod, at Hampton Beach, New Hampshire, and at Martha's Vineyard." The district's authority extended from the Canadian border on the north to Narragansett Bay in Rhode Island.[7]

In the early part of 1942, the U.S. Army Quartermaster Remount Branch established War Dog Reception and Training Centers at five locations around the country: Fort Royal, Virginia; Fort Robinson, Nebraska; Cat Island, Gulfport, Mississippi; Camp Rimini, Helena, Montana; and San Carlos, California, with "smaller temporary centers" at other locations. Later in the war, the War Department centralized all dog-training activities at Fort Robinson, Nebraska.[8]

The Quartermaster Corps trained both dogs and handlers. Clifford Welcome (F-181) says, the handlers in his company "were not local guys." The men "were miners from Arizona and Montana who volunteered to become trainers." After receiving the dogs, 26th Division Headquarters put out a call for volunteers to train as handlers. Battalion sent the men to a K-9 Corps training center in Oklahoma where they learned to work with the dogs.[9]

Initially, the program accepted more than 30 breeds. Later, however, the corps limited the types of dogs in the program to just five breeds: German shepherds (often referred to as "police dogs"), Belgian sheep dogs, Doberman pinchers, farm collies, and Giant Schnauzers. Of all the breeds, the "largest number passing the course," wrote Going, were German Shepherds. "This type is ideal for beach and guard work. They have size, strength, a hardy coat giving protection in nearly any weather, and an easy loping gait which will outlast a human opponent." Applicants admitted to the training program had to be between the ages of one and five years, more than 20 inches at the shoulder, weigh between 50 and 75 pounds, and be in top physical condition.[10]

Originally, the Army referred to the war dogs as "WAGS," but because it sounded too much like WACS, Major General Edmund B. Gregory, the Army's quartermaster general, decided "that they should have a more distinctive name." Going wrote, "Thus was born the term K-9 Corps."[11]

Upon arrival at the reception centers, a veterinarian gave the dogs "a quick examination to make sure they suffered no injury en route," then placed them in a run in a "quarantine section" where they were left alone "to recover from their journey and become accustomed to their strange surroundings." The next day, the veterinarian gave them a thorough examination and filled out a "record card" containing the "date of arrival, general description, weight," and "height from shoulder to ground." Quartermaster personnel assigned each dog "an official government serial number for identification purposes," which was tattooed "on the inside of the left ear" using the "Preston system ... a painless process." The induction process, which lasted anywhere from a week to 10 days, also included "injections and vaccinations." Once officially accepted into the program, the corps sent a letter to the owner signed by the quartermaster general expressing appreciation for his "patriotic action in donating [the] dog for use in connection with the armed forces of the United States."[12]

There were four specialized dog-training programs: sentry dogs, scout or patrol dogs, messenger dogs, or mine dogs. At the K-9 Corps centers, the dogs underwent military training for between 8 and 12 weeks, the length of time depending on a dog's particular specialty. The first phase of the program was a "basic training" period, where the dogs "began a rigid military routine." The primary "objectives" of basic training, wrote Going, were "to develop in dogs obedience that is a necessary preliminary to learning specific military duties, and to

"Wags at Canine Reception Center. Induction of dogs into the Army, Q.M. Depot, Fort Royal, Va., August 25, 1942, U.S. Army Signal Corps photograph by Charles Ray."

determine by a study of the reactions and temperament of the dogs during this period" their eventual assignments in one of the specialized training programs.[13]

During the first two weeks, Quartermaster Corps personnel trained the dogs "to carry out certain fundamental commands such as sit, stay, come, etc." Bishop says the training "was conducted by two 'handlers,' who commanded the dogs on the training fields under the direction of regular trainers." All commands were "by voice and hand signals." Next, trainers "accustomed the dogs to muzzles, gas masks, riding in military vehicles, and to gunfire."[14]

The final part of basic was the "attack training" phase. Dogs, working at night and on leash, learned to attack "shouting strangers, 'known as aggravators,'" who "made quick and unexpected" advances against the dogs from concealed positions. The aggressors wore heavy padded garments and wore special protective bite pads on their arms to prevent injury.[15]

During one of the exercises, the aggravator would fire a pistol loaded with blanks at the animals. Trainers taught the dog to respond instantly, "which was to seize the pistol arm" and "fight the opponent until he was 'conquered.'" After the handler disarmed the man, he would then order the dog to "let go." The dog "would stand guard over the 'prisoner,' while the patrolman went for help." Bishop says, "The dog was always allowed to win over 'the enemy'" in these training exercises. Training personnel changed aggravators frequently, "in order for the dogs to be suspicious of all, except their handlers." Noble wrote, "As both man and dog became more proficient, the human-animal team became one."[16]

If, at any point during the program, personnel deemed a dog "unsuited for training," the animal was mustered out of the program and returned to its owner or put up for adoption. The program rejected about 45 percent of the approximately 19,000 dogs procured between 1942 and 1945.[17]

Upon completion of the basic training phase, both dogs and trainees (handlers) had to pass an examination to show that they were "thorough masters of the fundamental lessons," wrote Going. The staff then evaluated the dogs and divided them into groups "by quality and personality traits," which determined their placement into one of the four specialty classes. Following this evaluation, the canines were ready to begin their period of advanced or specialized training.[18]

Most of the dogs trained by the military eventually became sentry dogs (approximately 9,300 of the 10,425 dogs). Trainers chose these specialty dogs to accompany military personnel or civilian guards on patrol of designated rounds to detect the presence of intruders. Trainers taught the dogs to work on a short leash and to give advance warning by growling, barking, or otherwise alerting their handlers of the presence or approach of strangers within a protected area. The Quartermaster Corps "issued" sentry dogs "to hundreds of military organizations such as coastal fortifications, harbor defenses, arsenals, ammunition dumps, airfields, depots, and industrial plants."[19]

For the second category, scout or patrol dogs, Born says the training staff selected "only dogs with superior intelligence and quiet disposition." Quartermaster handlers trained the canines as sentry dogs with one major difference: they taught the dogs to work in silence. When a scout dog detected the presence of someone in the restricted area, or an enemy, it "would stiffen its body, raise its hackles, prick its ears, and hold its tail rigid." The presence of these dogs "greatly lessened the danger of ambush and tended to boost morale." Through its keen sense of smell and hearing, scout dogs "could often detect the presence of the enemy at distances of up to 1,000 yards," long before a man would become aware of them, and possibly before it would be too late. In combat, "the scout dog and his Quartermaster handler normally walked point ... well in front of the infantry patrol."[20]

"The most desired quality" of the third category, messenger dogs, wrote Born, "was loyalty, since the dogs must be motivated by the desire to work with two handlers." These dogs carried messages from one handler to the other. Trainers taught the animals in this group to "travel silently and take advantage of natural cover when moving between the two handlers." The Quartermaster Corps trained the fourth category of canines, mine detection dogs, or M-Dogs, to detect "trip wires, booby traps, metallic, and non-metallic mines."[21]

A number of Quartermaster trained dogs "established outstanding records in combat" in both the Pacific and European theaters. Overseas commands awarded combat medals to several of the dogs. "These medals were later revoked," wrote Born, "because presenting these decorations to animals was contrary to Army policy." The War Department relaxed the restrictions in January 1944, "and allowed publication of commendations in individual unit General Orders."[22]

* * *

It is likely, as the following testimony indicates, the dogs used by troops of the 26th Division in New England were scout or patrol dogs. Clifford Welcome (F-181), who patrolled with the dogs in Maine, confirmed this. "The ones we worked with did not make a sound. When they detected someone, they would bristle up and point," he said. "The dogs we had in Maine," Welcome noted, "were mostly German shepherds and a few retrievers." He described the dogs as "very intelligent animals."[23]

Late one night, Welcome was walking patrol when the dog stopped in its tracks, went rigid, and pointed down the beach. He then walked very slowly forward, leading the patrolman until he came upon the form of a man lying down near the upper edge of the beach, partially concealed by some overhanging bushes. Welcome prodded the man with the barrel of his weapon only to discover he was sleeping off a night of hard drinking at one of the local pubs.[24]

When on duty, the patrol dogs lived with the patrolmen at the outpost huts. Most of the time, the handlers tied the dogs up outside and allowed them inside only during inclement weather. The dogs were on a strict diet of raw horsemeat and biscuits, delivered to the outposts on a periodic basis (see below). Bishop says, "The handlers took complete care of the animals and no one else was permitted to make friends with the dogs." Some of the men became very close to the animals and treated them like pets. Clifford Welcome said, "Sometimes the men would feed the dogs table scraps or leftovers and the handlers would get very angry."[25]

John J. Voellings was with Company B, 181st Infantry, stationed at the Burlingame State Forest. Voellings said, "The types of dogs we worked with were German shepherds, Doberman pincers, and one collie." The dogs "were on a short leash, if you got down and crawled, they would crawl with you. If a dog detected the presence of someone at night, they pulled up. They did not make a sound." Some of the dogs were "very vicious," he said. "They were very temperamental animals; you had to be careful the way you handled them because they would turn on you." "One time," Voellings remembered, "several dogs were tied up outside the barracks and one of the German shepherds attacked the collie and tore him to pieces before the handlers could pull them apart."[26]

* * *

One afternoon, while Ross Rajotte (D-181) and another member of his squad were walking patrol in Westerly, Rhode Island, a wealthy gentleman who owned a big summer home on the ocean approached them. He told the men he needed some steaks for a big barbecue his family was planning for guests the following weekend. In exchange, he offered them champagne, whiskey, or any other type of liquor they preferred. Beef was a rationed item and was very hard to get in any quantity during the war. The two men told him they would see what they could do.[27]

The next day, the crafty Rajotte volunteered for duty at the dog kennel, located at Camp Burlingame. Handlers fed the pampered canines a strict diet of fresh horsemeat that came packaged in large 25-pound boxes. He removed the original label from one of the boxes and replaced it with a USDA inspection tag that he carefully peeled from a discarded box near the mess hall stating the meat was prime beef for human consumption. The two men made the exchange the following day.

About a week later, the gentleman was sitting on his porch when he spotted the patrolmen on their rounds and came running down to the beach to greet them. The man was all smiles and told them, "The party was a huge success." He said, "The meat was the best he ever tasted and wanted more."[28]

* * *

In many areas of the East Coast, steep descents onto the beach created an extremely hazardous situation, especially during inclement weather or on dark, moonless nights. The July 1997 issue of *The Coast Guard Reservist* reported two incidents where dogs possibly saved the lives of their handlers. One such night "near Plymouth, Mass., a patrolman was prevented from walking over a cliff ... when his dog refused to advance."²⁹

The second took place on a cold, bitter night in November 1943, while Coast Guardsman Evans E. Mitchell was patrolling an isolated stretch of the coast near Oregon Inlet, North Carolina, with his dog, Nora, a German shepherd. Mitchell was at the far end of his patrol when he collapsed in an isolated spot. Nora grabbed Mitchell's cap and ran to the station to summon help. After alerting Chief Boatswain's Mate Thomas J. Harris, the officer of the day (OD), she then raced ahead to another Coast Guardsman patrolling the beach and led him to Mitchell, who by this time was suffering from exposure. Corpsmen rushed him to the Marine Hospital in Norfolk, Virginia, where he eventually recovered. The official Coast Guard report stated, "Nora's timely discovery and summoning of aid quite probably saved the Coast Guardsman from probable death from cold and exposure at the ocean's edge."³⁰

The "Oregon Inlet Coastie" had purchased Nora seven months prior to the incident for 50 cents from a neighborhood family. "She proved to be a smart and alert dog and it was decided to train her for patrol work. The decision was well made," commented Going (for a picture of Mitchell and Nora see *Dogs at War* by Clayton G. Going).³¹

"Chinook Kennels for U.S. Army Dogs, Wonalancet, New Hampshire. S/Sgt. Stanley Novak, stops with his dog for a short rest. November 1942. U.S. Army Signal Corps photograph by Charles Ray." Chinook Kennels bred Siberian huskies for use as sled dogs. The Army trained the dogs for search and rescue missions. Notice the dog's pack.

Sometimes, Noble noted, the dogs "were not quite as helpful. On three occasions, in the same area," the dogs led "their handlers on what appeared to be the trails of suspicious persons" only to "find skunks instead!"[32]

* * *

Eleanor C. Bishop says that the Coast Guard began cutting back dog patrols in the autumn of 1943, "reducing them to a quarter of their maximum strength." At this time, the Coast Guard closed its canine training schools and turned all surplus patrol dogs "over to the Army or Navy for duty at air bases or shore establishments." Two days after D-Day on June 6, 1944, the Coast Guard discontinued all beach patrols. The only arm of the Coast Guard beach patrol that remained was the lookout tower system. Clifford Welcome says that when the 2nd Battalion (181st) ended the dog patrols in 1943, "the animals were returned to their owners."[33]

Going wrote, "When the Coast Guard curtailed its beach patrol it sent the surplus dogs to the Army Quartermaster Corps for 'refresher courses,' prior to combat duty overseas." The corps "mustered out" those "found not suited for the battlefront ... with certificates of honorable discharge."[34]

Before discharging the dogs, the Quartermaster Corps put the animals through a program known as "processing in reverse," which, "in the majority of cases," removes "all traces of viciousness." This "system," Going says, "has proved most successful with most of the dogs." During the program, "military routine is discontinued" and the dogs were "allowed to associate and play with a number of the men" who provide them with "plenty of affection." Over time, this "does the trick," he said. After completing the "detraining program," corps trainers consider the dogs "no longer dangerous." They do, however, "retain their obedience training and ... still respond to the elementary commands such as Heel, Come, Sit, Down, and Stay."[35]

Owners who stated on their application that they wanted their dogs back at the end of the hostilities were "notified when their former pets" were "in condition to return home." The corps tried to place dogs not wanted by their former owners, or in cases where they could not be located, in a good home with a loving family. When news of the discharges appeared in the media, the public "deluged" the Quartermaster Corps "with some five thousand letters from dog lovers—all wanting to "adopt a dog." Many were placed with seeing-eye organizations, "as prospective blind leading dogs"; police departments; and companies who would employ them as guard dogs. The Marine Corps allowed handlers to keep their dogs if they so wished. A spokesperson for the Corps explained, "Such strong attachments develop between men and dogs, that it would be a tragedy to break them up."[36]

22

Provisional Military Police Unit

At some point during his tour of duty in Saco, my father, Joe Connole, volunteered for duty with the provisional military police (MP) unit headquartered at the High Shoe Company factory. Richard W. "Dick" Brill of Leominster, the 1st sergeant of H Company, wrote, "Many of the men in the unit came from the mortar platoon." Francis D. Donovan of Battery C, 211th Field Artillery Battalion, remembers that the MPs were billeted on the first floor of the building and "controlled the main gate."[1]

Capt. John S. Gerety, 2nd Battalion S-3 Section leader, says that shortly after the 181st arrived in Maine the local governments in many of the coastal resort towns began asking for help in dealing with unruly GIs, Merchant Marines, and Navy sailors who crammed the local bars and clubs every night of the week. The off-duty seamen would drift down from the Portland area in search of fun and excitement — as Brill put it, "to raise a little hell." The servicemen did some heavy drinking and carousing. Arguments and inter-service rivalries often erupted into brawls, resulting in injuries and much damage to private property. Gerety said in his final remarks, "These crewmen were not Boy Scouts, booze and women were all they had in mind."[2]

In January 1941, the U.S. Navy designated Casco Bay a fleet anchorage and established a naval section base in Portland. Many ships of the fleet docked in Portland Harbor to stock up on needed supplies before leaving to patrol the waters of the North Atlantic. Casco Bay was also a port of assembly for huge convoys bound for the United Kingdom or Soviet Union transporting lend-lease equipment and supplies. In April 1942, an average of 63 vessels passed in and out of Casco Bay every day. By 1944, the number was in the hundreds. On August 12, 1944, a record 539 ships entered and 558 departed the anchorage. Merchant seamen and U.S. Navy gun crews manned the cargo vessels. Early in the war, German U-boats were active just off the coast and sank many ships each month outside the harbor.[3]

Local police forces had neither the manpower nor the facilities to handle the large numbers of incidents and arrests. Every night, the local jails were filled to overflowing. Gerety wrote, "Concerned city and town officials approached the commander of the 2nd Battalion with a request to form a provisional MP Unit to assist local police departments in maintaining order." Brill's version of how the unit came into being is slightly different. He wrote, "To the best of my knowledge, the civil police approached the Commanding Officer of the army troops, a Lt. Col. [John A. Amberg], and demanded relief." The battalion commander was aware of the need and readily agreed to comply.[4]

The call went out for volunteers. Those chosen to serve attended the division MP school, conducted periodically at Camp Framingham, Massachusetts. Gerety wrote, "Since I was six four and with a reputation to go with it, I was selected as the leader" (provost officer). "It was mean rough duty," according to Gerety, and "everyone in the unit was hand picked."[5]

Gerety appointed Raymond Freeman, a police officer from Gardner, Massachusetts, to the position of provost sergeant. Freeman was in charge of the day-to-day operations of the MP unit. Brill wrote, "The unit was composed of members of Company H only—probably twenty or twenty-five men" (out of a total of approximately 185). "The MP units patrolled the Saco-Biddeford-Old Orchard Beach area in jeeps." An MP's "equipment consisted of arm brassards—MP, night sticks, and .45 cal. Pistols. Unloaded. To the best of my recollection, they did not carry ammo. Their leggings and roundabout cartridge belts were whitened," he wrote.[6]

A photograph from the collection of Mrs. Dorothy M. Orrizzi, whose husband, Orlando "Tutor" Orrizzi, was a member of the MP unit, shows Sgt. James J. "Joseph" Rahilly, Jr., in a dress shirt and tie, dress pants and shoes. On his head is an overseas or garrison cap with the regimental pin on the left side. He is wearing a short khaki-colored field jacket and a five-inch black armband on the left sleeve with bold white MP letters. Around his waist is a web belt with holster and .45-caliber automatic pistol. Hanging behind the weapon is a long black night stick or baton, which extends well below his knee (see photograph p. 134).

Robert F. Gallagher, of Chicago, who served with an MP unit in Germany shortly after the war, wrote that the club "was lead weighted" and "was a very lethal weapon, and we were instructed to use it with care." Gallagher was a member of the Battery D, 815th Antiaircraft Artillery Battalion (AAA), Automatic Weapons Battalion (40mm guns).[7]

An MP's "main challenges," Gallagher explained, "was to check passes, stop fights, pick up GIs who could not navigate on their own, soothe abused saloonkeepers, and try to keep the peace in general." Most of the problems, Gallagher said, occurred on the days "right after payday when the money flowed freely and drinking was at its peak."[8]

Gallagher realized that putting on the symbols of an MP "automatically" made them "unpopular with most GIs," and that "this dislike (or hatred in some cases) resulted from personal experiences and from horror stories about harsh treatment being handed out."[9]

It did not take long for Gallagher and his fellow police officers to discover that "the easiest way to get through an evening without some physical confrontation was to practice the art of diplomacy and not rule with an iron hand." The majority of the MPs, he noted, "liked the challenges of keeping men from fighting and mediating the sometimes chaotic experiences in the bars." Sometimes, this policy did not always meet with success "and we had to enforce the law." It was an "unwritten rule" that only a minimum effort be used to enforce minor infractions. There "were a few" MPs, he says, who harassed or brought soldiers into the station for minor infractions of the rules, outdated passes, violations of the dress or other codes, lack of military courtesy, etc. Members of this minority, he said, "were soon labeled the chicken s--- detail." Gallagher stated that "the rest of us felt our major assignment was limited to keeping law and order."[10]

Capt. Gerety, affectionately known as "Long John," was well respected and admired by the men of the battalion. Gerety wore his .45-caliber automatic "low on the hip" and had, as several veterans of Company H related, "a reputation for being fast on the draw." Apparently, the men engaged in quick-draw contests to see who was the fastest. My next letter to Mr. Gerety went unanswered. I later spoke with him on the telephone and he said that his health was failing and he had difficulty writing.

One interesting story about Gerety, as told by one of the veterans of H Company, was that at Saco he somehow acquired a used motorboat. Gerety made some minor repairs and mounted a .30 cal. machine gun with tripod on the foredeck. The lieutenant and a couple of his men would cruise the waters off Saco-Biddeford shooting harbor seals, presumably for

Left: Jim Dineen. *Right:* Joe Macuga with pregnant seal shot for bounty — pregnant seals counted for two kills. Crane's Beach, Ipswich. Joe was killed in Italy (both photographs from Dorothy E. Dineen Collection — Massachusetts National Guard Archives & Museum, Worcester).

sport. In a conversation I had with Dorothy E. Dineen of Worcester, whose husband, Jim, was a private first class with Company L, 181st Infantry, stationed at Ipswich, Massachusetts, she related that there was a bounty on seals at the time. Jim and two or three of his buddies would go seal hunting for a little extra cash between paydays. Dorothy has a picture of one of Jim's buddies, Joe Macuga, kneeling next to the body of a pregnant female. "Pregnant females counted as two kills and paid a double bounty," she explained. Possibly, this was Gerety's motivation.[11]

As a member of the MP unit, Joe Connole received a promotion to the rank of buck sergeant (three stripes). Several times he told me the story of how, when I was born on February 9, 1943, he came home from Maine on a 48-hour pass to see me for the first time. He visited my mother and me in St. Vincent's Hospital in Worcester, staying as long as he possibly could, and then started thumbing a ride back to Saco.

Usually, motorists would not hesitate to pick up a soldier in uniform, and many times would go miles out of their way to see that they arrived at their destination. However, during this point in the war the government had rationed gasoline and tires resulting in few cars traveling on the major roadways, what were then the highways of New England, down east to Saco. My father did not make it back in time for reveille on Monday morning and the commanding officer had him busted. He expressed his bitterness about the incident and felt the CO should have taken his circumstances into consideration. After that, he said, he never wanted another promotion, which would place him in a position of responsibility.

23

The Rockland Sector

The commanding officer of the 2nd Battalion, 181st Infantry, stationed several units in the more northern outposts of Maine, as far north as Machias near the Canadian border. This group, commanded by 1st Lt. Salvi J. Laquidara of Framingham, Massachusetts, became known as the Rockland Sector, with headquarters at Searsport, Maine. The following is a list of units and stations:

One platoon of "H" Company, Searsport, Maine (the platoon moved to Camden, Maine, in the fall of 1942).
"C" Company, 1st Battalion (less one platoon — see below), Searsport, Maine.
Detachment "E" Company, 22nd Quartermaster Regiment, Searsport, Maine.
26th Division Cavalry Reconnaissance Troop, Ellsworth, Maine.
Detachment Platoon 26th Division Cavalry Reconnaissance Troop, Machias, Maine.
One platoon of "C" Company, 1st Battalion, Wiscasset, Maine.

From north to south, the assigned areas, as far as is known, are as follows: the platoon from Company H was responsible for the stretch of coast from Bucksport south to Waldoboro (see Ruuska below); Company C, 1st Battalion, patrolled from Waldoboro south to Freeport; Company E, 22nd Quartermaster Regiment, comprised of "colored" troops, did not patrol; the 26th Division Cavalry Reconnaissance Troop, stationed at Ellsworth, patrolled the area from Bar Harbor south to Bucksport (see Fecteau and Adams below); Detachment Platoon, 26th Recon Troop, covered the coast from the Canadian border south to Ellsworth; the extent of the area covered by the platoon from Company C, 1st Battalion, is not known.[1]

Because of northern Maine's "innumerable small islands, bays and inlets," Eleanor C. Bishop says, it was "impossible" to guard the area as closely as the southernmost portion of the state. The rocky, wooded coast in parts of New England, especially in Maine, differed markedly from the sandy beaches farther down the Atlantic seaboard — the rocks were covered with a slippery algae and littered with slimy kelp, strewn with broken lobster pots, and flotsam and jetsam, and in some instances an oily sludge from ships sunk just off the coast by German U-boats, making the patrols extremely hazardous. Troops of the 181st Infantry stationed in the Rockland Sector used jeep and truck patrols to cover the coast north to Machias. From Little Machias Bay north to Quoddy, the Coast Guard used the "long truck patrol." Beach patrol personnel also used long truck patrols "along the resort areas of Mt. Desert Island, Southwest Harbor, and Cranberry Islands."[2]

Engineers constructed a network of lookout towers, some with searchlights, to guard the most inaccessible areas and isolated points. Both Coast Guard and 181st Infantry personnel manned the towers. Toward the end of 1944, the Army and Coast Guard phased out more and more of the beach and dog patrols and relied on greater use of the watchtower system.³

In the "more isolated and less populated" areas, "in the neighborhood of Quoddy Roads, Owl's Head, Heron Neck, Head Harbor Lubec Narrows, Friar Roads, the Western Passage," and around the adjacent islands of "Franklin, Mosquito, Long Moose, Petit Manon, Mark, Cross, and Machias," the Coast Guard patrolled by boat, called "picket patrols." "These were long patrols, known as the 'Vagabond' patrol," wrote Bishop. "Picket patrol boats covered the areas which the foot patrolman ... and dog patrolman could not physically reach due to water, swamps, or natural hazards." One picket patrol out of Rockland "went around Long Island." A second, went from the "Lubec Station" in "West Quoddy Head through Lubec Narrows and Friars Road, around Moose Island northward through the Western Passage." As early as June 1942, the Coast Guard "added numerous civilian boats" to its already "existing fleet ... of vessels."⁴

* * *

Many of the men of the 181st Infantry "were not thrilled to be stationed in that part of the country," wrote Marc P. Fecteau. Marc's father, Phillip Fecteau, was a member of the 3rd Platoon, 26th Division Cavalry Reconnaissance Troop, stationed in the sleepy coastal town of Ellsworth, with headquarters at the "old Ellsworth Hotel" on School Street.⁵

Today, Ellsworth is a thriving community, located only 15 to 20 minutes from Acadia National Park, "but," the younger Fecteau says, "in 1942, there wasn't much to do in the area." The city of Bangor, approximately 40 miles south, "was the only city that offered much in the way of entertainment. There was a lounge in Ellsworth called the Hancock House on Main Street, that appears to have been a popular hang-out," Marc said, "since many of my dad's photos of that time were taken on the porch of the establishment."⁶

Edward J. Adams was another member of the 26th Reconnaissance Troop stationed in Ellsworth. Adams says that the unit "was an entirely new outfit." Division Headquarters called for volunteers and he transferred from the 101st Field Artillery. "We were responsible for patrolling all the seaport towns between Ellsworth and the Canadian border," wrote Adams. He described the unit's arrival in Ellsworth in May 1942:

> When we first arrived it was during the summer and the day we entered the town we scared the hell out of the natives. They didn't know what was hitting them, our motor-cycle section, Harley Davidsons, were leading the convoy and making a hell of a racket. Some were showing off. We had a wild bunch in the bike section. The bikes were followed by armored half-track troop carriers.

The troop "billeted in field-tents on the fringe of the town [near the causeway to Mt. Desert Island] not far from Bar Harbor, but with winter coming on we took over the Ellsworth Hotel that sat on a hill as you enter the town on the main road."⁷

There were "several U-boat sightings," Adams said, and "one time authorities issued an alert that several Germans had escaped from a Canadian POW camp and might be heading in our direction." FBI agents eventually picked up the escapees in the Detroit area. "But all in all it was a rather boring assignment," Adams commented.⁸

* * *

At this time, there was a lot of paranoia about German sub landings and spies that might be in the area. While stationed in Camden, James V. Carnivale (H-181), a "sectional sergeant" who was in command of the machine gun platoon, says he received a number of complaints from the locals about "a strange light coming from a nearby small island." He witnessed the light himself, and decided to investigate. A civilian loaned the sergeant a small boat, and he

Above: Headquarters, Camden, Maine, 1942. *Below:* Jack Smith, Company H, 181 Infantry, of Raven, Virginia — at the shore near Camden, Maine (both photographs from Sulo O. Ruuska Collection).

and two of his men rowed the mile or so out to the supposedly deserted island. He said, "We walked all over that island and saw nothing but four deer."[9]

"Another time," Carnivale wrote, "I was on patrol in a jeep with one of my men near Christmas Cove" (just south of Bristol), "when several people hailed us down and said there was a suspicious woman on the beach." They reported that "she had a typewriter, parasol and a small folding table and chair and thought she might be a spy." Carnivale said he parked the jeep and walked down the path to the beach area. "I questioned her about what she was typing, when she pulled the piece of paper out of the roll and would not give it to me." The woman spoke with a heavy German accent. He then ordered her to come with him back to the cottage where she was staying. He said, "I posted my buddy at the foot of the stairs with orders that no one goes up or down and escorted her up to the porch."[10]

"Once inside the cottage," Carnivale says, "I asked her for her passport. Her name was Herta Knute." After checking the document closely, he discovered that "it had expired." He called headquarters on the telephone and the officer in charge said, "Stay there. We'll be right down." When the detail arrived, Carnivale said, "they told us to leave and they would handle it."[11]

Carnivale wrote, "Days later, I found out she had left Germany in Early 1941. She worked for our side, writing down everything she could remember so our people could use whatever was important." Carnivale closed, "Well, that's it Dennis, we did have our moments."[12]

* * *

Antonio J. "Tony" Tata (H-181), Lieutenant Colonel, retired, Massachusetts National Guard, of Leominster, Massachusetts, was a member of the .50-caliber machine gun platoon of Company H, consisting of four squads (one gun each). During the summer of 1942, battalion transferred Tata's squad to Brunswick, Maine, in the Rockland Sector. One day, Tata was on duty at a permanent gun emplacement near Freeport in Casco Bay. The time was late afternoon and the sun was close to the horizon when the crew spotted a German U-boat moving slowly on the surface about two hundred yards off shore. It was a very hazy day and visibility was restricted, Tata said.[13]

The squad leader ordered the gun crew to open fire. The gunner fired several long bursts before the vessel moved out of range. Tata said that he is not sure if any of the rounds hit the sub, or if they caused any damage. The squad leader put a telephone call through to the duty officer at Battalion Headquarters, who notified Naval Headquarters in Portland. Tata says the outfit "later received word that Navy destroyers had sunk the sub."[14]

Maine historian Joel W. Eastman reported that on June 22, 1942, a telescope watch station spotted a German submarine on the surface off Jewell Island in Casco Bay. The U.S. Army Coast Artillery Commander ordered the mobile coast defense battery stationed at Fort Baldwin near Popham Beach (near the mouth of the Kennebec River) to fire on the U-boat as soon as it came into range. The battery, located atop nearby Sabino Hill, consisted of four 155mm Howitzers.[15]

When two U. S. Navy destroyers approached, Naval Headquarters in Portland countermanded the order (see below). Eastman says that the "submarine dived, was depth-charged, but escaped." It is quite possible that this was the submarine fired on by Tata's squad. Tata claims the incident happened in 1942, but cannot recall the date.[16]

Joint research by commercial diver Edward R. Michaud, the president of Trident Research & Recovery, Inc., Framingham, Massachusetts, and Greg Brooks, president of Sub Sea Recovery (now Sub Sea Research) of Portland, Maine (Trident is no longer in operation), uncovered various log entries regarding the incident at the National Archives & Records Administration (NARA) New England regional facility at the Waltham Repository in Waltham, Massachusetts. Under Record Group 181, "Records of Naval Districts and Shore Establishments," and "War Diary, Commander Portland Section," and Record Group 242, "Collection of Foreign Records Seized, Records relating to U-Boat Warfare, 1939–1945," are a series of reports by both the Navy and Army confirming the presence of a German U-boat (and possibly two) in the "area around Bailey Island in Casco Bay," between June 22 and June 26, 1942.[17]

The records include reports of "Magnetic Loop Signatures," picked up by the Bailey Isle and Cape Elizabeth Receiving Station indicating an incoming vessel. The U.S. Navy installed "the highly secret anti-submarine indicator loops" at the entrances to Portland Harbor one month earlier in May 1942. The Royal Navy developed the indicator loop technology during

World War I, and during the 1930s U.S. Navy personnel modified and refined the detection system. When a submarine approaches a loop receiving station, the receiver picks up an "incoming magnetic signature." As the vessel passes out of the area, the station records an "outgoing signature." Steel magnetic detection loops, laid along the bottom of a passage or shipping lane, detect anomalies in the earth's magnetic field created by the passage of a metal hull over the loop. An instrument, called a fluxmeter, picks up the distortions and feeds the data to a recording device.[18]

The NARA documents also contain reports of a number of visual sightings by several vessels operating in the area and by observers at the Bailey Isle Loop Receiving Station. Eyewitnesses reported a U-boat "traveling on the surface within the waters of Casco Bay, close to the shore and ranging between Bailey Isle and Cape Small."[19]

Beginning at 4:38 P.M., the naval commander of the Portland Sector dispatched five destroyers and two escorts to conduct "an anti-sub sweep" of the waters off Bailey Island ("War Diary"). National Archives Record Group 181 contains a report that at "1720 [5:20 P.M.] on 22 June" the U.S. Navy Command ordered the Army Coastal Defense Command artillery 155 battery at Popham Beach to open fire when enemy submarine is sighted as it clears the Cape Small Range" (see below). Navy Headquarters "advised" the battery commander of "DD'S [Destroyers] IN VICINITY." This was the battery mentioned by Eastman above. The historian says the Navy rescinded the order to fire for fear of the large caliber rounds bouncing off the water on their trajectories and possibly hitting the approaching destroyer intercepts.[20]

"Records of the German Navy," contained in National Archives Record Group 242, "reflect the fact that two separate U-boats are known to have been operating within operational strike-range of the Casco Bay area during this time frame," wrote Edward R. Michaud. These have been identified as U-754 and U-458. At the time, the two U-boats were "maintaining radio silence ... which is very indicative of a 'special operation' being conducted by both of these vessels," he says. The submarines in question, were on "Lonewolf Patrol," *U-458* from "Cape Hatteras thence to the coast of New Foundland," and *U-754* from "St Lawrence, Nova Scotia, [to] New England." *U-754* "was sunk on 31 July 1942, by aircraft of the RCAF (Royal Canadian Air Force) Squadron 113 ... approximately 20 miles southeast of Cape Sable, Nova Scotia, with the loss of all hands."[21]

The following is a chronology of the sequence of events beginning at 12:40 P.M. on June 22, 1942:

1240	(12:40 P.M.) "Bailey Island Loop Receiving Station reports a strong inbound signature to H.E.C.P. [Harbor Entrance Control Post] — Portland"
1258	(12:58 P.M.) Bailey Isle "reports another strong inbound signature."
1415	(2:15 P.M.) "Strong inbound signature reported by Cape Elizabeth Loop Receiving Station."
1638	(4:38 P.M.) Bailey Isle "Reports enemy submarine on the surface two and one-half miles south of Jaquish Island."
1638	(4:38 P.M.) Naval Headquarters in Portland orders the first of five destroyers and two "auxiliary vessels" to "search for and destroy enemy submarine in Casco Bay."
1720	(5:20 P.M.) "U.S. Army Coastal Defense Command advises H.E.C.P.— Portland that the Popham Beach 155 Batteries have been ordered to open fire when enemy submarine is sighted.... The Army Battery is immediately advised of the presence of destroyers in the area."

1815 (6:15 P.M.) one of the destroyers, USS *McCalla* (DD-488) "made good sound contact and conducted depth charge attack [forward fired hedgehogs]." The ship reported, "Results negative."

1925 (7:25 P.M.) a Navy "OS2U-3 patrol plane" (Vought-Sikorsky Kingfisher seaplane) from Lewiston reported that it had "sighted oil bubbling up from the bottom off Cape Small."

Was the German craft sunk at this time, or did it escape? Over the next two hours, reports of the submarine's presence in the area continued to come in to Naval Headquarters in Portland. There were two additional eyewitness sightings by personnel stationed at the Bailey Isle Magnetic Loop Station. The submarine was last reported seen one mile east of Brown Cow Island at 2115 hours (9:15 P.M.), "on a course of 120 degrees true." The "Sub Sea Recovery" website claims to have "imaged a Type VII German U-Boat resting on the bottom of Casco Bay" using "a sonic compression video imaging system." No recent information can be found.[22]

Never at any time, the records state, did the magnetic indicator loops record any outgoing signatures. Record Group 181, "Records of Naval Districts and Shore Establishments," reported that "due to faults in the other loop" (at the exit point) the monitoring station did not detect the submarine on its way out of the harbor. "The fault turned out to be from loose terminals." The "War Diary, Commander Portland Section," noted that the lack of outgoing loop signatures indicated the "necessity of [using patrol] vessels equipped with microphones for listening purposes" as a backup security measure.[23]

On an interesting aside, Michaud states, there is "documentation that four [German] bodies washed ashore within two months of the date of activity within Casco Bay," which "tend to concur with the probability that the two U-boats ranging within Casco Bay were most probably involved with a saboteur/spy insertion operation." Remember also that it was shortly before this incident (June 13 and June 17, 1942) that "two other Nazi U-Boats had landed 4-man saboteur teams at both Amagansett, Long Island, New York and Ponte Vedra, Florida."[24]

* * *

In June or July 1942, battalion transferred (Cpl.) Sulo Ruuska's machine gun platoon, Company H, from Saco to Searsport. The unit became part of the Rockland Sector stationed at Searsport. Ruuska says, the "platoon set up pyramidal tents in a meadow and ran patrols from there." The platoon's area of responsibility extended from Waldoboro (15 miles west of Rockport) on the south, north to Bucksport (20 miles south of Bangor).[25]

James V. Carnivale (H-181) wrote, "S/Sgt. [Alexander V.] Bartemo and I, a 'Buck' Sgt., were in command of the unit. No officers. There were about 48 men in the platoon." The men "were on duty for six hours daily around the clock."[26]

Sulo Ruuska expressed his feelings regarding the situation:

> My platoon, the second (2nd) was the step-child of the company. I say this because we were separated from the company and sent north to Searsport [from Saco]. Not only were we much farther from home with far poorer means of getting there, but a place where we had little to do on our off-time.

He explained the difficulty getting home from Searsport: "We would go to Belfast and take the Belfast-Moosehead Lake Line to Burnham Junction and then the Boston & Maine train to Boston. It was an unusual ride." Sulo lived in nearby Quincy. This was the roundabout way, since the train traveled northwest from Belfast approximately 30 miles to Burnham Junction (14 miles southeast of Skowhegan), which is in the opposite direction from his destination and probably added an additional 70 to 80 miles to the trip.²⁷

Ruuska related a number of incidents that occurred on one of the train rides home to Boston:

> Once the train stopped at a stream and a fisherman with waders, fly rod and creel got off. Presumably, the engineer would pick him up on the return trip to Belfast. Another time, after a long toot of the whistle the train stopped and the fireman got off with a package. The package was for a farmer's wife who came running across the meadow from her home to the tracks to pick it up. On another trip, the train stopped at Burnham Junction and there were two hunters loading a couple of deer and a black bear into the baggage car. The animals had ear tags showing their destination.

Ruuska's quaint descriptions provide a nostalgic view of rural Maine in the early 1940s.²⁸

One day, Sulo says he was talking with "one of the natives" who told him a story about how he once shot a bear during hunting season in the fall and

George Ruberti and Sulo Ruuska, Company H, 181 Infantry, "on top of mountain behind Camden" (Sulo O. Ruuska Collection).

brought it home to clean and butcher. He said he got tied up with other things and before he knew it the bear "got sort of ripe, in fact," he admitted, "it stunk." Well, before he could dispose of the carcass, "the weather turned cold and it froze." The local man said, "Along came a city slicker from Boston who had not bagged anything and offered to buy the bear." Sulo says, "The deal was made and the bear went away tied to the roof of the hunter's car." The storyteller let out a hearty laugh and said, "When that bear thawed out, the smell must have been so bad all of Boston would have had to be evacuated."²⁹

"Sometimes," Ruuska wrote, "if the schedule of a patrol was convenient, we would hitch a ride to Rockland and take the train to Boston from there." Other times, Ruuska said he would "thumb a ride" to Rockland, but "this was not at all that easy, as tires and gasoline were rationed so the traffic in that part of Maine was mighty light."³⁰

Ruuska's company did not man permanent gun emplacements or walk the beaches; instead, units covered their assigned areas using motor patrols. "A patrol consisted of a non-commissioned officer, [either a] sergeant or corporal, one or two men, and a driver." The group rode in a ½-ton weapons carrier. "Shifts were of six hours duration, the first beginning at 6 A.M.," he wrote. Sector Headquarters "did not assign patrols to the men of the platoon every day, so they had a lot of free time on their hands, with very little to do." For the

George Ruberti, Company H, 181 Infantry — Motor Pool, Camden, Maine (Sulo O. Ruuska Collection).

troops in Camden, Ruuska related, "Monotony was the enemy." This was a common sentiment voiced by many of the veterans of the 181st stationed in Maine.[31]

"We did a lot of firing our weapons at the range while stationed in Searsport," Ruuska wrote, "the machine guns would be steaming, the fore stock on my rifle would be smoking." Sulo said he "did not know if it was for firing practice or to use up old ammunition, there was so much of it. If it was the latter it was a shame because one time in Italy ammunition was rationed."[32]

* * *

In a letter dated November 5, 1999, Sulo Ruuska wrote about an incident involving himself and his friend Nick Renzetti which took place near Searsport one day in the fall of 1942. He said that he and Nick were reminiscing about their days in Maine over the phone earlier in the week. After the war, the two men became lifelong friends. One of them recalled the incident, and they enjoyed a good laugh. "It's funny now," he said, but not then. I could have ended up in the stockade, because I was the patrol leader. Not only that, but a statement of charges would have meant my pay would have been garnished and maybe I would still be paying for an army truck." Sulo provided the following narrative:

> It was deer season, so we [the three man patrol] thought a small island on the coast near Searsport would be full of deer; no matter where we shot we would hit one. We drove onto the island over a narrow strip of land, which separated it from the mainland. We could only drive in a few yards

because it was so heavily wooded. It was a struggle to walk through the underbrush. We saw no deer and neither did we, being the nimrods we were, shoot ourselves. Time to return, but how, the tide had come in and our return route was now under water. Heck, full throttle, full speed ahead — right up to the hubs and stuck. The truck had a winch and on the far shore was something that might have been called a tree, because it was so scrawny, a poor excuse for even a bush. Nick volunteered to go in the water. He took off his shoes, socks, rolled up his pant legs, and waded in. It was already late fall and the water was cold. He pulled the winch cable along while me and the driver hoped it was long enough. It was — barely. Nick had hardly enough to wrap it around the base of the tree. With the winch turning and four wheels driving, we moved slowly as we got out of the mud onto firm ground.

Sulo, in his final remarks, said, "We were lucky twice in that we got out and secondly that we did not shoot a deer. I have always had reverence for life, even more so in my later years. Had we shot a deer, I'm sure I would have many times felt badly."[33]

* * *

Sulo Ruuska and George Ruberti, Company H, 181 Infantry, in front of barracks at Camden, Maine (Sulo O. Ruuska Collection).

After the summer of 1942, Ruuska's platoon moved to a CCC Camp in Camden, Maine, 25 miles south of Searsport. Sulo Ruuska described Camden as "a beautiful town." According to Jim Carnivale, the unit "patrolled from the area of Camden to Bucksport and around Rowena Island."[34]

The men stayed in tarpaper barracks, similar to those constructed by the engineers in Saco, "heated with two pot-bellied coal stoves." The shower room at the CCC Camp "was a challenge," Ruuska says, "the water heater provided hot water for only about three or four showers, and there were probably about one hundred fifty men in the camp."[35]

Besides Ruuska's platoon, there were two rifle platoons and a group of Quartermaster drivers with 10-wheelers (deuce-and-a-halfs), part of E Company, 22nd Quartermaster Regiment. The men of the Quartermaster Corps were "colored," Ruuska noted, and "the Army was not integrated then."[36]

"It was cold riding that mid-night to 6 A.M. shift, the temperature often well below zero," Ruuska recalled. The trucks were not equipped with heaters and had an open cab covered only by a canvas top with attached side curtains that were far from being airtight. These were Dodge ½-ton 4WD light duty pick-up trucks built from 1940 to 1947. "We took our blankets and quilts to wrap up in, the poor driver couldn't do this." On some night patrols, the men would have to "travel 60 miles or more, especially if your patrol was at the extreme end of our area."[37]

"Summers were pleasant enough if you had a daytime or early evening patrol," Ruuska remembered. The detail "would stop at a seaside lobster shack and get a chicken lobster for 25 cents, or two for 25 cents if they were culls" (one claw). On occasion, Ruuska would "requisition a truck and get some volunteers to go digging clams. They were so good steamed," he commented. While at Camden, the men on patrol "would stop at some of the coastal streams to scoop out a bushel or two of Atlantic herring during the seasonal runs." The men "would sell the fish at the local sardine factory for a little extra spending money." Ruuska closed, "We thought we would stay in Maine for the duration, but this was not to be."[38]

Conclusion

Foot and motor patrols remained in effect until the fall of 1943, when both the Army and the Coast Guard began to gradually phase them out. United States military forces "had successfully carried the war to the enemy" to the point "where the maintenance of a domestic defensive force was no longer necessary."[1]

The U.S. Army eventually replaced regular beach patrols with "mechanized cavalry reconnaissance groups ... which served as a mobile reconnoitering and striking force." These units remained on standby duty and were called upon when needed. "The 16th Cavalry Group served in New England, the 101st in the Chesapeake Bay and later in the New York–Philadelphia Sector as well, and 11th in Carolina, Georgia, and Florida." Shortly thereafter, the Army further reduced "even these small forces" leaving only the 143rd and 144th Cavalry Reconnaissance Troops (released in April 1945).[2]

Most accounts written about the U.S. Army, Navy, and Coast Guard beach patrol activities have deemed the program a tremendous success. The goal of the beach patrol, Bishop writes, was "the prevention of any further landings by the enemy." In her opinion, this objective "was achieved." She elaborates, "Two years after the patrol was founded to prevent a repeat of the landings at Long Island and Florida, the achievements [of the Beach Patrols] were measured, not by major incidents, but by no record of a major incident." The only other publicized landing took place on November 29, 1944, at Hancock Point, south of Bangor in Maine by two Nazi saboteurs, this occurring after the Army discontinued patrols by the 181st Infantry, the last of the 26th Division units on coast patrol. The evidence shows that the troops of the Army and Coast Guard "aided the FBI" in the "round-up" of a number "of suspicious persons ... on the beaches" during this period. As mentioned in an earlier chapter, the FBI decided against reporting these incidents to the press. Bishop pronounced the beach patrols a "great success," and stated, that "this success was achieved because the men who manned the patrol did their job well."[3]

Dennis L. Noble, also writing about the measure of success attributed to the patrols, provided the following appraisal:

> The value of the Beach Patrol ... is difficult to assess. On the one hand, no known saboteur landings were successful. The record clearly shows that in surprise drills, Coast Guard Patrolmen inevitably located and reported the enemy. On the other hand, as the service's [Coast Guard] official history clearly notes, "there is no way of knowing how many spies, despite all possible precautions, eluded the patrols by slipping into the country via the route of the eight apprehended saboteurs of 1942." We will probably never know whether the beach patrols actually made Germany rethink its plans on putting spies into the United States.

He closed with the following comment: "The beach patrol must have helped allay the fears of a nervous population during the first confused and hectic months of the war," and the "sight of armed [servicemen] patrolling the beaches must have made seaside residents feel safer."[4]

* * *

On November 30, 1943, after 21 months, the War Department relieved the 181st Infantry from Coast Patrol duty within the New England Sector and assigned the enlisted men of the unit to "AGF & XIII Corps," Fort Dix, New Jersey, for overseas assignments.[5]

The troops of the 181st Infantry Regiment proceeded from their original stations by motor transport and assembled at Fort Devens, in Ayer, Massachusetts, on December 4, 1943. The unit left Fort Devens the same day and proceeded by rail to Fort Dix, arriving at their destination on December 5, 1943.[6]

Division issued many of the men a 30-day "delay en route" order which allowed them to go home and spend the Christmas holidays with their families before reporting to their units at Fort Dix. Twenty-four year-old Pfc. Dennis "Joe" Connole was one of the lucky ones and this was the last time he would see his family until after the war.

In February, the Army ordered all enlisted men (EMs) from the 181st to report to Replacement Depot #1 (known to American servicemen as a repple-depple), at Fort Meade, Maryland. "The majority," Antonio J. Tata (H-181) says, "went to Italy as replacements." Among this group was my father. As mentioned in the Introduction, he ended up serving with Company D, 141st Infantry, 36th "Texas" Division, from March 1944 until June 1945.[7]

The non-commissioned officers (NCOs) were sent to a replacement pool at Indiantown Gap, Pennsylvania, where they were "cataloged and 'held on the shelf'" until a unit had a particular need for their military occupation specialty (MOS), or assigned to various units below strength. A considerable number of non-coms received orders for movement overseas where they reported to replacement depots and segregated from the EMs. When a slot opened up due to battlefield losses, units selected NCOs from the pool. Tata, a non-com, reported to Indiantown Gap. He eventually ended up with the 90th "Tough 'Ombres'" Infantry Division (formerly called the "Texas-Oklahoma Division"), attached to Patton's 3rd Army. "We landed at Normandy on D-Day plus 2, and moved inland," he said. Tata received a battlefield commission on April 5, 1944, near Palatine, France. Among the medals Mr. Tata earned were the Purple Heart and the Bronze Star. After the war, he served in the Massachusetts National Guard attaining the rank of lieutenant colonel. Col. Tata retired on December 21, 1966, after 25 years of distinguished sevice.[8]

After a short stay at Indiantown Gap, Sulo O. Ruuska, a buck sergeant (three stripes) with Company H, 181st Infantry, shipped out for Italy in February 1944. He explained what it was like for the unattached non-commissioned officers. At the repple depple, he said he felt like an orphan. "Would you believe I was interviewed by officers from a number of companies? No one wanted me. Then again, why would a unit want someone green? A guy with stripes who had not heard a shot fired," he wrote. Sulo says he "finally received an assignment to Company D, 337th Infantry, 85th Division, a [heavy] weapons company such as 'H' was, as a reconnaissance sergeant." The 85th "Custer" Division was a combat outfit originally made up almost entirely of replacements.[9]

In a letter dated February 2, 2000, Ruuska related what the experience was like for him when he joined his new outfit:

> Boy was I resented. My predecessor had been killed in action. The fellow from all reports was a great guy, well liked, respected, and very intelligent. Letters from his father, which I found, indicated a wonderful father-son relationship, beautifully written. It was difficult. I was not accepted and treated poorly and why not. Here is a new guy with rank. Why couldn't the job have been given to one of their own? It took a long time before I became "one of them."

Knowing Sulo as I did, he earned their acceptance and respect.[10]

At Fort Dix, the U.S. Army officially inactivated the 181st Infantry Regiment, effective February 8, 1944.[11]

Appendix A.
Organizational List, National Guard of Massachusetts—1939

I. Headquarters Detachment, 26th Division Staff, Boston, Massachusetts

    A. Headquarters Company — Special Troops:
        26th Military Police Company, Boston
        26th Signal Company, Charleston
        26th Tank Company, Boston
        101st Ordinance Company, Natick
        Medical Department Detachment, Boston

II. 51st Brigade Headquarters, Quincy, Massachusetts

    A. Headquarters Company, Quincy, Massachusetts

    B. 101st Infantry Headquarters, Boston
        Headquarters Company, Boston
        Service Company, Boston
        Band Section, Boston
        Howitzer Company, Quincy
        Medical Department Detachment, Boston

        1st Battalion Headquarters, Boston
          Headquarters Company, Boston
          Company A, Boston
          Company B, Boston
          Company C, West Newton
          Company D, Cambridge

        2nd Battalion Headquarters, Boston
          Headquarters Company, Boston
          Company E, Boston
          Company F, Boston
          Company G, Norwood
          Company H, Cambridge

        3rd Battalion, Headquarters, Quincy
          Headquarters Company, Quincy
          Company I, Attleboro
          Company K, Hingham

Company L, Plymouth
Company M, Cambridge

C. 182nd Infantry Headquarters, Charleston
Headquarters Company, Charleston
Service Company, Charleston
Band Section, Charleston
Howitzer Company, Charleston
Medical Department Detachment, Wakefield

1st Battalion Headquarters, Lowell
Headquarters Company, Lowell
Company A, Haverhill
Company B, Lawrence
Company C, Lowell
Company D, Lowell

2nd Battalion Headquarters, Waltham
Headquarters Company, Waltham
Company E, Wakefield
Company F, Waltham
Company G, Woburn
Company H, Concord

3rd Battalion Headquarters, Melrose
Headquarters Company, Melrose
Company I, Stoneham
Company K, Malden
Company L, Malden
Company M, Everett

III. 52nd Brigade Headquarters, Worcester, Massachusetts

D. 104th Infantry Headquarters, Springfield
Headquarters Company, Springfield
Service Company, Springfield
Band Section, Springfield
Howitzer Company, Springfield
Medical Department Detachment, Springfield

1st Battalion Headquarters, Springfield
Headquarters Company, Springfield
Companies A, B, C, and D, Springfield

2nd Battalion Headquarters, Holyoke
Headquarters Company, Holyoke
Company E, Holyoke
Company F, Holyoke
Company G, Northampton
Company H, Westfield

3rd Battalion, Headquarters, Pittsfield
Headquarters Company, Pittsfield
Company I, Pittsfield
Company K, North Adams
Company L, Greenfield
Company M, Adams

E. 181st Infantry Headquarters, Worcester
Headquarters Company, Worcester

Organizational List, National Guard of Massachusetts—1939

      Service Company, Worcester
      Band Section, Worcester
      Howitzer Company, Worcester
      Medical Department Detachment, Worcester

          1st Battalion Headquarters, Worcester
            Headquarters Company, Worcester
            Companies A, B, C, D, Worcester

          2nd Battalion Headquarters, Fitchburg
            Headquarters Company, Fitchburg
            Company E, Fitchburg
            Company F, Orange
            Company G, Clinton
            Company H, Fitchburg

          3rd Battalion, Headquarters, Natick
            Headquarters Company, Natick
            Company I, Milford
            Company K, Marlborough
            Company L, Hudson
            Company M, Framingham

F. 51st Field Artillery, Brigade Headquarters, Boston
      Headquarters Battery, Boston

G. 101st Field Artillery Headquarters, Boston
      Headquarters Battery, Boston
      Service Battery, Boston
      Band Section, Boston
      Medical Department Detachment, Boston

          1st Battalion Headquarters, Boston
            Headquarters Battery, Boston
            Batteries A, B, and C, Boston

          3rd Battalion Headquarters, Bedford
            Headquarters Battery, New Bedford
            Battery D, New Bedford
            Battery E, Brockton
            Battery F, Taunton

H. 102nd Field Artillery Headquarters, Lawrence
          Service Battery, Salem
          Band Section, Salem
          Medical Department Detachment, Salem

          1st Battalion Headquarters, Lowell
            Headquarters Battery, Lowell
            Battery A, Gloucester
            Battery B, Lowell
            Battery C, Lawrence

          2nd Battalion Headquarters, Salem
            Battery D, Salem
            Battery E, Lynn
            Battery F, Salem

I. 101st Engineers Headquarters and Service Company, Cambridge
      Medical Department Detachment, Cambridge

Band Section, Cambridge

1st Battalion Headquarters, Cambridge
  Company A, Somerville
  Company B, Somerville
  Company C, Cambridge

2nd Battalion Headquarters, Lynn
  Company D, Lynn
  Company E, Medford
  Company F, Lynn

J. 101st Medical Regiment, Boston
  Band Section, Boston
  Service Company, Boston
    Company A, Boston
    Company D, Worcester
    Company E, Boston
    Company G, Boston

K. 101st Quartermaster Regiment Headquarters, West Newton
    Headquarters Company, West Newton

  1st Battalion, Natick
    Company A, Natick
    Company B, Woburn

  2nd Battalion, Framingham
    Company C, Framingham
    Company D, Lawrence

  3rd Battalion, Natick
    Company E, Natick
    Company E, Everett

L. 26th Division Aviation, Boston Airport (now Logan), East Boston
  Medical Department Detachment
  101st Observation Squadron, East Boston
  101st Photo Section, East Boston
  101st Medical Department Detachment, East Boston

M. 241st Coast Artillery Headquarters, Boston
  Headquarters Battery, Boston
  Band Section, Boston
  Medical Department Detachment, Boston

  1st Battalion
    Batteries A, B, M, and I, Fall River

  2nd Battalion
    Batteries C, D, G, and K, Boston

  3rd Battalion
    Battery E, New Bedford
    Battery F, New Bedford
    Battery H, Chelsea
    Battery L, Boston

N. 211th Coast Artillery AA (anti-aircraft) Headquarters Detachment, Boston
  Band Section, Boston
  Service Battery, Boston
  Medical Department Detachment, Boston

1st Battalion Headquarters, Boston
  Batteries A, B, and C, Boston

2nd Battalion Headquarters, Boston
  Battery F, Boston
  Battery H, Boston

O. 21st Cavalry Division Headquarters, Lawrence
  Troop A, Lawrence

  121st Quartermaster Squadron Headquarters, Boston
    Troop F, Boston

  21st Reconnaissance Squadron Headquarters, Boston
    Troop A, Boston

P. 110th Cavalry Headquarters Troop, Boston

  Band Section, Boston
  Medical Department Detachment, Boston

  2nd Squadron
    Troop E, Boston
    Troop F, Boston

  3rd Squadron
    Troop I, Boston
    Troop K, Boston

Q. 372nd Infantry Headquarters, Boston

  Medical Department Detachment, Boston

  3rd Battalion Headquarters, Boston
    Headquarters Company, Boston
    Companies I, K, L, and M, Boston

Source: Historical and Pictorial Review: National Guard of the Commonwealth of Massachusetts (26th Division), published in 1939.

Appendix B. Organizational List, 181st Infantry Regiment, 26th Division—1941

I. **Headquarters and Headquarters Company, 181st Infantry, Worcester, Massachusetts**

        Service Company, Worcester
        Howitzer Company, Worcester
        Band Section, Worcester
        Medical Department Detachment, Worcester

II. **181st Infantry Regiment — Worcester, Massachusetts**

    A. Headquarters Company, 1st Battalion, Worcester, Massachusetts:
        Companies A, B, C, D, Worcester

    B. Headquarters Company, 2nd Battalion, Fitchburg, Massachusetts:
        Company E — Fitchburg
        Company F — Orange
        Company G — Clinton
        Company H — Fitchburg

    C. Headquarters Company, 3rd Battalion, Natick, Massachusetts:
        Company I — Milford
        Company K — Marlborough
        Company L — Webster
        Company M — Gardner

    D. Antitank Unit (A/T) — Hudson.

Source: Monthly Rosters ("Form No. 703, A.G.O., Monthly Roster, 16 Jan. 1941").

Appendix C.
Station List,
181st Infantry Combat Team

(Corrected to July 19, 1942)

Headquarters, 26th Infantry Division
A.P. Hill, Fredericksburg, Va.

Headquarters, New England Sector
150 Causeway Street, Boston, Mass.

Headquarters, 181st Infantry Combat Team, Camp Framingham, Massachusetts
Commanding Officer   Colonel James P. Powers
Executive Officer   Lt. Col. William F. Bigelow

Headquarters and Headquarters Company, First Battalion, 181st Infantry, Burlingame State Forest, Charlestown, Rhode Island
Commanding Officer   Lt. Col. William E. McBride
Executive Officer   Major Wiley M. Mangum

Battalion Headquarters Company, Burlingame State Forest
Commanding Officer   1st Lt. John J. Gagen

"A" Company, Fort Rodman, New Bedford, Massachusetts
Commanding Officer   Capt. Cornelius F. O'Leary

"B" Company, Burlingame State Forest
Commanding Officer   Capt. Thomas B. McKoan

"C" Company, Searsport, Maine
Commanding Officer   1st Lt. Francis J. Kret

"D" Company, Fort Adams, Newport, Rhode Island
Commanding Officer   1st Lt. John E. Baudin

"A" Battery, 211 F.A., Burlingame State Forest
Commanding Officer   1st Lt. Benjamin Beale

"C" Company, 132nd Engineers, Fort Kearney, Rhode Island
Commanding Officer   Capt. George R. Snyder

Detachment 22nd Quartermaster Regiment, Burlingame State Forest
Commanding Officer   Lt. Nagle

Headquarters and Headquarters Company, 2nd Battalion, 181st Infantry, High Shoe Factory Building, Saco, Maine

Commanding Officer	Lt. Col. John A. Amberg
Executive Officer	Major Joseph P. Kelly

Battalion Headquarters Company, High Shoe Co., Saco, Maine
Commanding Officer 1st Lt. Hugh J. Hawkins

"E" Company, Morley Button Factory, Portsmouth, New Hampshire
Commanding Officer   Capt. John F. Lane

"F" Company, High Pine, Sanford, Maine
Commanding Officer   Capt. John F. Asselta

"G" Company, Town Hall, Old Orchard Beach, Maine
Commanding Officer   Capt. Russell W. Vinton

"H" Company, High Shoe Company, Saco, Maine
Commanding Officer   1st Lt. B.C. O'Connor

"C" Battery, 211th F.A., High Shoe Company, Saco, Maine
Commanding Officer   Capt. Joseph P. Hayes

"A" Company, 132nd Engineers, Saco, Maine
Commanding Officer   Capt. Orlan A. Johnson

1st Platoon, "A" Company, 22nd Quartermaster Regiment, Saco, Maine
Commanding Officer   1st Lt. Richard A. Crain

Headquarters, Rockland Sector, Second Battalion, 181st Infantry, Searsport, Maine
Commanding Officer   1st Lt. Salvi Laquidara

"C" Company, Searsport, Maine
Commanding Officer   1st Lt. Francis J. Kret

Detachment "E" Company, 22nd Quartermaster Regiment, Searsport, Maine
Commanding Officer   Lt. Fernander Kirby

26th Division Cavalry Reconnaissance Troop, Ellsworth, Maine
Commanding Officer   Capt. Arthur S. Marcoullier

Detachment Platoon, 26th Division Cavalry Reconnaissance Troop, Machias, Maine
Commanding Officer   1st Lt. Bernardier

Platoon of "C" Company, 181st Infantry, Wiscasset, Maine

Headquarters and Headquarters Company, Third Battalion, 181st Infantry, South Hingham, Massachusetts
Commanding Officer	Lt. Col. Armand Ruby
Executive Officer	Major George A. Mildonian

Battalion Headquarters Company, South Hingham, Massachusetts
Commanding Officer   1st Lt. Joseph C. Dine

"I" Company, South Hingham, Massachusetts
Commanding Officer   Capt. Earl D. Van Alstyne

"K" Company, Plymouth, Massachusetts
Commanding Officer   Capt. John H. Wagner

"L" Company, Ipswich, Massachusetts
Commanding Officer   1st Lt. Peter S. Wondolowski

"M" Company, South Hingham, Massachusetts
Commanding Officer   Capt. William J. Gannon

"B" Battery, 211th F.A., Ipswich, Massachusetts
Commanding Officer   1st Lt. George F. Cassin

"D" Battery, 211th F.A., Plymouth, Massachusetts
Commanding Officer   1st Lt. Philip K. Allen

"B" Company, 132nd Engineers, South Hingham, Massachusetts
Commanding Officer   Capt. Steele

Source: "Station List, 181st Infantry Combat Team (Corrected to July 19, 1942)." Provided by: Theodore Simmington, Jr., 88 Old Farm Road, Needham, Massachusetts 02192

Appendix D.
History of the 181st Infantry

The 181st Infantry was organized originally as the 6th Infantry, Massachusetts Volunteer Militia, from companies which were organized as early as 1781, and later, in townships that furnished the "Minute Man" for Revolutionary War Service.

Several of these companies were in continuous existence for more than one hundred years. In this original organization were included companies which in turn were originally "Minute Men" companies — Veterans of Concord, Lexington and Bunker Hill.

These companies came, as do present companies of the regiment, from towns in Worcester and Middlesex Counties — and the regiment was known from the time of its organization as the Minute Man Regiment. It has as its special insignia a Colonial Powder Horn, which has been perpetuated in the present regimental badge — a silver powder horn on a blue shield.

The 6th Massachusetts Infantry was re-organized by the consolidation of previously existing companies under General Order Number 4, dated February 26, 1855.

Civil War Service 1861–1864

1st Service: 3 months— during which time it was called the Minute Man [regiment]. Tendered its services to Governor Andrews, January 21, 1861. Arrived in Boston, Mass. April 16, 1861.

Entrained for Washington, D.C., April 17, 1861 and was the first armed regiment to reach Washington in response to President Lincoln's first call for troops on April 19, 1861. While en route to Washington it was fired on in the streets of Baltimore, Md. and suffered a number of casualties. The regiment was mustered into service in Washington, April 22, 1861 and served in the vicinity of Washington and Virginia during this period of the war. Mustered out of service at Boston, Mass. August 2, 1861.

2nd Service: 9 months— Companies and officers were mustered in on various dates between August 31st and September 8, 1862. The regiment was stationed at Fort Monroe, and did service at Deserted House, Va., January 30, 1863, and in the siege of Suffolk in May of the same year. It was again mustered out of service at Lowell, Mass. June 3, 1863.

3rd Service: 100 days— Companies were mustered on various dates from July 14th to 19th, 1864. The regiment did guard duty at Arlington Heights and Fort Delaware. It was mustered out at Readville, Mass. on October 27, 1864.

Spanish American War Service, 1898–1899

Reported at State Camp Ground, "Camp Dewey," South Framingham, Mass., May 6, 1898, in response to S0 #45, A.G.O. Mass. Dated April 29, 1898. It was mustered into the United States Service as United States Volunteers, May 13, 1898. Entrained for Falls Church, Va., May 20, 1898. Paraded in Baltimore, Md., while en route and at its destination "Camp Alger," May 22, 1898. On July 5th, 1898 it entrained for Charlestown, S.C., en route for Cuba, embarked on USS "Yale," July 8th, 1898, arrived off coast of Cuba, July 14th and anchored in Guautonomo [sic] Bay. On July 20th it sailed for Porto [sic] Rico. On July 25th landed near Guanico on the road to Yauco. Participated in all the activities of the Porto [sic] Rican Campaign. From October 18 to 21 it embarked on the USS Mississippi, for the home voyage. Arrived in Boston Harbor, October 27, 1898. Mustered out of the Service January 21, 1899.

World War I

Shortly after March 30, 1917, the 6th Infantry Regiment was broken up and approximately 1500 officers and [enlisted] men were transferred to various units of the 26th (Yankee) Division which was then being formed. These officers and men took part in the World War as members of the Yankee Division.

A number of officers and enlisted men from the 6th and 8th Infantry Regiments formed the new 104th Infantry. Another group of officers from the 6th, 5th, and 9th Infantry Regiments formed the new 101st Infantry. All that was left of the 5th, 6th, and 9th Infantry Regiments were, on February 10, 1918, organized into what was known as the 4th Pioneer Infantry and this regiment saw service in the United States and France, being mustered out of service February 8, 1919.

In the re-organization of the National Guard during 1919–1920, this regiment was organized as the 103rd Field Artillery on March 15, 1920, under the command of Colonel John D. Murphy.

On September 1, 1920, the designation was changed from the 103rd Field Artillery to the 3rd Field Artillery.

On August 31, 1921, the designation was again changed, this time, from the 3rd Field Artillery to the 3rd Infantry.

On November 30, 1921, the 3rd Infantry was re-organized and the designation changed to the 181ST INFANTRY and Federal recognition was granted on this date.

Colonel Murphy was promoted to Brigadier General, Command of the regiment passed to Colonel Frank L. Converse. Colonel Converse retired in 1931 after commanding the regiment for seven years and was succeeded by Colonel Edgar C. Erickson. Colonel Erickson was promoted to Brigadier General in 1937 and command of the regiment was assumed by Colonel Roy W. Smith.

The War Department has authorized the Regiment to wear on its colors, battle streamers, with inscriptions as follows:

Civil War
Virginia 1862–1863

Spanish-American War
Porto [sic]-Rico 1898

World War No. I
Without inscription
Coat of Arms: Approved by the War Department, 17 November 1923
Shield: Azure, a colonial powder horn, gold trim (border)
Motto: "Keep your powder dry"

Since 1921 the 181st Infantry has participated in all Federal Tours of Field Duty, including all large scale maneuvers. During First Army Maneuvers at Potsdam, N.Y., in 1940, the 181st Infantry was commended by the Commanding General 1st Army for the excellent and efficient manner in which it performed during the maneuvers.

It also performed duty during the flood and hurricane in 1936 and 1938.

The regiment won the General John J. Pershing Trophy in 1939 for its excellence in Marksmanship. This competition in which all National Guard Units of the United States participated.

World War II

On January 16, 1941, the 181st Infantry, as part of the 26th Infantry Division was inducted into the active military service of the United States for one year under Presidential Order #8613, dated December 23, 1940 and GO#6, A.G.O., Mass., dated December 30, 1940.

On January 24, 1941 the units of the regiment moved from their various stations in Central Massachusetts to Camp Edwards, Mass., where intensive Military Training was taken up.

The regiment was increased to near war strength by the influx of Selective Trainees during the months of February, March, April and May, 1941, and spent a period of thirteen weeks in the basic training of these recruits.

The regiment participated in the VI Army Corps Maneuvers in the vicinity of Fort Devens, Mass. during the months of August and September and then proceeded to McLeod, N.C., where it took part in the First Army Maneuvers during the period from September 28 to December 6, 1941. During this time the regiment was rated one of the best Infantry regiments in the First Army.

On December 7, 1941, war was declared on Japan, Germany, Italy and their allies and the Military service of the regiment was extended for the duration of the war plus 6 months per Bulletin #37, Par[a] III, dated December 12, 1941.

Shortly after the formal declaration of War, the 2nd Bn. of the regiment was dispatched to the Eastern Coast as part of the Coastal Defense, extending from Woods Hole, Mass. to Montauk Point, Long Island, N.Y. The 2nd Bn. was relieved by the 104th Infantry and returned to Camp Edwards on February 1, 1942.

On February 5, 1942, the 26th Infantry Division was "streamlined" and re-designated from a square to a triangular division and the 181st Infantry was authorized to go to it's [sic] full war strength, 123 officers and 3325 men.

On December 31, 1941, Colonel Roy W. Smith was transferred from the regiment to the 1114th [sic] C.A.S.U. and Colonel James P. Powers, a veteran for many years, assumed command.

On May 11, 1942, the regiment with 211th FA Bn., two Co's of 22nd QM Regiment (C), one company of 132nd Combat Engineers, a detachment of 114th Medical Regiment comprising Combat Team 181 were ordered on Coastal Patrol of Coastal area between Higgins Beach, Maine and Watch Hill, Rhode Island. Command Post of CT 181 stationed at 150 Causeway St., Boston, Mass., of the 1st Bn. CT 181, Burlingame State Reservation, Charlestown, R.I., of the 2nd Bn. CT 181, Saco, Me., and of the 3rd Bn. CT 181, Blue Hills Reservation, Milton, Mass. At later dates the C.P.'s were changed to facilitate tactical handling of troops as follows:

CP CT 181—Camp Framingham, Mass.
CP 1st Bn—Camp Burlingame, Westerly, R.I.
CP 3rd Bn—So. Hingham, Mass.
CP 2nd Bn—Remained as originally located

In accordance with Special Orders #125 and 126, Hq. 26th Inf. Div., the regimental strength was increased by 824 enlisted men who had received their basic training at Camp Wheeler, Ga. Total enlisted strength as of 20 May 1942 was 3260 men.

On June 24, 1942, the specialists of the regiment were disrated [reduced to a lower rank] and appointed to technician grade pursuant to instructions contained in Ltr., Hq., 1st Army, "Abolishment of Specialist Ratings and Reappointment to Technician Grades" dated 19 June 1942 and WD Radiogram, same subject, dated 18 June 1942.

In accordance with T/O 7–11, Inf. Regt., WD, Washington, April 1, 1942 and GO XIII, Hq. 181st Inf., 6 July 1942 the regiment was reorganized. Such reorganization consisting of an increase of strength of certain units and redesignation of these units as listed below:

Hq. Det. 1st Bn. redesignated Hq. Co. 1st Bn.
"   " 2nd   "   "   " 2nd "
"   " 3rd   "   "   " 3rd "

A Cannon Company was formed, but later disbanded due to the prevailing War Department policy.

Six Warrant Officers were assigned to the Regiment effective 9 October 1942 pursuant to authority contained in SO 248, Hq., 26th Inf. Div., 9 October 1942. All six were drawn from the enlisted strength of the 181st Infantry by means of competitive examinations.

During the month of December, 1942, 263 enlisted men (selectees) were assigned this organization per SO 88 and 89, IRTC, C[am]p Wheeler, Ga. 21 enlisted men (SS) were assigned to this organization per SO 30, IRTC, Cp Wolters, Texas, 14 December 1942 and 28 enlisted men (SS) were assigned per SO 159, Hq., 76th Div., Ft. Geo. G. Meade, Md., 28 Dec. 1942, bringing the strength of the regiment up to 3329.

The regiment was detached from the 26th Infantry Division on January 14, 1943 per letter Hq., EDC & FA, file G-3370.5, Subject: Movement Orders #595, and reassigned to New England Sector on February 8, 1943 per letter, Hq., EDC & FA, file G-3 320.2/906, dated 8 Feb. 1943, Subject: Assignments and Attachment of CT Elements.

Field Order #3, Hq., NES, dated 25 January 1943 assigned Battalion Combat Teams to Subsectors as follows:

Hq., CT 181—Boston Subsector
CT 181-1 (1st Bn)—Newport Subsector
CT 181-2 (2nd Bn)—Portland Subsector
CT 181-3 (3rd Bn)—Boston Subsector

On 20 March 1943, the regiment received a new Table of Organization for an Infantry Regiment as follows: T/O 7–11, Inf., Regt., W.D., Washington, D.C., 1 Mar 43 with a total strength of 3088, a difference of 384 less than the old T/O. However, the regiment because of the nature of its duties along the coast was not reorganized to conform with the new T/O and therefore, remained as organized under the old T/O. Shortly thereafter, a Tank Detachment, under the Hq. Co. was formed; made up from commissioned and enlisted personnel of the regiment. After the necessary training was completed, the Tank Detachment was divided up among the various Battalions and entered upon its duties.

On 27 August 1943, the 181st Infantry was reorganized PAC Sec I & II, GO 16, Hq., NES, 25 August 1943, in accordance with T/O 7–11, 15 July 1943, In order to conform with the new T/O, 100 EM were transferred within the regiment to various units of the regiment, being however, retained on Special Duty with their original units. Concurrently, with the reorganization, a Cannon Company was activated PAC Ltr WD, AGO, file AG 322 (7 Aug 43) OB-I-GNGCT-M, Subject: Reorganization of Infantry Regiment under new T/O, dated 10 Aug 43. The personnel of the Cannon Company (113 EM—5 Officers) were drawn from other units of the Regiment.

On 12 September 1943, the 132nd Engr (C) Bn. was withdrawn from the combat team and asgd AGF, XIII Corps at Fort Dix, NJ PAC Ltr WD, AGO file 370.5 (1 Sept 43) OB-S-GNGCT-M 1 Sept 43.

On 26 Sept 43, the regiment was brought up to proper NCO strength by the promotion of EM per SO 200, Hq., 181 CT, dated 26 Sep 43.

On 21 Oct 43, the 211th FA Bn was rel[ieved]d fr asgmt with CT 181 and asgd AGF, XIII Corps, FT Dix, NJ PAC Ltr WD file AG 370.5 (1 Oct 43) OB-S-GNGCT-M, 10 Oct 43.

On 30 Nov 43, the regiment was relieved from duty with the New England Sector and asgd to AGF & XIII Corps, Fort Dix, NJ. The regiment, less 1st Bn (less Co C) assembled at Fort Devens, Mass. by motor and on 4 Dec 43 proceeded by rail to Fort Dix, NJ arriving 5 Dec 43. The 1st Bn. (Less Co C) proceeded from original stations by motor and rail to Ft Dix, on 3 Dec 43, arriving 5 Dec 43. Auth: SO 254, Hq., NES, Boston, Mass., 24 Nov 43, as amended by par 5, SO 259, Hq., NES, Boston, Mass., 30 Nov. 43.

The 181st Infantry is inactivated at Fort Dix, NJ, effective 2359, 8 Feb 44, per Ltr Hq., XIII Corps, Ft Du Pont [sic], Delaware, file 322 (Inf) (GNNMC) Subj: Inactivation of the 181st Infantry, dated 1 February 1944 & G.O. #12, Hq., XIII Corps, Fort Du Pont [sic], Delaware, dated 2 February 1944.

Source: Paper on file at the Massachusetts National Guard Military Museum & Archives, Worcester, Mass.

Appendix E.
Résumé of Regimental Activities, 181st Infantry, Since Induction on January 16, 1941

Headquarters, 181st Infantry (Rifle)
Office of the Regimental Commander

Fort Dix, N.J.
7 December 1943

TO: Commanding General, XIII Corps, Fort Dupont, Del.

1. a. The 181st Infantry Regiment was inducted into Federal service on January 16, 1941 as a regiment of the 26th Infantry Division.

   b. It came into service with approximately 1057 EM and 123 officers and had its basic training at Camp Edwards, Mass. Early in March, the organization received the first fillers of selective service men direct from reception centers and conducted its own basic training for these men.

   c. Training of all elements of the command was carried on during the spring and summer of 1941 and in August the Division moved to Fort Devens and vicinity for extended maneuvers. It then returned to Camp Edwards until the later part of September when it moved with the division to North Carolina to attend the First Army maneuvers, returning to Camp Edwards in December.

2. From January, 1942 until May, platoon, company, battalion and regiment was subjected to a series of tests conducted with the Sixth Army Corps.

3. a. On May 11, 1942, the regiment was ordered into position along the entire coastline of New England from the Connecticut — Rhode Island state line to Canada with the mission of observing, by having men stationed in hutments along the coast from which foot patrols would operate and a complete system of motor patrols. Strong points where small reserves were held alerted at all times were established throughout the regimental area.

   b. The regiment was further strengthened by the attachment of the 211th FA Bn, 105 How., 132nd Eng. Bn. and the 675th Medical Collecting Co. with Co. E, 22nd QM Regiment (Truck) (Colored) attached for transportation.

   c. Because of the tremendous distances and necessity of long hauling distances, one hundred and fifty extra vehicles were supplied the regiment.

   d. During this tour of duty it became the regiment's duty to operate some thirty M1 light tanks, hence it has a number of tank operators and crews; however, these men were members of rifle and MG units and have now returned to their former assignments.

4. The following figures represent schools attended by officers of this command:

Ft. Benning, Ga.	Officers Basic Course	46
Ft. Benning, Ga.	Officers Advance Course	18
Ft. Benning, Ga.	Communications	13
Ft. Benning, Ga.	Motor Maintenance	19
Ft. Benning, Ga.	O.C.S.	62
Ft. Benning, Ga.	Cannon Course	7
Ft. Benning, Ga.	Special Methods	1
Ft. Leavenworth	Bn Command & Staff Officers	7
Carlisle Barracks	Med. Fld Serv Sch	8
Mayo Foundation	Medicine, Internal	2
Ft. Washington, Md.	AGO Administration	2
Hollidaysburg, Pa.	Keystone Radio Sch	1
Holabird QM Depot	Motor Mech & Maintenance	1
Holabird QM Depot	Motor Transportation	1
Cp Hood, Texas	Tank Destroyer	5
Ft. Meade, Md.	Special Service Off	1
Wash. & Lee Univ.	Special Service Off	2
Fort Knox, Ky.	Tank Maintenance	2
Aberdeen, Md.	Bomb Maintenance	2
Harvard Univ.	Chaplains Sch	3
Ft. Sill, Okla.	Btry Off.	2
Brooksfield, Texas	AAFAF Aircraft Observers	2
Edgewood Arsenal	Chemical Warfare Sch	1
Carlisle Barracks	Med Fld Serv Dental	1
Washington, D.C.	Trop. Mil. Med.	1
Richmond, Va.	First FC Aircraft Identification	1
Cp Picket, Va.	MRTC Military Medicine	1
Fort Knox, Ky.	Training Tank Personnel	2
Cp Ritchie, Md.	Military Intelligence	1
Cp Ritchie, Md.	Language Sch	1
Ft. Washington, Md.	MRU TAC Sch	1
	Chemical Warfare 20th UGO	2
Ft. Wayne, Ind.	Motor Transportation	2

5. During the regiment's duty on coast Defense, a great many schools were conducted by the regiment at East Douglas, Mass. by the splendid cooperation of the Commanding General of the New England Sector, Major Gen. K.T. Blood and his staff. This tactical school of instruction for all enlisted men and officers was in constant operation. It was patterned after the Infantry School, Fort Benning, Ga. and had for its purpose the physical conditioning and hardening of all and a complete, detailed familiarization of all infantry weapons as to nomenclature and functioning as well as tactical application. Further, to teach the men in ranks exactly what his particular duty consisted of, his cooperation with other members of his squad and platoon and why these many times mysterious things were done.

The school faculty consisted of selected officers and non-commissioned officers who developed into experts and were a credit to the organization. The work was strenuous but interesting and each class was constituted as a complete rifle company, reinforced by an 81mm Mortar section and Heavy MG platoon. The rifle platoons were drawn from various units along the coast as were the weapons sections and platoons; officers were assigned platoons as was the company commander from some units not then attending so that both the officers and men were strange to each other, the then being [?] all would learn the lessons offered without embarrassment and also for the welding together of the regiment and for uniform instruction within the regiment.

The duration of the tactical school was fourteen consecutive days, Saturday and Sunday included; no passes or time out was allowed; and the training day commenced at 0430 and continued throughout the day with four overnight problems. During this two week period 184 hours of training were given with many graded tests to assure the instruction was getting over.

A complete file with schedules and instruction lectures is on file at this headquarters.

Every man and officer except the headquarters units were subjected to training at the tactical training school.

6. A very extensive school for NCO's and Junior Officers for a 6 weeks duration was planned but not carried into execution because of the movement into Fort Dix, however, the instructors, lectures and training aids are all prepared and it is anticipated much of this already prepared data will be used during our stay here.

7. At Ellsworth, Maine, during July and August of 1943, a very thorough Anti-Tank School was operated. Here, the entire Anti-Tank personnel of the regiment attended, in several sessions, by detailing one half of the Battalion AT Platoon with a platoon of AT Co. at each semester. This, it is felt, was an excellent school and much benefit derived, however, the unit was then only equipped with 37mm and only theory of the 57mm and such nomenclature as was possible from charts was given. The school included AT mines and personnel mines with booby traps.

8. Three combat intelligence schools and counter-intelligence training schools were conducted at Framingham, Mass. where all intelligence men were in attendance under the regimental S-2. In addition, many have attended the Intelligence School at Camp Ritchie, Md. and twenty-four men are now at Camp Ritchie.

9. Other schools of instruction were constantly being conducted for all officers and enlisted men under the supervision of Battalion C.O.'s.

10. Because of the nature of the mission, only a small percentage of men were allowed time off—10 percent on pass and 5 percent on leave which would give a man forty-eight hours of free time in twenty-one days.

11. During the coast duty, each battalion was assembled, less actual patrols for a twenty-four hour battalion exercise based on defense of the coastline in which it was necessary to destroy an enemy beachhead by a counterattack; artillery and tanks were used during the exercise. The assembling of these Battalions required a move in some cases of several hundred miles, but it was felt much benefit came from these exercises, in that they gave the Battalion C.O. an opportunity to see and work his battalion as a unit the first time in many months.

12. a. Known distance ranges were constructed all along the coast where it was too far to reach National Guard of State ranges by units, and as a result some 95 percent of the regiment have fired the familiarization course and 75 percent have fired Practice Record Modified C[ourse] with the M1 and '03 with a large majority qualifying.

b. The carbine has not been fired in that these weapons were just received and arrangements have been completed to begin firing on Monday next.

Other weapons are covered in the attached resume, paragraph #29.

c. Much training along the lines of intelligence has been given consistent with the recent assignment on identification of planes, ships, suspicious persons, etc.

d. The regiment has a number of trained patrol dog men in that some 150 dogs were employed during the beach duty.

13. It is felt that the regiment is in need of a refresher course of individual, squad and platoon training as well as an opportunity to conduct Company and Battalion training with associated arms in that it has been nineteen months since any of this training has been accomplished.

All men should, if possible, fire a familiarization course with all individual and crew-fired weapons, and men who have not qualified with individual weapons fire for qualification.

14. At the present time the unit is approximately 150 men understrength, but has been notified that 82 men, caliber unknown, are already at Fort Dix and a requisition for the remaining shortage is now being framed. If these men are direct from the reception center, a training company will

be immediately organized to conduct their proper basic training. Men already trained will be, after interview and test, assigned to various units now below strength.

> For the Regimental Commander:
> Antonio F. Antalek
> Captain, Infantry
> Adjutant

Source: Paper on file at the National Archives and Records Administration (NARA), Modern Military Records, Textual Archives Services Division College Park, Maryland (5 pages).

Chapter Notes

Introduction

1. The Piersall Collection of Orders, Decorations, and Medals From Around the World: "The Bronze Star Medal 1944–Present," http://www.marksmedals.com/us_medals_files/bronze_star.html.
2. Ibid.
3. Mark Melady, "They rose to defend the home front: 26th Yankee Division kept watch in New England," (Worcester, MA) *Sunday Telegram*, September 30, 2001, All.
4. Ibid.
5. Ibid.

Chapter 1

1. Louis L. Snyder, "World War II," *Academic American Encyclopedia*, 20: 251 (Granby, CT: Groliers, 1993); Kenneth Macksey, "Blitzkrieg," *Oxford Companion to World War II*, I.C.B. Dear, general editor, and M.R.D. Foot, consultant editor (New York: Oxford University Press, 1995), 140; James L. Stokesbury, "World War II," *World Book Encyclopedia* 21: 468, 472 (Chicago: World Book, 2001).
2. Ibid.; Stokesbury, 472–473; Keith Sword, "Poland," *Oxford Companion to World War II*, 891.
3. Ibid.; 254–255; Stokesbury, 468, 475–476; Alfred Price, "Blitz," *Oxford Companion to World War II*, 138–139.
4. Stokesbury, 477; Kimball Warren, "Lend-Lease," *Oxford Companion to World War II*, 677–679; "Lend-Lease," *World Book Encyclopedia* 12: 190; James T. Patterson, "Roosevelt, Franklin Delano," *World Book Encyclopedia* 16: 459–460.
5. "Selective service system," *Oxford Companion to World War II*, 996; "Army, United States, World War II (1939–1945)," *World Book Encyclopedia* 1: 739; Lee B. Kennett, *G.I.: The American Soldier in World War II* (New York: Scribner, 1987), 4; Michael D. Doubler, "Guard Century — Not So Calm, Before the Storm: 1920 to 1940," *National Guard Magazine* 53, no. 10 (October, 1999), 35.
6. Kennett, 7–8; Chris Pope, "Draft for WWII recalled: Worcester men in '158 Club'" (Worcester, MA) *Sunday Telegram* (October 14, 1990), A1.
7. Pope, A1.
8. Raymond A. Fitzpatrick, "10,000 Hear FDR Talk Briefly on Defense Here," *Worcester [MA] Telegram* (October 31, 1940), 1, 11.
9. Ibid.; Pope, A1.
10. Doubler, 34–35.
11. Yankee Division Veterans Association (YDVA), *The History of the 26th Yankee Division: 1917–1919 and 1941–1945* (Salem, MA: Deschamps, 1955), 19. Hereafter cited as YDVA.
12. YDVA; Richard P. Taffe, "As War Clouds Gathered," *Army Magazine* 41, no. 12 (December 1991), 27.
13. YDVA, 19; "History of the 104th [Infantry]," Robert M. Mackintosh (Captain), et al., eds. (c. 1942) Massachusetts National Guard Military Museum & Archives, Worcester, MA, pages not numbered.
14. John D. Turini (G-181 and Hq. Co., 2nd Bn.-181), "Recollections," *Worcester's Vanishing Veterans, Worcestertalks: Oral History Project*, Worcester Historical Museum (August, 2002), pages not numbered.
15. Taffe, 27; Doubler, 35.
16. Ibid.; YDVA, 19.
17. "History of the 104th [Infantry]."
18. "City Bids Farewell to Departing Troops," (Worcester, MA) *Sunday Telegram* (January 26, 1941). 8; Joseph H. Gauthier, "500 City Soldiers Head for Falmouth," (Worcester, MA) *Evening Gazette* (January 25, 1941), 1, 3.
19. Ibid.; Gauthier, 1, 3.
20. Ibid.; Gauthier, 3.
21. Ibid.; Gauthier, 3.
22. Ibid.
23. Ibid.; Gauthier, 3.
24. Ibid.; Gauthier, 1.
25. Ibid.; Gauthier, 3.
26. Joseph H. Gauthier, "Guardsmen of Area Start Basic Training" (Worcester, MA) *Evening Gazette* (January 27, 1941), 8.
27. Ibid.
28. YDVA, 19; "History of the 104th [Infantry]."
29. YDVA, 19–20; "History of the 104th [Infantry]."
30. Dennis J. Connole, U.S. Army "Enlisted Record and Report of Separation, Honorable Discharge, 27 June 45," Form WD AGO 53–55, November 1944.
31. Nathaniel Mencow (M-181), interview on February 6, 2002; Nathaniel ("Nate" or "Gus") Mencow left the 181st Infantry in early 1942, shortly after the U.S. entered the war. He applied for and received acceptance into the Army Air Corps Cadet Training Program. Assigned to the flight training school at Mather Army Air Field in Sacramento, California, Mencow trained as a navigator. Based in England, Mencow flew 25 missions over Europe in a B-17 Flying Fortress, part of a squadron of the 390th Bomb Group with the 8th Air Force, eventually attaining the rank of captain. This was early in the war, before fighter air cover. Later, the Air Corps increased the number of missions to 35 and eventually to 50 missions. The name of his ship was "Betty Boop/Pistol Packin' Mama," the subject of a 1991 Kenwood Productions American Hero Series video, which aired on the Public Broadcasting System (PBS)—see Kenwood Productions, Inc., *Pistol Packin' Mama: The Missions of a B-17*, VHS, Director: Tom Jenz (1991). Two months after Mencow finished his

tour of duty, antiaircraft fire destroyed the airplane over Berlin. Of a crew of 10, only three members survived. After completing his required 25 combat missions, the Air Corps appointed Mencow wing navigator for the 13th Combat Wing, which included the 95th, 100th, and 390th bomb groups, "in charge of mission planning and training of personnel." He flew one additional mission before the war ended. Nate Mencow was awarded the Distinguished Flying Cross and Air Medal with four oak leaf clusters. He retired a lieutenant colonel in the U.S. Air Force Reserve.
    32. Ibid.
    33. YDVA, 19.

Chapter 2

1. "History of the 104th [Infantry]," Robert M. Mackintosh (Captain), et al., eds. (c. 1942), Massachusetts National Guard Military Museum & Archives, Worcester, MA. Pages not numbered.
    2. Ibid.
    3. Roger Larsen, "Out in Front from France to Czechoslovakia," *The Columbus* [Ohio] *Packet* (December 27, 2001), reprinted in *Yankee Doings*, September 2002, 15.
    4. "History of the 104th [Infantry]"; Lee B. Kennett, *G.I.: The American Soldier in World War II* (New York: Scribner, 1987), 26.
    5. Ibid.
    6. Richard P. Taffe, "As War Clouds Gathered," *Army Magazine* 41, no. 12 (December 1991), 28.
    7. Ibid.
    8. "History of the 104th [Infantry]."
    9. Ibid.
    10. Ibid.
    11. Ibid.
    12. Ibid.
    13. Kennett, 23.
    14. Ibid., 33; "History of the 104th [Infantry]"; Taffe, 28.
    15. "History of the 104th [Infantry]"; Taffe, 30.
    16. Taffe, 30.
    17. Kennett, 34–35.
    18. Ibid., 35.
    19. Taffe, 29.

Chapter 3

1. Richard P. Taffe, "As War Clouds Gathered," *Army Magazine* 41, no. 12 (December, 1991), 29.
    2. Francis D. Donovan (C-211), letter dated October 8, 1999.
    3. John D. Turini (G-181 and Hq. Co., 2nd Bn.-181), "Recollections," *Worcester's Vanishing Veterans, Worcestertalks: Oral History Project*, Worcester Historical Museum (August 2002), pages not numbered.
    4. Lorenz F. Bading, "36th Division Band," *The Fighting 36th Historical Quarterly*, supplement to the *T-Patcher Newsletter* (Summer 1997), 3.
    5. Taffe, 28.
    6. Ibid.
    7. "History of the 104th [Infantry]," Robert M. Mackintosh (captain), et al., eds. (c. 1942), Massachusetts National Guard Military Museum & Archives, Worcester, Massachusetts, pages not numbered.
    8. Ibid.
    9. Ibid.
    10. Ibid.; Taffe, 29; Yankee Division Veterans Association (YDVA), *The History of the 26th Yankee Division: 1917–1919 and 1941–1945* (Salem, MA: Deschamps, 1955), 19–20, hereafter cited as YDVA.
    11. Ibid.; Lee B. Kennett, *G.I.: The American Soldier in World War II* (New York: Scribner, 1987), 32.
    12. Ibid.; Taffe, 29; Robert W. Brickman (D-141), letter dated May 13, 2000.
    13. Clifford P. Welcome, telephone interview on October 5, 1999.
    14. "History of the 104th [Infantry]."
    15. Ibid.; YDVA, 20.
    16. YDVA, 20.
    17. "History of the 104th [Infantry]."
    18. Ibid.; Mark M. Boatner III, *Military Customs and Traditions* (Westport, CT: McKay, 1956), 88–89.
    19. Ibid.
    20. Ibid.
    21. Ibid.
    22. Ibid.
    23. Ibid.
    24. Ibid.
    25. Nathaniel Mencow (M-181), telephone interview on May 23, 2006.
    26. Ibid.
    27. Ibid.
    28. Ibid.
    29. Ibid.
    30. YDVA, 20.
    31. Ibid.
    32. "History of the 104th [Infantry]."
    33. Robert W. Brickman (D-141), letter dated May 13, 2000.
    34. Ibid.
    35. "History of the 104th [Infantry]."
    36. Ibid.
    37. Ibid.
    38. Ibid.
    39. Ibid.
    40. Ibid.
    41. Ibid.

Chapter 4

1. Ian V. Hogg, "Mortars," *Oxford Companion to World War II*, I.C.B. Dear, general editor, and M.R.D. Foot, consultant editor (New York: Oxford University Press, 1995), 758; Ian V. Hogg, *The Encyclopedia of Infantry Weapons of World War II* (Northbrook, IL: Arms and Armour Press, 1977), 102, 108–109; U.S. Government Printing Office, *81-MM Mortar M1, Basic Field Manual, FM 23–90* (Washington DC, May 7, 1942), 1; IRTC [Infantry Replacement Training Center], "I am a Doughboy," see "I member of a Heavy Weapons Company," Pamphlet (c. 1943), 14, 18.
    2. Ibid., 760; IRTC, 18; Bill Mauldin, *Up Front 50th Anniversary Edition* (New York: Norton, 1995), 97–98.
    3. IRTC, 18.
    4. Headquarters, Department of the Army, *Mortar Gunnery, FM 23–91* (Washington, DC, 1971), 1–1, 1–2.
    5. Hogg, *Encyclopedia of Infantry Weapons of World War II*, 102, 108; IRTC, 18.
    6. Ibid., 108.
    7. Hogg, "Mortars," 759; *FM 23–90*, 19–20, 23–29.
    8. U.S. War Department, *Table of Organization and Equipment (TO&E)*, No. 7-8, "Infantry Heavy Weapons Company" (Washington, DC, 15 July 1941), 2–5.
    9. Guido J. Fratturelli (H-181), Company H Reunion September 10, 2002; Sulo O. Ruuska (H-181), Company H Reunion September 10, 2002.
    10. Ibid.; TO&E, 5, 8.
    11. Ibid.; TO&E, 5, 8.
    12. *FM 23–90*, 43.

13. Ibid.
14. Ibid., 43, 49.
15. Guido J. Fratturelli, Company H Reunion.
16. Guido J. Fratturelli (H-181), letter received on May 1, 2000 (not dated).
17. Ibid.
18. Ibid.
19. Ibid.

Chapter 5

1. "History of the 104th [Infantry]," Robert M. Mackintosh (Captain), et al., eds. (c. 1942), Massachusetts National Guard Military Museum & Archives, Worcester, Massachusetts, pages not numbered.
2. Richard P. Taffe, "As War Clouds Gathered," *Army Magazine* 41, no. 12 (December, 1991), 28.
3. "History of the 104th [Infantry]."
4. Ibid.
5. Ibid.
6. Ibid.
7. Helen G. Palumbo.
8. Nathaniel Mencow (M-181), telephone interview on November 12, 2002; "History of the 104th [Infantry]."
9. Ibid.
10. "U.S.O. Club," *Falmouth Enterprise* (March 6, 1942), 6.
11. "USO Here Holding Open House Program Sunday," *Biddeford Journal* (February 5, 1944); Matt Grills, "Until Everyone Comes Home: The USO Celebrates 65 Years of Serving U.S. Military Personnel," *American Legion Magazine* (August 2006), 15.
12. Helen G. Palumbo.
13. "Soldiers Bring Songs of West and South to Song-Fests at U.S.O.," *Falmouth Enterprise* (September 18, 1942), 3.
14. Ibid.
15. Ibid.
16. Ibid.
17. Ibid.

Chapter 6

1. Frank J. Boyce, "Boys of 181st Home for Weekend Bivouac," *Worcester Telegram* (August 1, 1941), 1, 10; Frank J. Boyce, "40,000 Watch 181st Inf. Parade," *Worcester Telegram* (August 2, 1941), 1, 4; "181st Infantry Arrives Here for Three-day Stay," (Worcester) *Evening Gazette* (August 1, 1941), 12.
2. Ibid.; "10,000 to See 181st Nine and Nortons Under Lights," *Worcester Telegram* (August 1, 1941), 23–24.
3. Ibid., 10; Boyce, "40,000 Watch 181st Inf. Parade."
4. Ibid., 1, 10.
5. Ibid.; Boyce, "40,000 Watch 181st Inf. Parade," 1, 4.
6. Ibid., 10.
7. Ibid.
8. Ibid.; Boyce, "40,000 Watch 181st Inf. Parade," 4.
9. Ibid., 1, 10.; Boyce, "40,000 Watch 181st Inf. Parade."
10. Ibid., 10.; Boyce, "40,000 Watch 181st Inf. Parade," 1; John F. Houlihan, "More Than 15,000 See Nortons Beat Soldiers Nine," *Worcester Telegram* (August 2, 1941), 11–12; "181st Infantry Arrives Here for Three Day Stay," 12.
11. Ibid.; Houlihan, "15,000," 11–12; Boyce, "40,000 Watch 181st Inf. Parade," 4.
12. Boyce, "40,000 Watch 181st Inf. Parade," 4; Houlihan, "15,000," 11–12; "181st Infantry Arrives Here for Three-Day Stay," 12.
13. Houlihan, "15,000," 11–12.
14. Boyce, "181st Home for Weekend," 10; Boyce, "40,000 Watch 181st Inf. Parade," 4; Frank J. Boyce, "181st Breaks Camp Here This Afternoon" (Worcester) *Sunday Telegram* (August 3, 1941), 14.
15. Ibid.; Boyce, "40,000 Watch 181st Inf. Parade," 4; Frank J. Boyce, "181st Returns to Edwards," *Worcester Telegram* (August 5, 1941), 1, 5.
16. Ibid.; Boyce, "181st Returns to Edwards," 1.
17. "181st Infantry Arrives Here for Three Day Stay," 12; Clifford P. Welcome (F-181), telephone interview on February 17, 1999.
18. Boyce, "40,000 Watch 181st Infantry Parade," 4; William H. Moiles, "Soldiers Left at Park are Content," *Worcester Telegram* (August 2, 1941), 4.
19. Ibid.
20. Boyce, "181st Breaks Camp," 1, 14.
21. Ibid.
22. Boyce, "40,000 Watch 181st Inf. Parade," 4; Boyce, "181st Returns to Edwards," 5.
23. Ibid.; Boyce, "181st Returns to Edwards," 5.

Chapter 7

1. "History of the 104th [Infantry]," Robert M. Mackintosh (Captain), et al., eds. (c. 1942), Massachusetts National Guard Military Museum & Archives, Worcester, Massachusetts, pages not numbered.
2. Ibid.
3. Ibid.
4. Ibid.
5. Yankee Division Veterans Association (YDVA), *The History of the 26th Yankee Division: 1917–1919 and 1941–1945* (Salem, MA: Deschamps, 1955), 22, hereafter cited as YDVA; Richard P. Taffe, "As War Clouds Gathered," *Army Magazine* 41, no. 12 (December, 1991), 29.
6. YDVA, 22; Taffe, 29; Paul Fussell, *Wartime: Understanding and Behavior in the Second World War* (New York: Oxford University Press, 1989), 259.
7. YDVA, 22.
8. "History of the 104th [Infantry]"; Nathaniel Mencow (M-181), interview on November 12, 2002; Paul T. Metcalf (G-101), "What We Did Back in 1941," *Yankee Doings* (September 2001), 27.
9. C. Lincoln Christensen, "The 1941 Carolina Maneuvers found America Unprepared for World Conflict," *World War II Magazine* 16, no. 6 (February 2002): 20, 22.
10. YDVA, 18–19; "History of the 104th [Infantry]."

Chapter 8

1. "History of the 104th [Infantry]," Robert M. Mackintosh (Captain), et al., eds. (c. 1942), Massachusetts National Guard Military Museum & Archives, Worcester, Massachusetts, pages not numbered; Yankee Division Veterans Association (YDVA), *The History of the 26th Yankee Division: 1917–1919 and 1941–1945* (Salem, MA: Deschamps, 1955), 21, hereafter cited as YDVA.
2. Ibid.
3. Ibid.
4. Ibid.
5. Ibid.
6. Ibid.
7. Ibid.
8. Ibid.
9. Ibid.
10. Ibid.
11. Ibid.
12. Ibid.
13. Ibid.

14. Ibid.
15. Ibid.
16. YDVA, 21–22; Christopher R. Gable, *The U.S. Army General Headquarters (GHQ) Maneuvers of 1941* (Washington, DC: Government Printing Office, 1991), 59.
17. YDVA; Gable, 59.
18. "History of the 104th [Infantry]."

Chapter 9

1. Christopher R. Gable, *The U.S. Army General Headquarters (GHQ) Maneuvers of 1941* (Washington, DC: Government Printing Office, 1991), 5, 45.
2. Ibid., iii.
3. Ibid., 4–5.
4. Ibid., 5.
5. Ibid., 5, 9.
6. Ibid., 5, 14, 44.
7. Ibid., 5; Yankee Division Veterans Association (YDVA), *The History of the 26th Yankee Division: 1917–1919 and 1941–1945* (Salem, MA: Deschamps, 1955), 22.
8. Ibid.
9. Ibid., 22–23.
10. Ibid., 23–24.
11. Ibid., 24.
12. Ibid., 26–27.
13. Ibid., 24–25, 27–28.
14. Ibid., 26–27.
15. Ibid., 30–31, 49.
16. Ibid., 31, 49.
17. Ibid., 31–32.
18. Ibid., 32.
19. Ibid., 33.
20. Ibid.

Chapter 10

1. "History of the 104th [Infantry]," Robert M. Mackintosh (Captain), et al., eds. (c. 1942), Massachusetts National Guard Military Museum & Archives, Worcester, Massachusetts, pages not numbered.
2. Ibid.
3. Ibid.
4. Ibid.
5. Ibid.
6. Ibid.
7. Ibid; Lincoln C. Christensen, "The 1941 Carolina Maneuvers found America unprepared for World Conflict," *World War II Magazine* (February 2000), 18; Christopher R. Gable, *The U.S. Army General Headquarters (GHQ) Maneuvers of 1941* (Washington, DC: Government Printing Office, 1991), 50.
8. Ibid.
9. Ibid.
10. Ibid.
11. Gable, 136.
12. Ibid., 55–56.
13. Ibid., 48–49, 134, 136.
14. Ibid., 133.
15. Ibid., 134.
16. Ibid., 155–156.
17. Ibid., 45–47.
18. Ibid., 47–49.
19. Ibid., 47.
20. Ibid., 47–48.
21. Ibid., 47; Christensen, 18.
22. Ibid., 136; Christensen, 20; "History of the 104th [Infantry]."
23. Christensen, 18.
24. Ibid., 18, 20; Henry Parrott, *The History of a Combat Regiment, 1939–1945 — 104th Infantry Regiment* (Baton Rouge, LA, 1960), pages not numbered.
25. Ibid., 20, 22.
26. "History of the 104th [Infantry]."
27. Ibid.
28. Ibid.
29. Ibid.
30. Ibid.
31. Ibid.
32. Ibid.; Yankee Division Veterans Association (YDVA), *The History of the 26th Yankee Division: 1917–1919 and 1941–1945* (Salem, MA: Deschamps, 1955), 22, hereafter cited as YDVA.
33. Lee B. Kennett, *G.I.: The American Soldier in World War II* (New York: Scribner's, 1987), 72.
34. "History of the 104th [Infantry]"; YDVA, 22.
35. Ibid.
36. Earl Mayan, "Excerpts from the war letters 1941–1945," http://home.earthlink.net/~klavir/WWII/War_Letters_Main_Page.html, letter dated October 11, 1941.
37. Ibid., letter dated November 30, 1941.
38. Ibid.
39. Ibid., letter dated October 19, 1941: e-mails to the author dated December 15, 2002, December 19, 2002, and December 25, 2002.
40. Ibid., letters dated November 18, 1941, and November 30, 1941.
41. "History of the 104th [Infantry]."
42. Ibid.
43. Ibid.
44. Ibid.
45. Ibid.
46. Ibid.
47. Ibid.
48. Ibid.
49. Ibid.
50. Ibid.

Chapter 11

1. Christopher R. Gable, *The U.S. Army General Headquarters (GHQ) Maneuvers of 1941* (Washington, DC: Government Printing Office, 1991), 148–149.
2. Ibid.
3. Ibid.
4. Ibid., 149.
5. Ibid., 149, 165.
6. Ibid., 149–150.
7. Lincoln C. Christensen, "The 1941 Carolina Maneuvers Found America Unprepared for World Conflict," *World War II Magazine* (February 2000), 20.
8. Ibid.
9. Ibid.
10. Ibid.
11. "History of the 104th [Infantry]."
12. Christensen, 20.
13. Ibid.
14. Ibid., 18, 20.
15. "History of the 104th [Infantry]."
16. Gable, 166.
17. Yankee Division Veterans Association (YDVA), *The History of the 26th Yankee Division: 1917–1919 and 1941–1945* (Salem, MA: Deschamps, 1955), 23.

Chapter 12

1. "History of the 104th [Infantry]," Robert M. Mackintosh (Captain), et al., eds. (c. 1942), Massachusetts

National Guard Military Museum & Archives, Worcester, Massachusetts, pages not numbered.
  2. Ibid.
  3. Ibid.; Yankee Division Veterans Association (YDVA), *The History of the 26th Yankee Division: 1917–1919 and 1941–1945* (Salem, MA: Deschamps, 1955), 22.
  4. Ibid.
  5. Ibid.
  6. Ibid.
  7. Richard P. Taffe, "As War Clouds Gathered," *Army Magazine* 41, no. 12 (December 1991), 27.
  8. "History of the 104th [Infantry]."
  9. Ibid.

Chapter 13

  1. John S. Gerety, Col., USA-Ret. (S-3, 2nd Bn.-181 and H-181), Letter to Major Theodore Simmington, Jr., Ret. (April 27, 1988).
  2. Ibid.
  3. Hugh A. Drum "The Eastern Defense Command: A Review of Its Operations," *Army & Navy Journal*, December 7, 1943, 152, hereafter cited as Drum; U.S. Army, Eastern defense Command, G-3, "History of the Eastern Defense Command, and the Defense of the Atlantic Coast of the U.S. in the Second World War," photostatic typescript (New York, 1945), 52, hereafter cited as EDC.
  4. EDC, 52; "History of the 181st Infantry [Regiment]," paper on file at the Massachusetts National Guard Military Museum & Archives, Worcester, Massachusetts, 5–6.
  5. EDC, 53.
  6. "History of the 181st Infantry [Regiment]," 5–6.
  7. Sulo O. Ruuska (H-181), letter dated November 14, 1999; James V. Carnivale (H-181), telephone interview on January 15, 2000.
  8. Ibid.
  9. Ibid.; Guido J. Fratturelli (H-181), letter received on December 5, 1999.
  10. Ibid.
  11. Ibid.
  12. Ibid.
  13. Romeo C. LeBlanc (H-181), telephone interview on November 12, 1999.
  14. Ibid.; Guido J. Fratturelli (H-181), letter received on December 5, 1999.
  15. Clifford P. Welcome (F-181), telephone interviews on April 20, 1999, and October 5, 1999.
  16. John D. Turini (G-181 and Hq. Co., 2nd Bn.-181), "Recollections," *Worcester's Vanishing Veterans, Worcestertalks: Oral History Project*, Worcester Historical Museum (August 2002), pages not numbered.
  17. Peter Blute (Cong.), letter to David L. Petree, director of the National Personnel Records Center (NPRC), Special Inquiries Room, St. Louis, Missouri, written on behalf of John J. Voellings (August 21, 1996), Voellings file, January 4, 2002, *Worcester's Vanishing Veterans, Worcestertalks: Oral History Project*, Worcester Historical Museum, Worcester, Mass.
  18. Carl P. DeVasto (Hq. Co., 2nd Bn.-101), e-mail to the author dated December 6, 1999.
  19. Paul T. Metcalf (G-101), e-mail to the author dated September 18, 2001.
  20. Ibid.
  21. Ibid.
  22. Francis H. McGinnis (M-101), telephone interview on December 6, 1999.
  23. Henry Parrott, *The History of a Combat Regiment 1939–1945 — 104th Infantry regiment*, Chapter 4 (pages not numbered); Edward J. Griffin (L-101), *Diary* (1944).
  24. "History of the 181st Infantry [Regiment]," 6.
  25. Yankee Division Veterans Association (YDVA), *The History of the 26th Yankee Division: 1917–1919 and 1941–1945* (Salem, MA: Deschamps, 1955), 23, 145, 147, hereafter cited as YDVA.
  26. YDVA, 23, 145–146.
  27. YDVA, 23, 145, 147.
  28. YDVA, 146–148; Francis D. Cronin, *Under the Southern Cross: The Saga of the Americal Division* (Washington, DC: Combat Forces Press, 1951), 29.
  29. YDVA, 145–147.
  30. Drum, 57.
  31. Drum.
  32. Drum.
  33. Drum, 152.
  34. Drum.
  35. Shelby L. Stanton, *Order of Battle, U.S. Army, World War II* (Novato, CA: Presidio Press, 1984), 34–37; see also Coast Artillery Patches (Frontispiece); Clifford P. Welcome (F-181), telephone interview on October 5, 1999.
  36. Ibid.

Chapter 14

  1. "Sentries Watch Our Shores: Outposts Move From Porches and Beach Houses to Their Own Huts," *Falmouth Enterprise* (March 6, 1942), 1, 7.
  2. Ibid., 1.
  3. Ibid., 7.
  4. Ibid.
  5. Ibid.
  6. Ibid.
  7. Ibid., 1.
  8. Ibid.
  9. Ibid., 1, 7.
  10. Ibid., 7.
  11. Ibid.
  12. Ibid., 1, 7.
  13. Ibid., 7.
  14. Ibid.
  15. Ibid.
  16. Ibid.
  17. Ibid.
  18. Ibid.
  19. Ibid.
  20. Ibid.
  21. Ibid.; "Resume of Regimental Activities, 181st Infantry, since induction January 16, 1941, Headquarters, 181st (Rifle), Office of the Regimental Commander" (Fort Dix, New Jersey, December 7, 1943), 1, among the records pertaining to the 181st Infantry at the National Archives and Records Administration (NARA), College Park, Maryland.
  22. John D. Turini (G-181 and Hq. Co., 2nd Bn.-181), "Recollections," *Worcester's Vanishing Veterans, Worcestertalks: Oral History Project*, Worcester Historical Museum (August, 2002), pages not numbered.
  23. Ibid.; "Sentries," 7; Walter E. Whitney (L-181), telephone interview on November 17, 1999.
  24. Rinaldo M. Delsignore (A-181), "Military Experiences of LTC Rinaldo Delsignore, Ret., *Newsletter No. 15 — For Former WWII 181st Infantry Officers* (September 16, 1998), 1–2, provided by Theodore Simmington, Jr.; Rinaldo M. Delsignore, telephone interview on November 22, 1999.
  25. Ibid.
  26. Ibid.
  27. Ibid.
  28. "Sentries," 1, 7.
  29. Henry Parrott, *The History of a Combat Regiment,*

1639–1945 — 104th Infantry Regiment (Baton Rouge, LA, 1960), pages not numbered; "History of the 181st Infantry [Regiment]," paper on file at the Massachusetts National Guard Military Museum & Archives, Worcester, Massachusetts, 5–6; Clifford P. Welcome, telephone interview on October 5, 1999.
  30. Ibid.
  31. "History of the 181st Infantry [Regiment]," 6.

Chapter 15

  1. "Warns Against Spies Landing in N. E. From Subs," *Worcester Telegram* (April 10, 1942), 1.
  2. Yankee Division Veterans Association (YDVA), *The History of the 26th Yankee Division: 1917–1919 and 1941–1945* (Salem, MA: Deschamps, 1955), 23, hereafter cited as YDVA; U.S. Army, Eastern Defense Command, G-3, "History of the Eastern Defense Command, and the Defense of the Atlantic Coast of the U.S. in the Second World War," photostatic typescript (New York, 1945), 52, hereafter cited as EDC.
  3. YDVA; "Resume of Regimental Activities, 181st Infantry, since induction January 16, 1941, Headquarters, 181st (Rifle), Office of the Regimental Commander" (Fort Dix, New Jersey, December 7, 1943), 1, among the records pertaining to the 181st Infantry at the National Archives and Records Administration (NARA), College Park, Maryland; Henry Parrott, *The History of a Combat Regiment, 1939–1945 — 104th Infantry Regiment* (Baton Rouge, LA, 1960), pages not numbered.
  4. "History of the 181st Infantry [Regiment]," paper on file at the Massachusetts National Guard Military Museum & Archives, Worcester, Massachusetts, 6; see also "Station List, corrected to July 19, 1942," Appendix C.
  5. YDVA, 20–21; "History of the 181st Infantry [Regiment]," 5; "Resume of Regimental Activities," 1.
  6. Rosaire J. Rajotte (D-181), telephone interview on May 11, 2000.
  7. Ibid., telephone interview on February 21, 1999.
  8. Ibid., telephone interview on February 7, 1999.
  9. Paul J. Turini (G-181), telephone interview on January 30, 2003.
  10. Edwin P. Hoyt, *U-Boats Offshore: When Hitler Struck America* (New York: Stein and Day, 1978), 150–151.
  11. W.A. Swanberg, "The Spies Who Came in from the Sea," *American Heritage* 21, no. 3 (April 1970): 67; Stan Cohen, and Don DeNevi, with Richard Gay, *They Came to Destroy America* (Missoula, MT: Pictorial Histories, 2003), 47, 50.
  12. Ibid.; Cohen and DeNevi, 47, 50, 55.
  13. Cohen and DeNevi, 47, 56–60.
  14. Ibid., 60, 63; Swanberg, 66; Hoyt, 150–151; George J. Dasch, *Eight Spies Against America* (New York: McBride, 1959), 98.
  15. Swanberg, 66; Hoyt, 150–151; EDC, 53; Dasch, 97–98.
  16. Ibid.; Hoyt, 151; Dasch, 98.
  17. Dasch, 96, 98.
  18. Ibid., 98–99; Hoyt, 151.
  19. Ibid.; Hoyt, 151–152.
  20. Ibid.; Hoyt, 152; Swanberg, 66.
  21. Ibid., 99–100; Hoyt, 152; Swanberg, 66.
  22. Ibid.; Hoyt, 152; Swanberg, 66.
  23. Hoyt, 153; Swanberg, 66.
  24. Ibid.; EDC, 54.
  25. Ibid., 152–153; Swanberg, 67; EDC, 54.
  26. Ibid., 153; EDC, 54.
  27. Ibid.; EDC, 54.
  28. Ibid., 152–153, 155; EDC, 54–55.
  29. Ibid., 153–154; Swanberg, 67, 69; Dasch, 100; Cohen and DeNevi, 60.
  30. Ibid., 154–155.
  31. Dasch, 103–105.
  32. Swanberg, 69; Cohen and DeNevi, 70.
  33. Ibid., 67–68; Cohen and DeNevi, 50.
  34. Ibid., 68, 89; Dasch, 111–112.
  35. Ibid., 69, 87; Cohen and DeNevi, 70–71; Dasch, 115, 117–118; Hoyt, 156.
  36. Cohen and DeNevi, 65; Hoyt, 155–156.
  37. Ibid., 81–82; Swanberg, 87–89.
  38. Ibid.; Swanberg, 89–90.
  39. Ibid.; Swanberg, 90–91.
  40. Ibid., 71, 129.
  41. EDC, 54–55.
  42. Ibid.
  43. Edward J. Griffin (L-101), Diary (1944); Edward J. Griffin, letter dated July 6, 2000.
  44. Ibid.

Chapter 16

  1. Theodore Simmington, Jr. (F-181 and K-181), letter dated March 5, 1999.
  2. Ibid.
  3. Ibid.; Michael Stubinski (K-181), letter not dated (c. 2002), letter dated February 26, 2002.
  4. Ibid.
  5. Romeo C. LeBlanc (H-181), Company H reunion on September 12, 2000.
  6. Joel W. Eastman, "Casco Bay During WWII: An Illustrated Lecture Presented as Part of a Series on Maine in the Twentieth Century by the Maine Historical Society," paper on file in the Maine History Room at the Dyer Library, Saco, Maine (April 19, 1988), 4.
  7. Marc P. Fecteau, son of Philip Fecteau (26th Recon. Troop), letter dated September 20, 1999.
  8. Randy Seaver, "Allen plans a reunion," *Biddeford-Saco-OOB Courier* (August 24, 2000), 4.
  9. John J. Voellings (B-181), telephone interview on February 7, 2003; Peter Blute, letter to David L. Petree, director of the National Personnel Records Center (NPRC), Special Inquiries Room, St. Louis, Missouri, written on behalf of John J. Voellings (August 21, 1996), Voellings file, January 4, 2002, *Worcester's Vanishing Veterans, Worcestertalks: Oral History Project*, Worcester Historical Museum, Worcester, Mass.
  10. Barry L. Zerby, National Archives and Records Administration (NARA), College Park, Maryland, letter to John J. Voellings (February 21, 1997), Voellings file, January 4, 2002, *Worcester's Vanishing Veterans, Worcestertalks: Oral History Project*, Worcester Historical Museum, Worcester, Mass.

Chapter 17

  1. U.S. Army, Eastern Defense Command, G-3, "History of the Eastern Defense Command, and the Defense of the Atlantic Coast of the U.S. in the Second World War," photostatic typescript (New York, 1945), 53, hereafter cited as EDC.
  2. EDC.
  3. Dennis L. Noble, *The Coast Guard in World War II: The Beach Patrol and Corsair Fleet* (Washington, DC: Coast Guard, 1992), 15–16; Eleanor C. Bishop, *Prints in the Sand: The U.S. Coast Guard Beach Patrol During World War II* (Missoula, MT: Pictorial Histories, 1989), 3; "The WWII Beach Patrol," *Coast Guard Reservist* (July 1997), 7.

According to the *Reservist*, "The bulk of this article is a reprint of Dennis L. Noble's *The Beach Patrol and Corsair Fleet*."

4. Ibid., 13; Bishop, 2–3; EDC, 53; Henry Parrott, *The History of a Combat Regiment, 1939–1945 — 104th Infantry Regiment* (Baton Rouge, LA, 1960), pages not numbered, hereafter cited as Parrott.
5. EDC, 53.
6. Parrott.
7. Yankee Division Veterans Association (YDVA), *The History of the 26th Yankee Division: 1917–1919 and 1941–1945* (Salem, MA: Deschamps, 1955), 24, hereafter cited as YDVA.
8. YDVA.
9. YDVA.
10. YDVA.
11. YDVA.

Chapter 18

1. Roy P. Fairfield, *Sands, Spindles, and Steeples* (Portland, ME: House of Falmouth, 1956), vii, viii, 391.
2. Ibid., ix, 371; Michael Hughes, "The Beach Booms in the Wake of WWII," *Old Orchard Beach Times* (August 3–17, 1983), 10.
3. Hughes, 10–11.
4. Randy Seaver, "Allen plans a reunion," *Biddeford-Saco-OOB Courier* (August 24, 2000), 1, 4; Jillian Carle Jakeman, e-mail to the author dated August 27, 2006.
5. Fairfield, 355.
6. Ibid., "Park Street Lofts dig into history," *Biddeford-Saco-OOB Courier* (April 6, 2006), 21.
7. John D. Turini (G-181 and Hq. Co., 2nd Bn.-181), "Recollections," *Worcester's Vanishing Veterans, Worcestertalks: Oral History Project*, Worcester Historical Museum (August 2002), pages not numbered; Francis D. Donovan (C-211), letter dated October 8, 1999; Sulo O. Ruuska (H-181), letter dated November 14, 1999.
8. Ibid.
9. Ibid.
10. Francis D. Donovan (C-211), letter dated October 8, 1999.
11. "Station List, 181st Infantry Combat Team — Corrected to July 19, 1942," provided by Theodore Simmington, Jr., 6.
12. Turini, "Recollections."
13. Paul J. Turini (G-181), telephone interview on January 30, 2003.
14. Clifford P. Welcome (F-181), letter dated February 1, 1999, and telephone interview on April 20, 1999.
15. "Station List," 7.
16. Seaver, 4; Fairfield, 377; Jillian Carle Jakeman, "Saco in World War II: The 132nd Engineer Battalion, 77th Infantry Division," paper on file in the Maine History Room at the Dyer Library, Saco Maine; Jillian Carle Jakeman, e-mails to the author dated November 29, 1999, and December 6, 2000.
17. Turini, "Recollections."
18. Seaver, 4; Talmadge Allen (A-132), photographs on file in the Maine History Room at the Dyer Library in Saco, Maine. Shortly before his death, Talmadge Allen turned over his photograph and memorabilia collection to the Army National Guard Museum at Camp Keyes in Augusta, Maine.
19. Jakeman, "Saco in World War II"; Jakeman, e-mail to the author dated August 27, 2006.
20. James V. Carnivale (H-181), Company H reunion on September 14, 1999; telephone interview on October 5, 1999.
21. Ibid.

Chapter 19

1. John J. Voellings (B-181), telephone interview on February 7, 2003; Dennis L. Noble, *The Coast Guard in World War II: The Beach Patrol and Corsair Fleet*, (Washington, DC: Coast Guard, 1992), 12–13.
2. Eleanor C. Bishop, *Prints in the Sand: The U.S. Coast Guard Beach Patrol During World War II* (Missoula, MT: Pictorial Histories, 1989), ix, 25; Noble, 8, 10, 12–13; "The WWII Beach Patrol," *Coast Guard Reservist* (July 1997), 5. According to the *Reservist*, "The bulk of this article is a reprint of Dennis L. Noble's *The Beach Patrol and Corsair Fleet*."
3. Clifford P. Welcome (F-181), telephone interviews on February 17, 1999, and April 20, 1999; Rosaire J. Rajotte (D-181), telephone interview on February 7, 1999.
4. Paul J. Turini (G-181), telephone interview on January 30, 2003.
5. Ibid.
6. Clifford P. Welcome (F-181), telephone interview on April 20, 1999; Bishop, 25.
7. Romeo C. LeBlanc (H-181), Company H reunion on September 12, 2000.
8. Ibid.
9. Ibid.
10. Antonio J. Tata (H-181), telephone interview on February 11, 1999.
11. Ibid.; LeBlanc, reunion.
12. Sulo O. Ruuska (H-181), letter dated November 14, 1999.
13. Ibid.
14. Romeo C. LeBlanc (H-181), letter received on July 7, 2004 (not dated).
15. Clifford P. Welcome (F-181), telephone interview on April 20, 1999.
16. Francis D. Donovan (C-211), letter dated October 8, 1999.
17. Randy Seaver, "Allen plans a reunion," *Biddeford-Saco-OOB Courier* (August 24, 2000), 4; Jillian Carle Jakeman, "Saco in World War II: The 132nd Engineer Battalion, 77th Infantry Division," paper on file in the Maine History Room at the Dyer Library, Saco Maine; Talmadge Allen (A-132), interview at his home in Ocean Park, Maine, on July 14, 1999.
18. LeBlanc, reunion.
19. "Plane Makes Crash Landing Kinney Shores," *Biddeford Daily Journal* (March 25, 1943), 1.
20. LeBlanc, Company H reunion on September 11, 2001; Jillian Carle Jakeman, e-mail to the author dated January 28, 1999.
21. LeBlanc, Company H reunion on September 11, 2001; "Plane Makes Crash Landing," 1.
22. Letter from N.W. Timmerman, wing commander, for Group Captain (not named) Commanding 34.T.U., Royal Canadian Air Force, to Lt. Col. John A. Amberg, Commanding Officer, 2nd Battalion, 181st Infantry ("27 March 1943"), among the records pertaining to the 181st Infantry at the National Archives and Records Administration (NARA), College Park, Maryland.
23. Clifford P. Welcome (F-181), telephone interview on October 5, 1999.
24. Ibid.
25. LeBlanc, Company H reunion on September 12, 2000.
26. Seaver, 4.
27. Shelby L. Stanton, *U.S. Army Uniforms of World War II* (Harrisburg, PA: Stackpole Books, 1991), 164–165, 188–189.

28. Ibid., 165.
29. Ibid., 164–165; Clifford P. Welcome (F-181), telephone interview on October 5, 1999; Sulo O. Ruuska (H-181), telephone interview on February 8, 2000.
30. Stanton, 254–255.
31. Ibid.
32. Ibid., 165, 192.
33. Rinaldo M. Delsignore (A-181), "Military Experiences of LTC Rinaldo Delsignore, Ret., *Newsletter No. 15 — For Former WWII 181st Infantry Officers* (September 16, 1998), 1–2, provided by Theodore Simmington, Jr.
34. Noble, 13–14; Bishop, 25; "The WWII Beach Patrol," 8.

Chapter 20

1. Francis D. Donovan (C-211), letter dated October 8, 1999.
2. "USO Here Holding Open House Program Sunday," *Biddeford Daily Journal* (February 5, 1944), 6.
3. Ibid.; Frank Coffey, *50 Years of the USO — Always Home: The Official Photographic History* (Washington, DC: Brassey's, 1991), 5–6.
4. Donovan, letter.
5. Cascade Lodge and Cabins Menu (c. 1942), now the Cascade Inn Restaurant, Route 1, Saco, Maine.
6. Clifford Welcome (F-181), telephone interview on February 17, 1999.
7. John D. Turini (G-181 and Hq. Co., 2nd Bn.-181), "Recollections," *Worcester's Vanishing Veterans, Worcestertalks: Oral History Project*, Worcester Historical Museum (August 2002), pages not numbered.
8. Roy P. Fairfield, *Sands, Spindles, and Steeples* (Portland, ME: House of Falmouth, 1956), 371.
9. Paul J. Turini (G-181), telephone interview on January 30, 2003; Clifford P. Welcome (F-181), telephone interview on February 17, 1999.
10. Welcome, telephone interview.
11. John D. Turini (G-181 and Hq. Co., 2nd Bn.-181), "Recollections."
12. Ibid.
13. Ibid.
14. Ibid.
15. Ibid
16. Ibid.
17. Ibid.; Paul J. Turini (G-181), e-mail to the author dated March 17, 2004.
18. Guido J. Fratturelli (H-181), telephone interview on July 17, 2006.
19. Clifford P. Welcome (F-181), telephone interviews on February 17, 1999, and October 5, 1999.
20. Ibid., telephone interview on October 5, 1999.
21. Rosaire J. Rajotte (D-181), telephone interview on February 7, 1999.
22. Ibid.
23. Edward J. Adams (26th Recon. Troop), letter dated March 16, 2000.

Chapter 21

1. Dennis L. Noble, *The Coast Guard in World War II: The Beach Patrol and Corsair Fleet* (Washington, DC: Coast Guard, 1992), 14; Eleanor C. Bishop, *Prints in the Sand: The U.S. Coast Guard Beach Patrol During World War II* (Missoula, MT: Pictorial Histories, 1989), 4; "The WWII Beach Patrol," *Coast Guard Reservist* (July 1997), 8. According to the *Reservist*, "The bulk of this article is a reprint of Dennis L. Noble's *The Beach Patrol and Corsair Fleet*."; "History of the 181st Infantry [Regiment]," paper on file at the Massachusetts National Guard Military Museum & Archives, Worcester, Massachusetts, 4.
2. Ibid.; Clayton G. Going, *Dogs at War* (New York: Macmillan, 1945), 14.
3. Major Kevin M. Born, "War Dogs— A resource for information on the Army's use of dogs 1942–Present," U.S. Army Quartermaster Museum, Fort Lee, Virginia (Last Update, June 17, 2003), http://www.qmfound.com/War_Dogs.htm.
4. Going, 9–10.
5. Ibid., 3–4, 7–9.
6. Born, "War Dogs."
7. Ibid.; Bishop, 23.
8. Ibid.
9. Clifford P. Welcome (F-181), telephone interview on April 20, 1999.
10. Going, 15, 136; Born, "War Dogs."
11. Ibid., 28.
12. Ibid., 17–18.
13. Ibid., 19–21; Born, "War Dogs"; Bishop, 16.
14. Ibid.; Bishop, 16.
15. Ibid., 21–22; Bishop, 16.
16. Bishop, 16; Noble, 14.
17. Born, "War Dogs."
18. Ibid.; Going, 21.
19. Ibid.
20. Ibid.
21. Ibid.
22. Ibid.
23. Clifford P. Welcome (F-181), telephone interview on February 17, 1999.
24. Ibid.
25. Ibid.; Bishop, 16.
26. John J. Voellings (B-181), telephone interview on February 7, 2003.
27. Rosaire J. Rajotte (D-181), telephone interview on February 7, 1999.
28. Ibid.
29. Noble, 12–14; "The WWII Beach Patrol," 8.
30. "The WWII Beach Patrol," 8; Going, 138–139.
31. Ibid.; Going, 138.
32. Ibid.; Noble, 14.
33. Ibid.; Noble, 20–21; Bishop, 73–74; Clifford P. Welcome (F-181), telephone interview on February 17, 1999; Going, 136–137.
34. Going, 178.
35. Ibid., 177–178.
36. Ibid., 178–179.

Chapter 22

1. Richard W. Brill (H-181), letter dated December 8, 2000; Francis D. Donovan (C-211), letter dated October 8, 1999.
2. Ibid.; John S. Gerety (S-3, 2nd Bn.-181 and H-181), letter dated March 19, 1999.
3. Joel W. Eastman, "Casco Bay During WWII: An Illustrated Lecture Presented as Part of a Series on Maine in the Twentieth Century by the Maine Historical Society," paper on file in the Maine History Room at the Dyer Library, Saco, Maine (April 19, 1988), 3, 5.
4. Gerety, letter; Brill, letter.
5. Ibid.
6. Ibid.; Brill, letter.
7. Robert F. Gallagher, "Scratch One Messerschmitt" (2005), http://gallagher.com/ww2/chapter28.html.
8. Ibid.
9. Ibid.
10. Ibid.

11. Dorothy E. Dineen, widow of James F. Dineen (L-181), conversation at her home (c. 2000).

Chapter 23

1. "Station List, 181st Infantry Combat Team — Corrected to July 19, 1942," provided by Theodore Simmington, Jr., 7.
2. Eleanor C. Bishop, *Prints in the Sand: The U.S. Coast Guard Beach Patrol During World War II* (Missoula, MT: Pictorial Histories, 1989), 22–24.
3. Ibid., 22–23.
4. Ibid.
5. Marc P. Fecteau, son of Philip Fecteau (26th Recon. Troop), letter dated September 20, 1999.
6. Ibid.
7. Edward J. Adams, (26th Recon. Troop), letter dated March 16, 2000.
8. Ibid.
9. James V. Carnivale (H-181), letter dated December 14, 1999.
10. Ibid.
11. Ibid.
12. Ibid.
13. Antonio J. Tata (H-181), telephone interview on February 11, 1999.
14. Ibid.
15. Joel W. Eastman, "Casco Bay During WWII: An Illustrated Lecture Presented as Part of a Series on Maine in the Twentieth Century by the Maine Historical Society," paper on file in the Maine History Room at the Dyer Library, Saco, Maine (April 19, 1988), 5.
16. Ibid., 5; Tata, telephone interview.
17. Edward R. Michaud, e-mail to the author dated September 14, 2000; Edward R. Michaud, "Internal Recorder Assessments" (July 1997), from Records Group 181: "Naval Districts and Shore Establishments — June 1942," and Records Group 242: National Archives Collection of Foreign Records Seized — June and July 1942," *National Archives and Records Administration* (NARA), Waltham Repository, Waltham, Massachusetts (July 1997) 10; Greg Brooks, Sub Sea Recovery, "Special Report," http://subsearecovery.com/u233.htm (website is no longer active).
18. Edward R. Michaud, Records Group 181, "War Diary, Commander Portland Section, 1st Naval District, June 16–22," 138, 146; Edward R. Michaud, Records Group 181, "Records of Naval Districts and Shore Establishments," Naval Unit 1-A, Loop Receiving Station, Bailey Isle, "Verbatim Extracts from 22, 23, 24 June [1942]," 2. See also, "WW 2 Comes to Casco Bay," http://home.iprimus.com.au/waldingr/peaks.htm
19. Edward R. Michaud, Records Group 181, "War Diary, Commander Portland Section, 1st Naval District, June 16–22," 138, 151; Edward R. Michaud, Records Group 181, "Records of Naval Districts and Shore Establishments," Naval Unit 1-A, Loop Receiving Station, Bailey Isle, Maine, "Verbatim Extracts from 22, 23, 24 June [1942]," 2.
20. Edward R. Michaud, Records Group 181, "War Diary, Commander Portland Section, 1st Naval District, June 16–22," 139, 146; Eastman, 5.
21. Michaud, "Internal Recorder Assessments" (July 1997), 6, 8; Edward R. Michaud, Doc. 030, "Correspondence File, Research details of U-754" (June 10, 1997), 2.
22. Ibid., 5, 8–9; Edward R. Michaud, "Various log entries from Record Group 181 regarding incidents within Casco Bay, during June of 1942" (July 4, 1997), 2; Sub Sea Recovery Website, "Special Project," http://subsearecovery.com/u233.htm (website no longer active).
23. Records Group 181, "War Diary, Commander Portland Section, 1st Naval District, June 16–22." 137, 139, 148; "WW 2 Comes to Casco Bay," see "Source Material," http://home.iprimus.com.au/waldingr/peaks.htm.
24. Michaud, "Internal Recorder Assessments" (July 1997), 6; Sub Sea Recovery Website, "Special Project," http://subearecovery.com/u233.htm (no longer active).
25. Sulo O. Ruuska (H-181), letter dated November 14, 1999.
26. James V. Carnivale (H-181), letter dated December 14, 1999.
27. Sulo O. Ruuska (H-181), letter dated November 5, 1999.
28. Ibid.
29. Ibid.
30. Ibid.
31. Ibid., letter dated November 14, 1999.
32. Ibid., letter dated November 5, 1999.
33. Ibid.
34. Ibid; letter dated November 14, 1999.
35. Ibid.
36. Ibid.
37. Ibid.
38. Ibid.

Chapter 24

1. U.S. Army, Eastern defense Command, G-3, "History of the Eastern Defense Command, and the Defense of the Atlantic Coast of the U.S. in the Second World War," photostatic typescript (New York, 1945), 55, hereafter cited as EDC.
2. EDC, 55; Eleanor C. Bishop, *Prints in the Sand: The U.S. Coast Guard Beach Patrol During World War II* (Missoula, MT: Pictorial Histories, 1989), 75.
3. Bishop, 75; "The WWII Beach Patrol," *Coast Guard Reservist* (July 1997), 11. According to the *Reservist*, "The bulk of this article is a reprint of Dennis L. Noble's *The Beach Patrol and Corsair Fleet*" (Washington, DC: Coast Guard, March 1992).
4. Dennis L. Noble, *The Coast Guard in World War II: The Beach Patrol and Corsair Fleet* (Washington, DC: Coast Guard, 1992), 21.
5. "History of the 181st Infantry [Regiment]," paper on file at the Massachusetts National Guard Military Museum & Archives, Worcester, Massachusetts, 9.
6. Ibid.
7. Ibid.
8. Ibid.; Antonio J. Tata (H-181), telephone interview on February 11, 1999.
9. Sulo O. Ruuska (H-181), letters dated November 14, 1999, and February 2, 2000.
10. Ibid.
11. "History of the 181st Infantry [Regiment]," 9.

Bibliography

Books

Bishop, Eleanor C. *Prints in the Sand: The U.S. Coast Guard Beach Patrol During World War II.* Missoula, MT: Pictorial Histories, 1989.

Boatner, Mark M., III. *Military Customs and Traditions.* Westport, CT: McKay, 1956.

Coffey, Frank. *Always Home: 50 Years of the USO—The Official Photographic History.* Washington, DC: Brassey's, 1991.

Cohen, Stan, and Don DeNevi, with Richard Gay. *They Came to Destroy America.* Missoula, MT: Pictorial Histories, 2003.

Cronin, Francis, D. *Under the Southern Cross: The Saga of the Americal Division.* Washington, DC: Combat Forces Press, 1951.

Dasch, George J. *Eight Spies Against America.* New York: McBride, 1959.

Dear, I.C.B., general editor, and M.R.D. Foot, consultant editor. *Oxford Companion to World War II.* New York: Oxford University Press, 1995.

Fairfield, Roy P. *Sands, Spindles, and Steeples.* Portland, ME: House of Falmouth, 1956.

Fussell, Paul. *Wartime: Understanding and Behavior in the Second World War.* New York: Oxford University Press, 1989.

Gable, Christopher R. *The U.S. Army GHQ Maneuvers of 1941.* Washington, DC: Government Printing Office, 1991.

Going, Clayton G. *Dogs at War.* New York: Macmillan, 1945.

Hogg, Ian V. *The Encyclopedia of Infantry Weapons of World War II.* Northbrook, IL: Arms and Armour Press, 1977.

Hoyt, Edwin P. *U-Boats Offshore: When Hitler Struck America.* New York: Stein and Day, 1978.

Kennett, Lee B. *G.I.: The American Soldier in World War II.* New York: Scribner, 1987.

Mauldin, Bill. *Up Front 50th Anniversary Edition.* New York: Norton, 1995.

Noble, Dennis L. *The Coast Guard in World War II: The Beach Patrol and Corsair Fleet.* Washington, DC: Coast Guard, 1992.

Stanton, Shelby L. *Order of Battle, U.S. Army, World War II.* Novato, CA: Presidio Press, 1984.

_____. *U.S. Army Uniforms of World War II.* Harrisburg, PA: Stackpole Books, 1991.

This Fabulous Century, 1940–1950, Vol. 5, by the editors of Time-Life Books. Alexandria, VA: Time-Life, 1969.

Yankee Division Veterans Association. *The History of the 26th Yankee Division: 1917–1919 and 1941–1945.* Salem, MA: Deschamps, 1955.

Newspaper and Other Articles

"Army, United States, World War II (1939–1945)." *World Book Encyclopedia.* 1: 730–741. Chicago: World Book, 2001.

Bading, Lorenz F. "36th Division Band." *The Fighting 36th Historical Quarterly,* supplement to the *T-Patcher Newsletter.* Summer 1997, 1–3.

Boyce, Frank J. "Boys of 181st Home for Weekend Bivouac." *Worcester* [MA] *Telegram.* August 1, 1941, 1, 10.

_____. "40,000 Watch 181st Infantry Parade." *Worcester* [MA] *Telegram.* August 2, 1941, 1, 4–5.

_____. "181st Returns to Edwards." *Worcester* [MA] *Telegram.* August 4, 1941, 1, 5.

_____. "181st Breaks Camp Here This Afternoon." (Worcester, MA) *Sunday Telegram.* August 3, 1941, 1, 14.

_____. "Worcester Troops Begin Fitting Out Camp Quarters" (Worcester, MA) *Sunday Telegram.* January 26, 1941, 1, 8.

Christensen, C. Lincoln. "The 1941 Carolina Maneuvers found America unprepared for world conflict." *World War II Magazine* 16, no. 6 (February 2002), 18, 20, 22, 24.

"City Bids Farewell to Departing Troops" (Worcester, MA) *Sunday Telegram.* January 26, 1941, **8.**

Doubler, Michael D. "Guard Century—Not So Calm, Before the Storm: 1920 to 1940." *National Guard Magazine* 53, no. 10 (October 1999), 32–35. Available online at http://www.ngaus.org/ngmagazine/guardcentury1940to1960-1199.asp.

Drum, Hugh A. "The Eastern Defense Command: A Review of Its Operations." *Army & Navy Journal* 81 (December 7, 1943), 57, 152.

Fitzpatrick, Raymond A. "10,000 Hear FDR Talk Briefly on Defense Here." *Worcester* [MA] *Telegram.* October 3, 1941, 1, 11.

Gauthier, Joseph. "500 City Soldiers Head for Falmouth." (Worcester, MA) *Evening Gazette.* January 26, 1941, 1, 3.

_____. "Guardsmen of Area Start Basic Training." (Worcester, MA) *Evening Gazette.* January 27, 1941, 8.

Grills, Matt. "Until Everyone Comes Home: The USO Celebrates 65 Years of Serving U.S. Military Personnel." *American Legion Magazine* 161, no.2. (August 2006), 14–22.

Hogg, Ian V. "Mortars," *The Oxford Companion to World War II.* I.C.B. Dear, general editor, and M.R.D. Foot, consultant editor. New York: Oxford University Press, 1995, 759–760.

Houlihan, John F. "More Than 15,000 See Nortons Beat Soldiers Nine, 11–4." *Worcester* [MA] *Telegram.* August 2, 1941, 11–12.

Hughes, Michael. "The Beach Booms in the Wake of WWII." *Old Orchard Beach* [ME] *Times* 3, no. 6 (August 3–17, 1983), 9–11.

Kimball, Warren. "Lend-Lease." *Oxford Companion to World War II.* I.C.B. Dear, general editor, and M.R.D. Foot, consultant editor. New York: Oxford University Press, 1995, 677–679.

Larsen, Roger. "Out in Front from France to Czechoslovakia." *The Columbus* [Ohio] *Packet.* December 27, 2001. Reprinted in *Yankee Doings* 83, no. 3 (September 2002), 15–16.

"Lend-Lease." *World Book Encyclopedia.* 12: 190. Chicago: World Book, 2001.

Macksey, Kenneth. "Blitzkrieg," *Oxford Companion to World War II.* I.C.B. Dear, general editor, and M.R.D. Foot, consultant editor. New York: Oxford University Press, 1995, 140.

Melady, Mark. "They Rose to Defend the Home Front: 26th Yankee Division Kept Watch in New England." (Worcester, MA) *Sunday Telegram.* September 30, 2001, A1, A11.

Metcalf, Paul T. "What We Did Back in '41." *Yankee Doings* 82, No. 3 (September 2001), 27–28.

Moiles, William H. "Soldiers Left at Park are Content." *Worcester* [MA] *Telegram.* August 2, 1941, 4.

"Nazi U-boat found 4 miles off Cape, German embassy tells divers to stay away." Associated Press, (Worcester, MA) *Sunday Telegram.* June 16, 1993, A4.

"181st Infantry Arrives Here for Three-day Stay." (Worcester, MA) *Evening Gazette.* August 1, 1941, 1, 12.

"Park Street Lofts dig into history." *Biddeford-Saco-OOB* [ME] *Courier.* April 6, 2006, 21.

Patterson, James T. "Roosevelt, Franklin Delano." *World Book Encyclopedia.* 16: 452–463. Chicago: World Book, 2001.

"Plane Makes Crash Landing Kinney Shores." *Biddeford* [ME] *Daily Journal.* March 25, 1943, 1.

Pope, Chris. "Draft for WWII recalled: Worcester men in '158 Club.'" (Worcester, MA) *Sunday Telegram.* October 14, 1990, A1, A14.

Price, Alfred. "Blitz." *Oxford Companion to World War II.* I.C.B. Dear, General Editor, and M.R.D. Foot, consultant editor. New York: Oxford University Press, 1995, 138–140.

Seaver, Randy. "Allen Plans a Reunion." *Biddeford-Saco-OOB* [ME] *Courier.* August 24, 2000, 1, 4.

"Selective service system." *Oxford Companion to World War II.* I.C.B. Dear, general editor, and M.R.D. Foot, consultant editor. New York: Oxford University Press, 1995, 996.

"Sentries Watch Our Shore: Outposts Move from Porches and Beach Houses to Their Own Huts." *Falmouth* [MA] *Enterprise.* March 6, 1942, 1, 7.

Snyder, Louis L. "World War II." *Academic American Encyclopedia.* 20: 248–281. Granby, CT: Grolier, 1993.

"Soldiers Bring Songs of West and South to Song-Fests at U.S.O." *Falmouth* [MA] *Enterprise.* September 18, 1942, 3.

Stokesbury, James L. "World War II." *World Book Encyclopedia.* 21: 468–499. Chicago: World Book, 2001.

Swanberg, W.A. "The Spies Who Came in from the Sea." *American Heritage* 21, no. 3 (April 1970), 66–69, 87–91.

Sword, Keith. "Poland." *Oxford Companion to World War II.* I.C.B. Dear, general editor, and M.R.D. Foot, consultant editor. New York: Oxford University Press, 1995, 891–903.

Taffe, Richard P. "As War Clouds Gathered." *Army Magazine* 41, no. 12 (December 1991), 27–30.

"10,000 to See 181st Nine and Nortons Under Lights." *Worcester* [MA] *Telegram.* August 1, 1941, 23–24.

"USO Here Holding Open House Program Sunday." *Biddeford* [ME] *Journal.* February 5, 1944, 3, 6.

"U.S.O. Club." *Falmouth* [MA] *Enterprise.* March 6, 1942, 7.

"Warns Against Spies Landing in N.E. from Subs." *Worcester* [MA] *Telegram.* April 10, 1942, 1.

"The WWII Beach Patrol." *Coast Guard Reservist* 44, no. 7 (July 1997), 4–11. According to the *Reservist,* "The bulk of this article is a reprint of Dennis L. Noble's 'The Beach Patrol and Corsair Fleet.'" Washington, DC: Coast Guard Historian's Office, 1992.

Sources at Worcester, MA, Historical Museum

Turini, John D. "Recollections." *Worcester's Vanishing Veterans, Worcestertalks: Oral History Project.* Worcester Historical Museum, Worcester, MA, August 2002.

Blute, Peter. Letter to David L. Petree, director of the National Personnel Records Center (NPRC), Special Inquires Room, St. Louis, Missouri, on behalf of John J. Voellings. August 21, 1996. Voellings file. *Worcester's Vanishing Veterans, Worcestertalks: Oral History Project,* Worcester Historical Museum, Worcester, MA, January 4, 2002.

Zerby, Barry L. Textual Archives Services Division, National Archives and Records Administration (NARA), College Park, Maryland. Letter to John J. Voellings, February 21, 1997. Voellings file. *Worcester's Vanishing Veterans, Worcestertalks: Oral History Project,* Worcester Historical Museum, Worcester, MA, January 4, 2002.

U.S. Government Publications—Pamphlets and Manuals

IRTC [Infantry Replacement Training Center]. "I am a Doughboy." Pamphlet (c. 1944). See "I am a member of a Heavy Weapons Company," 14–19.

U.S. Army. *81mm Mortar Instructional Pamphlet ST 7-191 FY 77.* United States Army Infantry School, Fort Benning, Georgia, 1977.

U.S. Government Printing Office. *81-MM Mortar M1, Basic Field Manual, FM 23-90.* Washington DC, 1942.

U.S. War Department. "Table of Organization and Equipment [TO&E], Infantry Heavy Weapons Company, no. 7–18." Washington, DC, July 15, 1943.

Headquarters, Department of the Army. *Mortar Gunnery, FM 23-9.* Washington, DC, 1971.

Unpublished Material

Delsignore, Rinaldo M. "Military Experiences of LTC Rinaldo Delsignore Ret." Newsletter No. 15—For Former WWII 181st Infantry Officers. September 16, 1998, 1–2. Provided by Maj. Theodore Simmington, Jr., Ret.

Eastman, Joel W. "Casco Bay During WWII: An Illustrated Lecture Presented as Part of a Series on Maine in the Twentieth Century by the Maine Historical Society, April 19, 1988." Paper on file at the Dyer Library, Saco, Maine. April 19, 1988, 1–6.

Edward J. Griffin. *Diary,* 1944. Provided by Edward J. Griffin.

Gerety, John S. Letter to Maj. Theodore Simmington, Jr., Ret. April 27, 1998. Provided by Maj. Simmington.

Jakeman, Jillian Carle. "Saco in World War II: The 132nd Engineer Battalion, 77th Infantry Division." No date. Paper on file in the Maine History Room at the Dyer Library, Saco Maine, 1–2.

Michaud, Edward R. "Document number 030, dated 10 June, 1997. Research Details of U-754. 2 pages of misc. notes with copies of actual U-boat command files (U-boat transmission logs)." National Archives and Records Administration, New England Division, Waltham Repository, Waltham, MA. Trident Research & Recovery, Inc., Framingham, MA.

_____. "General Research Document number 036, dated July 4, 1997. Various log entries regarding incidents within Casco Bay, Maine, during June of 1942." From Record Group 181: Naval Districts and Shore Establishments, National Archives and Records Administration, New England Division, Waltham Repository, Waltham, MA. Trident Research & Recovery, Inc., Framingham, MA.

_____. "Internal Recorder Assessments—various source references and assessments, along with chronological list of events related to June 1942 incident off Maine Coast." July 1997. Compiled from Records Group 181 and 242. National Archives and Records Administration, New England Division, Waltham Repository, Waltham, MA. Trident Research & Recovery, Inc., Framingham, MA.

"Station List, 181st Infantry Combat Team (Corrected to 19 July 1942)." Provided by Maj. Theodore Simmington, Jr., Ret.

Papers on File at the National Archives and Records Administration (NARA)

"History—181st Infantry (6th Massachusetts), 1781–1943." National Archives and Records Administration (NARA), College Park, MD, pages not numbered.

Timmerman, N.W. Letter to Lt. Col. John A. Amberg, commanding officer, 2nd Battalion, 181st Infantry, for wing commander, for group captain (not named) commanding 34.T.U., Royal Canadian Air Force ("27 March, 1943"). Letter is among records pertaining to the 181st Infantry at the National Archives and Records Administration (NARA), College Park, MD.

"Records Group 181." National Archives and Records Administration (NARA), Waltham Repository, New England Division, Waltham, MA.

"Record Group 242." National Archives and Records Administration (NARA), Waltham Repository, New England Division, Waltham, MA.

"Resume of Regimental Activities, 181st Infantry, since induction January 16, 1941, Headquarters, 181st Infantry (Rifle), Office of the Regimental Commander, Fort Dix, N.J., 7 December 1943." National Archives and Records Administration (NARA), Modern Military Records, Textual Archives Services Division College Park, MD, 1–5.

Sources at the Massachusetts National Guard Museum and Archives

"History of the 181st [Infantry]," 1–9.

"History of the 104th [Infantry]" (1939–1941). Robert M. Mackintosh (Captain), et al., eds. (c. 1942). Pages not numbered. A compilation of individual company histories prepared by unknown persons and typed by company clerks. Provides an excellent account of a 26th Division regiment during the period beginning with federalization to December 7, 1941.

"101st Infantry, World War II, September 7, 1944 — May 8, 1945." Pages not numbered.

Parrott, Henry. "History of a Combat Regiment, 1939–1945 —104th Infantry Regiment." Baton Rouge, Louisiana, 1960. Pages not numbered.

Government Documents and Records

Connole, Dennis J. U.S. Army "Enlisted Record and Report of Separation, Honorable Discharge, 27 June 45." Form WD AGO 53–55. November 1944.

"Executive Order 11046, Authorizing Award of the Bronze Star Medal, August 24, 1962." National Archives and Records Administration (NARA), College Park, MD.

U.S. Army, Office of the Chief of Military History. Eastern Defense Command, G-3, New York. "History of the Eastern Defense Command, and the Defense of the Atlantic Coast of the U.S. in the Second World War." Photostatic typescript. 1945. See Chapter IV, "Combat Teams and Reconnaissance Patrols," 52–55. Paper on file at the U.S. Army Military History Institute, Carlisle Barracks, Carlisle, PA.

Internet Sources

Born, Kevin M. "War Dogs—A resource for information on the Army's use of dogs 1942–Present." The U.S. Army Quartermaster Museum, Fort Lee, Virginia (accessed June 17, 2003). http://www.qmfound.com/War_Dogs.htm.

Brooks, Greg. Sub Sea Recovery, "Special Report." http://subsearecovery.com/u233.htm (Web site is no longer active).

Gallager, Robert F. "Scratch One Messerschmitt." 2005. http://gallagher.com/ww2/chapter28.html.

Mayan, Earl. "Excerpts from the war letters, 1941–1945." http://home.earthlink.net/~klavir/WWII/War_Letters_Main_Page.

"The Piersall Collection of Orders, Decorations, and Medals from Around the World: The Bronze Star Medal 1944–Present." http://www.marksmedals.com/us_medals_files/bronze_star.html.

"WW 2 Comes to Casco Bay." http://home.iprimus.com.au/waldingr/peaks.htm.

Interviews and Correspondence

Edward J. Adams (26th Recon. Trp.)
Talmadge Allen (A-132)
Robert W. Brickman (D-141)
Richard W. Brill (H-181)
James V. Carnivale (H-181)
Margaret M. Connole
Rinaldo M. Delsignore (A-181)
Carl P. DeVasto (Hq. Co., 2nd Bn.-101)
Dorothy E. Dineen, widow of James F. Dineen (L-181)
Francis D. Donovan (C-211)
Marc P. Fecteau, son of Philip Fecteau (26th Recon. Trp.)
Guido J. Fratturelli (H-181)
John S. Gerety, Col., USA-Ret. (S-3, 2nd Bn,-181 and H-181)
Edward J. Griffin (L-101)
Jillian Carle Jakeman
Romeo C. LeBlanc (H-181)
Francis H. McGinnis (M-101)
Earl Mayan
Nathaniel Mencow (M-181)
Paul T. Metcalf (G-101)
Edward R. Michaud
Helen G. Palumbo
Rosaire J. Rajotte (D-181)
Sulo O. Ruuska (H-181)
Theodore Simmington, Jr., Maj., Ret. (F-181 and K-181)
Michael Stubinski (K-181 and K-141)
Antonio J. Tata (H-181)
Paul J. Turini (G-181)
John J. Voellings (B-181)
Clifford P. Welcome (F-181)
Walter E. Whitney (L-181)

Index

1st Armored Division ("Old Ironsides") 68, 75, 90
1st Coast Artillery (CA) District (New England) 1, 5, 105–106, 125, 168, 169
1st Naval District Headquarters, Boston, Mass. 156
2nd Armored Division ("Hell on Wheels") 68, 75, 79
4th "Ivy" Motorized Infantry Division 75
16th Cavalry Reconnaissance Group 175
22nd Quartermaster Regiment 114, 133, 165, 173
26th Cavalry Reconnaissance Troop 71, 153, 165, 166
26th Infantry Division 1–2, 6–7, 13–19, 20–28, 29–46, 59–61, 62–65, 66–70, 71–89, 90–93, 94–97, 98–106, 107–112, 113–124, 125–126, 127–128, 129–138, 139–148, 149–153, 154–161, 162–164, 165–174, 175–176; 181st Infantry separated from division 128; deployment overseas 128; formation of 328th Infantry 128; loss of 182nd 128; reorganization 128; Special Troops Section 112; square division 14–15, 101, 104; triangular division 14–15, 42, 70, 101, 104, 128
31st "Dixie" Infantry Division 75
36th "Texas" Infantry Division 3, 6, 8, 29, 53, 176
43rd "Winged Victory" Division 75
51st Infantry Brigade 14, 104
52nd Infantry Brigade 14, 54
67th "Rebel" AA (antiaircraft) 29
81mm Mortar 42, 43, 47–50, 56, 60
84th Combat Engineer Battalion 85
85th Division 176

90th "Tough Ombres" Infantry Division 176
101st Cavalry Regiment (N.Y. Army National Guard) 84, 175
101st Combat Engineer Battalion 56–57
101st Field Artillery Battalion 113, 128, 166
101st Infantry 14, 20, 27, 29, 99, 100, 102–103, 104, 111, 113, 123–124, 128
101st Medical Regiment 14
101st Ordnance Company 112
102nd Field Artillery (FA) 56
104th Antitank Company 64, 89, 99
104th Infantry 14, 20–28, 29–46, 52, 59, 62–65, 71, 73, 74, 79, 80–81, 85, 88, 89, 92, 94–95, 96–97, 99, 103, 104, 111, 113, 114, 127–128
111th Cavalry Reconnaissance Group 175
113th Infantry Detachment 120
114th Medical Battalion 114
132nd Combat Engineers 114, 130, 133, 136, 143–144
141st Infantry 3, 6, 176
143rd Cavalry Reconnaissance Group 175
144th Cavalry Reconnaissance Group 175
180th Field Artillery (FA) Battalion 20
181st Antitank Company (Hudson, Mass.) 16
181st Infantry 1, 3, 7–8, 13, 14–16, 20, 29, 32, 33, 40, 42, 47–50, 54–58, 75, 77, 78, 80, 81, 99–100, 104, 106, 110, 111, 112, 113, 125–126, 129–138, 139–148, 154, 162–164, 165–174, 175–176; regimental band 15, 18, 24, 29, 52, 53, 54, 55, 57, 152; "Rhythm unit" 54

182nd Infantry 14, 20, 100, 104–105
211th Field Artillery Battalion 29, 114, 121, 131, 133, 142–143, 149, 162
328th Infantry 128
337th Infantry 176
502nd Parachute Battalion 77
815th Antiaircraft Artillery Battalion 163

Abwehr II 116–117, 122
Acadia National Park 166
Adams, Edward J. (26th Recon. Trp.) 153, 166
Advanced Infantry Training (AIT) 59–61
African-American ("colored") troops (22nd Quartermaster Regiment) 114, 115–116, 165, 173
aircraft 55, 59, 60, 75–76, 77, 81, 99, 103, 105, 150
Alexandria, Louisiana 68
Allen, Frances (wife of Talmadge) 130
Allen, Talmadge "Ted" (A-132) 126, 130, 136, 137, 138, 143–144, 146
Amagansett, L.I. 1, 101, 116–121, 170, 175
Amagansett Incident 116–121, 170, 175
Amberg, Lt. Col. John A. (CO, 2nd Bn.-181) 100, 129, 145, 162
Americal Division 104–105
American Red Cross 16, 147
Anderson, Rear Admiral Adolphus 120, 121
Andrews, Brig. Gen. Frank 68
Annetts, Pvt. Winthrop E. (A-181) 57
antitank units/weapons 41, 42, 55, 59, 68–70, 77, 89, 90, 140–141
armored fighting vehicles (tanks, armored half-track personnel

Index

carriers, self-propelled guns, etc.) 54, 59, 61, 64, 66, 67–70, 84, 90–92, 166
Army General Classification Test (AGCT) 27–28
Arnold, Maj. Gen. Henry H. "Hap" 75
artillery 1, 35, 55, 56, 59, 66, 168, 169
Assalta, Capt. John F. (F-181) 134
Athol, Mass. 145
AWOL problem (Camp Edwards) 43–44
Ayer, Mass. 62, 64, 115

Bading, Lorenz F. (36th Div. Band) 29
Bailey Island (Casco Bay) 168, 169, 170
Bar Harbor, Maine 165, 166
barbed wire entanglements 144
Barnes, Chief Boatswain's Mate 2nd Class Warren (USCG) 120
Bartemo, Alexander V. (H-181) 170
Bartula, Edward (L-181) 78
basic training 16–17, 29–46
beach huts or hutments (prefabricated living quarters) 107, 110–111, 115, 143, 144
beach patrols 98–106, 107–112, 113–124, 125–126, 127–128, 129–138, 139–148, 154–161, 162–164, 165–174, 175–176; cold weather gear 139, 144, 146–148; duty stations 98–99, 100–103, 113–114, 124, 125–126, 133–136, 142–143, 162, 165–166, 167, 173; flotsam and jetsam 148, 165; living quarters/accommodations 101, 102–103, 107–111, 130, 131, 133–134, 135–138, 143; pastimes 109–110; problems and developments 127–128
Bearsley, James P. (L-181) 78
Belfast, Maine 170
Belfast-Moosehead Lake Railroad Line 170
Belloli, Everett P. (F-181) 144
Berman, Alex (H-181) 33
Bethpage, L.I. 124
Biddeford, Maine 129, 149, 163
Biddeford Pool Coast Guard Station 145
Biddle, Francis B. (U.S. Attorney General) 122
Bishop, Eleanor C. 140, 148, 154, 156, 157, 159, 165, 166, 175
Bistany's Bombardiers 51
blitzkrieg 11, 59, 67–68

Block Island, R.I. 126
Blue Hills Reservation, Mass. 102
Blue Point, Maine 151
Blute, Congressman Peter (Mass.) 126
boat patrols 128–129, 166
Boatner, Maj. Mark M., III 38–39
Born, Maj. Kevin M. 154, 155, 158
Boston, Mass. 13, 56, 64, 99, 100, 102, 113, 114, 124, 128, 156, 171
Boston & Maine Railroad 4, 133, 170
Boston Army Base (now Logan Airport) 55
Bourne, Mass. 13, 59, 102
Boyce, Frank J. 54, 55, 56, 57, 58
Brickman, Robert W. (D-141) 34, 44
Brill, 1st Sgt. Richard W. "Dick" (H-181) 8, 162
Brisbane, Australia 104
Britton, Bobby 154
Bronze Star 4–5
Brooklyn Navy Yard, N.Y. 104
Brooks, Greg 168
Brown Cow Island, Maine 170
Brunswick, Georgia 127
Brunswick, Maine 150, 168
Bucksport, Maine 165, 170, 173
Burger, Ernest Peter 119, 121–123
Burke-Wadsworth Bill 112
Burlingame State Park/Forest (Charlestown, R.I.) 101, 143, 159
Burnham, Junction, Maine 170, 171

Camden, Maine 165, 166, 167, 171, 172, 173–174
Camden, S.C. 73, 74, 77, 79, 90, 91
Camp Blanding, Florida 128
Camp Bridgton, Auburn, Maine 138
Camp Burlingame, Westerly, R.I. 113, 115, 143, 159
Camp Drum (Pine Camp) N.Y. 146, 148
Camp Edwards, Mass. 3, 13, 15, 16–19, 20–28, 29–46, 51, 52–53, 59–61, 62, 63, 64, 65, 94–97, 98–99, 106, 111–112, 128
Camp Ellis, Maine 133, 145
Camp Framingham, Mass. 113, 152, 162; *see also* Framingham, Mass.
Camp Gordon, Georgia 128
Camp Mills, L.I. 124
Camp Shelby, Miss. 20
Camp Smith, Peekskill, N.Y. 71

Camp Wheeler, Georgia 112
Candor, N.C. 75
Cape Cod, Mass. 3, 13, 16–19, 20–28, 29–46, 51–53, 64, 94–97, 107–111, 125
Cape Cod Airport, 59
Cape Cod Canal 59, 99, 102, 125
Cape Elizabeth, Maine 168, 169
Cape Sable, Nova Scotia 169
Cape Small, Maine 169, 170
Cardillo, Guy (H-181) 73, 74
Carnivale, James V. "Pimple" (H-181) 100, 138, 166–168, 170, 173
Carolina Maneuvers (U.S. Army GHQ Maneuvers) 62, 65, 66–89, 90–93, 98; assessment and conclusions 90–93; dysentery 85; exercises 74–78; participating units/composition of troops 75; planning 66–70; social and recreational activities 83–84, 87–88; training area 71–74; umpires 77–78, 90; water supplies 81, 85; weather conditions 80, 85
Carthage, N.C. 88
Cascade Lodge & Cabins (Saco, Maine) 149
Casco Bay, Maine (fleet anchorage) 162, 168–170
Catawba River 76–77
Catman, Raymond G. (H-181) 72, 73
Cavalry Reconnaissance Troops (in relief of 181st) 175
Chaffee, Brig. Gen. Adna R. 68, 70
Chamberlain, Louis K. (H-181) 136
Chappelle, Harvey H., Jr. (H-181) 141
Charlestown, R.I. 101
Charlotte, N.C. 73, 88
Charon, Al (H-181) 73, 74, 81
Chester, S.C. 73
Christensen, C. Lincoln (Capt.) 60, 74, 79–80, 91–92
Christmas Cove, Maine 167
Cialone, Dominick J. (H-181) 30, 34, 73, 74
Civilian Conservation Corps (CCC) 114–115, 173
Clark, Col. Mark W. 67
Clinton, Mass. 17, 29, 40, 150, 151
Coakley, Maureen D. "Debbie" (Connole) 7
coast/shore patrol 98–106, 107, 112, 113–124, 125–126, 127–128, 129–138, 139–148, 149–153, 154–161, 162–164, 165–174, 175–176

Combat Infantryman Badge 4
Combat Task Force 6814 104
Company H, 181st Infantry (heavy weapons) 1, 7, 8–9, 29, 30, 31, 32, 33, 34, 42, 47–50, 57, 72, 73, 74, 80, 81, 98, 99, 100, 101, 140–142, 145–146, 162–164, 165, 168, 170–174
Company "J," 104th Infantry 38–39
Connole, Albert P. 18
Connole, Catherine F. (Wackell) 18
Connole, Dennis A. 4, 164
Connole, Dennis J. (H-181) 1, 3–6, 17–19, 27, 29, 42, 47, 55, 100, 162, 164, 176
Connole, Elizabeth A. "Bette" (Mitchell) 18
Connole, Helen G. (Palumbo) 18, 24, 52
Connole, Margaret M. "Peg" 18
Connole, Michelina C. "Mary" 3, 4, 5
Connole, Richard A. 4
Connole, Rita T. (Dean) 18
Coolidge Estate (Manchester, Mass.) 114
Coolidge Point (Manchester, Mass.) 114
Coonamessett Club (Falmouth, Mass.) 51
Costa, Manual J., Jr. "Manny" (H-181) 72, 73
Cramer, Maj. Gen. Myron C. 122
Cranberry Island, Maine 165
Crane's Beach (Ipswich, Mass.) 164
Cranston St. National Guard Armory (Providence, R.I.) 100–101
Cronin Francis, D. (Capt.) 104–105
Cullen, Seaman 2nd Class Seaman John C. 117–121

Daniels, Col. E.M. (Commander U.S. Army Quartermaster Remount Service) 155
Dasch, Georg Johann (a.k.a. George Davis) 117–119, 121–123
Delsignore, Lt. Col. Rinaldo M., Ret. (A-181) 110–111, 148
DeStefano, Louis (H-181) 31
DeVasto, Carl P. (Hq. Co., 2nd Bn.-101) 101–102
Dineen, Dorothy E. (wife of James F.) 116, 163–164
Dineen, James F. (L-181) 114, 163–164

dogs (patrol-scout) 115, 123, 126, 127, 154–161, 166; breeds 154–155, 156, 158; celebrities lend or donate pets 154–155; food 159; heroics 159, 160; medals awarded to 158; Nora 160; processing into program 156; procurement 154–155; return to civilian life/placement elsewhere 161; reverse processing (prior to discharge) 161; scout or patrol dogs 156, 158; specialty classes (sentry, scout or patrol, messenger, and mine detection dogs) 156, 158; training facilities 156; training programs (dogs and handlers) 154, 156–158, 160
Dogs for Defense 154–155
Donovan, Francis D. (C-211) 29, 131, 133, 142, 149, 162
Doubler, Michael D. (Lt. Col.) 13, 14
Dowell, Col. Cassius M. 122
Drum, Lt. General Hugh A. 49, 74, 77, 79, 90, 105
Duncan, Col. Asa N. 75
Dymek, Bernie (H-181) 31, 34, 72

Eames, 1st Lt. Owen W. (Protestant Chaplain, 104th) 81
East Amagansett Coast Guard Life Saving Station 117–118
East Dennis, Mass. 125
Eastern Defense Command (EDC) 105, 113, 120, 127, 128, 142
Eastern Military Area 105
Easthampton, Long Island 117
Eastman, Joel W. 126, 168, 169
Eckfeldt, Maj. Gen. Roger W. (CO, 26th Div.) 13, 43, 98–99
Edwards, Maj. Gen. Clarence R. 13
Eisenhower, Gen. Dwight D. 78, 92
Ellerbe, N.C. 74
Ellsworth, Maine 126, 141, 153, 165, 166
Ellsworth Hotel (Ellsworth, Maine) 126, 166
Erickson, Oscar H. (H-181) 31

F-4U Vought Corsairs 150
Fairfield, Roy P. 136
Fall River, Mass. 101
Falmouth, Mass. 21, 51, 52, 53, 59
Farmville, Virginia 71
Favreault, Charles 7
Fayetteville, N.C. 73
Fecteau, Marc P. (son of Philip) 126, 166

Fecteau, Philip (26th Recon. Trp.) 126, 166
Federal Bureau of Investigation (FBI) 101, 105, 118, 119, 120, 121, 122, 123, 125, 126, 166, 175
Fini, Wallace G. (H-181) 136
Fisher, Francis "Red" (L-181) 78
Fitchburg, Mass. 7–8, 16, 17, 21, 29, 64
Fitton Field (Holy Cross College) 54, 55–6
Fitzpatrick, Raymond A. 13
Florida Keys 1
flour sack bombs 60–61, 76, 81, 90
Fonesca, Pfc. David (26th Signal Co.) 105
Fort A.P. Hill Military Reservation (Fredericksburg, Virginia) 113, 128
Fort Adams, Newport, R.I. 99
Fort Baldwin, Maine 168
Fort Belvoir, Virginia 40
Fort Benning, Georgia 130
Fort Dawes, Deer Island, Boston Harbor 143
Fort Devens Maneuvers (VI Army Corps war games) 62–65, 176
Fort Dix, N.J. 176
Fort George G. Meade, Maryland 124, 176
Fort Jackson, S.C. 128
Fort Rodman (Fall River, Mass.) 101, 110
Fort Royal, Virginia 157
Foster, Stephen Collins 81
Framingham, Mass. 16, 162
Fratturelli, Guido J. (H-181) 7–8, 31, 47, 48, 49–50, 100, 136, 152
Freeman, Provost Sgt. Raymond (M.P. Unit, 2nd Bn.-131) 163
Freeport, Maine 36, 165, 168
Fussell, Paul 60

Gable, Christopher R. 65, 66–89, 90–93
Gallager, Robert F. (D-815) 163
Gardner, Mass. 17, 18
Garganigo, Paul P. "Whitey" (H-181) 32, 136
Gauthier, Joseph H. 17
Gerety, Col. John S. "Jack," USA-Ret. (S-3, 2nd Bn.-181; E and H-181) 7, 98–99, 162, 163–164
German agents land on east coast 99, 116–123, 125–126, 166, 173, 175; betrayal of 121–122; candidates for training 117; capture 122, 125, 126;

defense at trial 122–123; sabotage materials 119, 121, 122; sentenced to death 123; training 117; trial 122–123
Gibson, Robert A. (H-181) 34, 87
Goering, Hermann 11
Going, Clayton G. 154, 155, 156, 158, 160, 161
Goldberg, Richard (L-181) 78
Gordon, Frances 52
Greenough, George E. (H-181) 136, 141
Greensboro, N.C. 73, 88
Gregory, Maj. Gen. Edmund B. (U.S. Army Quartermaster General) 156
Griffin, Edward J. (L-101) 103, 123–124
Griswold, Maj. Gen. Oscar W. 75, 76, 77, 90
Guidette, Lt. Abdon F. (C-104) 33
gun emplacements/positions 141, 142–143, 149, 151, 168, 169

Hamilton, Mass. 143
Hancock House (Ellsworth, Maine) 166
Hancock Point, Maine 175
Hanover, Penn. 71
Harrington & Richardson Arms Company (Worcester) 15
Harris, Chief Boatswain's Mate Thomas J. (USCG) 160
Harvard, Mass. 151
Harvey, 2nd Lt. Walter (H-181) 31
Haynes, 2nd Lt. Donald (H-181) 31
heavy weapons 42, 43, 47–50, 56, 60, 80, 87, 101, 140, 141–142
Higgins, Col. John J. (CO, 104th Inf.) 38, 39
Higgins Beach (Scarborough, Maine) 133
High Pine (Wells), Maine 6–7, 133, 134, 150
High Shoe Factory (Saco, Maine) 7, 103, 130–133, 162
Hitler, Adolf 11, 64, 67, 117, 122
Hogg, Ian V. 47, 48
Holy Cross College 54, 55, 56
Holyoke, Mass. 20
Hoover, J. Edgar 122, 123, 126
horse patrols (USCG) 127
Horseneck Beach (R.I.) 101, 116
Hotel Thacher (Biddeford, Maine) 132, 149
Houlihan, John F. 55, 56
Howard, Mrs. Fred S. (USO) 53
Hoyt, Edwin P. 117, 120, 121
Hudson, Mass. 16

Hughes, Michael 129
Hull, Mass. 102, 103

Indiantown Gap, Penn. 176
Institute Park (Worcester) 52–58
Ipswich, Mass. 110–111, 115, 116, 118, 164

Jacksonville, Florida 1, 116, 122, 170, 175
Jamaica, N.Y. 121
Jennette, Boatswain's Mate 2nd Class Carl Ross (USCG) 119
Jewell Island (Casco Bay) 168
Jones Beach, L.I. 124

Kalva, Lt. Klemens (J-104) 39
Kelly, Francis (L-181) 78
Kennebunkport, Maine 133, 134
Kennedy, Joseph P. (H-181) 136, 141
Kennett, Lee B. 12, 21, 26, 27, 33, 84
Kerling, Edward John 122
Key West, Florida 1, 113
Kings Point, L.I. 124
Kinney Shores (Saco) 138, 144
Kirkwood Hotel (Camden, S.C.) 73–74, 80
Kirley, Pvt. Francis (104th) 20
Kittery, Maine 142, 149
Knute, Herta 168
Krock, Niilo E. (H-181) 136

Laconto, Peter (Band-181) 52
Lane, Capt. John F. (CO, E-181) 134
Laquidara, 1st Lt. Salvi J. (H-181) 136, 165
Lariviere, Joseph (H-181) 33
LeBlanc, Romeo C. "Ro" (H-181) 8, 101, 125, 140, 141, 144–145, 146–147
Lend-Lease Act of 1941 12
Leominster, Mass. 8, 140
Little Machias Bay, Maine 165
Lockheed B-34 Ventura medium bomber (RCAF) 144–145
Lofgren, 2nd Lt. James T. (H-181) 141
Logan, Brig. Gen. Francis V. 54, 55, 57
Long Island, New York 99, 111, 116–121, 124, 126, 148
Lowell, Mass. 24
Lunder Shoe Company (Saco, Maine) 131
Lunenburg, Mass. 64
Lynch, Maj. Gen. George A. 70

Machias, Maine 3, 126, 165
Machnick, Henry J. (H-181) 136

Mack, Charlie (Coonamessett Club) 51
Mackintosh, Capt. Robert M. (104th) 20
Macuga, Joseph S. (L-181) 164
magnetic loop stations 168–170
Magruder, Brig. Gen. Bruce 68
Maine National Guard Armory (Saco, Maine) 130, 136, 138, 143
Manchester, William 6
Manchester, Mass. 114
Marcoullier, Capt. Arthur S. (CO, 26th Recon. Trp.) 153
Marlborough, Mass. 17
Marshall, General George C. (U.S. Army Chief of Staff) 4, 64, 66–67, 68, 69, 70
Marshall Field, L.I. 124
Mashpee, Mass. 59
Mauldin, Bill 47
Mayan, Earl (84th Combat Eng. Bn.) 85–87
McBride, Lt. Col. William L. (CO, 1st Bn.-181) 98
USS *McCalla* (DD-488) 170
McCarter, Robert B. "Bill" (180th FA) 20
McEvoy, Frank (Coonamessett Club) 51
McGarry, Lt. Col. William (CO, 2nd Bn.-104) 103
McGinnis, Francis H. (M-101) 103
McLeod, N.C. 71, 73, 75, 76, 78
McNair, Lt. Gen. Leslie J. 67, 69, 70, 77, 90, 92–93
mechanization (employment of armored fighting vehicles) 59, 62, 64, 67–68, 70, 77, 84, 90–92
mechanized units *see* mechanization
Melbourne, Australia 104
Mencow, Nathaniel (M-181) 18, 41, 52, 60
Metcalf, Paul T (G-101) 60, 102–103
Michaud, Edward R. 168, 169, 170
Miles, Gen. Sherman 113, 126
Milford, Mass. 17
Military Police 5, 6, 55, 125, 134, 162–164
Milton, Mass. 102
Mitchell, Seaman 2nd Class Evans E. (USCG) 160
Moiles, William H. 57
Monroe, N.C. 88–89
Montauk Point, L.I. 100, 101, 126
Montgomery, Field Marshal Bernard 91

Index

Morley Button Factory (Portsmouth, N.H.) 103, 133, 134
motorized patrols 127, 140, 153, 165, 171, 173–174, 175
Mt. Desert Island, Maine 165, 166
Mullin, Arthur M. (M-104) 24, 26
Murphy, Robert (H-181) 136

Nantasket Beach (Hull, Mass.) 51, 102, 125
Narragansett, R.I. 115
Narragansett Bay 99, 156
Nashua, N.H. 62
Natick, Mass. 14, 17
National Archives & Records Administration (NARA), Waltham, Mass. 168–170
Neal, John C. (H-181) 136
Nelson, Brig. Gen. Harold W. 66
New Bedford, Mass. 98, 99, 101
New Caledonia, Melanesia 104
New England Frontier Defense Sector (Eastern Theater of Operations), headquartered at Fort Adams, Newport, R.I. 99–100
New London, Conn. 113
New York City, N.Y. 18, 104, 120, 121, 122, 124, 128, 154
New York, New Haven & Hartford Railroad (New Haven) 16, 18
Newport, R.I. 99, 100, 113
Noble, Dennis L. 127, 148, 154, 157, 161, 175
Novak, S/Sgt. Stanley 160

obstacle course (Camp Edwards) 36, 37, 38, 40–41, 42, 45
Ocean Park, Maine 126, 130, 145
O'Connor, 1st Lt. Bernard C. "B.C." (H-181) 133
Office of Price Administration (OPA) 150
OHIO (over the hill in October) 64–65
Old Orchard Beach (OOB), Maine 7, 126, 129, 130, 133, 138, 144–145, 150, 163; casino dance hall 142, 150, 151; pier 141, 142, 145, 150–151; town hall-fire station 133–134, 138, 139, 144, 150
Oliva, Andrew J. (H-181) 73
Oliver, James (H-181) 136
Operation Pastorius 117
Orange, Mass. 6–7, 17, 40
Oregon Inlet, N.C. 160
Orent, Lucy 116

Orrizzi, Dorothy M. (wife of Orlando) 163
Orrizzi, Orlando "Tutor," Jr. (H-181) 30, 31, 136, 138, 163
Owens, 1st Lt. George E. (104th) 96

Palumbo, Helen G. (wife of Matthew) see Connole, Helen
Palumbo, Matthew J. (Band-181) 15, 18, 24, 52, 53, 152
Panama Canal 104
Parker, Alice R. (Worcester, Mass.) 86
Patch, Maj. Gen. Alexander M., Jr. 104–105
Patton, Col. George S., Jr. 68, 79, 176
Pearl Harbor 31, 94–96, 98–99, 104, 138
Pee Dee River 74, 75, 76–77, 79, 80–81, 85
Pennfield Ridge, New Brunswick (RCAF Station) 144–145
Perreault, June (of Worcester, Mass., 181st regimental queen) 57
Philippines Division 105
Pine Camp see Camp Drum
Pine Point, Maine 151–152
Pinehurst, N.C. 88
Pittsfield, Mass. 115
Plymouth, Mass. 102–103, 125, 160
Point Judith, R.I. 115, 152–153
Ponte Vedra Beach, Florida 1, 116, 122, 170, 175
Popham Beach (Phippsburg, Maine) 168
Portland Harbor 162, 168–169
Portland, Maine 99, 100, 103, 113–114, 162, 168, 169–170
Portsmouth, N.H. 3, 7, 103, 133, 134
Powers, Col. James P. (CO, 181st Inf.) 104
Prouts Neck, Maine 133
Providence, R.I. 100
Purple Heart 3, 4, 5

Quaranta, Victor R. (H-181) 30, 57
Quentz Lake (Abwehr training facility) 117, 122
Quillia, Clarence H. (L-181) 110–111
Quonochontaug Beach (Charlestown, R.I.) 101
Quonset Point, R.I. 113

Rahilly, James J., Jr. (H-181) 134, 163

Rajotte, Rosaire J. "Ross" (D-181) 114–116, 139, 152–153
Raleigh, N.C. 71, 88
Record Group 181 168–170
Record Group 242 168–170
Regimental Combat Team (RCT) 114
Regis, John G. (H-181) 72, 73
Renzetti, Nicholas J. "Nick" (H-181) 172–173
Riley, Leonard (H-181) 34
Risley, Lt. Richard G. (J-104) 39
Riverhead, L.I. 101, 120
Rockingham, N.C. 74, 88
Rockland (Maine) Sector 126, 136, 165–174
Rocky Point, Plymouth, Mass. 102–103
Rommel, Field Marshal Erwin 91
Roosevelt, Franklin D. 4, 11–13, 52, 64, 67, 94, 105, 122, 123
Rose, Brig. Gen. William I. (Commander 51st Infantry Brigade) 104
Roseland Ballroom (Taunton, Mass.) 51
Rowena Island (Maine) 173
Royal Canadian Air Force (RCAF) 144–145, 169
Royall, Col. Kenneth C. 122–123
Ruberti, George J. (H-181) 171, 172, 173
Ruuska, Sulo O. (H-181) 8–9, 31, 48, 73, 81, 100, 101, 133, 141, 147, 170–174, 176

Saco, Maine 1, 3, 7, 49–50, 103, 114, 125, 129–138, 143, 145, 150, 152, 162–164
Saco-Biddeford ("twin cities"), Maine 129
Saco National Guard Armory see Maine N.G. Armory
Saco River 49, 129, 152
St. Lawrence, Nova Scotia 169
Sandwich, Mass. 13, 44
Sanford, Maine 134, 150
Scarborough, Maine 133
Schiavone, Lt. (C-211) 142
Scott, Maj. Gen. Charles L. 68
search light stations/towers 106, 142, 143, 165
Sears & Roebuck Shoe Factory 130–131
Searsport, Maine 165, 170, 172
Selective Service Board #167 (Worcester) 17
Selective Service draftees or trainees ("selectees") 12, 17, 19, 20–28
Selective Training and Service Act of 1940 12

Senior, Kathleen M. 4
Service Men's Mothers Club (Saco, Maine) 150
Simmington, Maj. Theodore "Simmy," Jr., Ret. (F-181 and K-181) 7, 99, 125, 133
simulated weapons 60–61, 79–80, 92
Smith, Dick 52
Smith, Jack B. (H-181) 167
Smith, Col. Roy W. (CO, 181st Inf.) 15, 55, 56, 57, 98, 104
social and recreational activities/off duty hours 42, 51–53, 64, 83–84, 87–88, 149–153
Soubble, John J. (L-181) 114
South Hingham 114, 125
South Portland, Maine 142, 149
Southampton, L.I. 101
Southern Pines, N.C. 88
Southwest Harbor, Maine 165
Stalin, Joseph 11
Stanton, Shelby L. 106, 146–148
Stimson, Harry L. (Secretary of War) 12
Stubinski, Michael (K-181 and K-141) 125
Sub Sea Recovery (Portland, Maine) 168–170
Swanburg, W.A. 122

Taffe, Lt. Col. Richard P., AUS, Ret. (Hq. Co., 3rd Bn.-181) 13–14, 23, 27, 28, 29, 30, 32–33, 34, 51, 60, 96
Tank Destroyer Battalions 70
Tata, Lt. Col. Antonio "Tony" J., Ret. (H-181) 140–141, 168, 176
Taunton, Mass. 42, 51
telescope stations 126, 142, 168
Thacher Hotel (Biddeford, Maine) 132, 149
Third Naval District command post (Riverhead, L.I.) 120, 121
Timmerman, Wing Commander N.W. (RCAF) 145
Toczko, Stanley A. (H-181) 33, 73
Tomasello, James (L-181) 77
Toomey, John M. (Mayor of Worcester) 16
Trident Research & Recovery, Inc. (Framingham, Mass.) 168–170
Trubenback, 1st Lt. Alfred E. (XO, F-181) 98
Truman, Harry S. 5, 123
Truro, Mass. 125

Trusedell, Maj. Gen. Karl (VI Corps Commander) 93
Turini, Arletta Skillings (wife of John D.) 151–152
Turini, John D. (G-181 and Hq. Co., 2nd Bn.-181) 14, 29, 101, 110, 131, 133, 136, 139–140, 150, 151–152
Turini, Paul J. (G-181) 115, 133, 139, 150

U-202 117, 120
U-458 169
U-584 122
U-754 169
U-boat sightings 103, 125–126, 166, 168–170
uniforms 15, 24, 26–27
United Services Organizations, Inc. (USO) 52–53, 88, 108, 111, 149
U.S. Army Air Corps 55, 75, 103, 105, 121
U.S. Army Coast Artillery Corps (CAC) 1, 106
U.S. Army Coastal Defense Command 168, 169
U.S. Army General Headquarters (GHQ) 66–67, 77–78, 79, 88–89, 90–91
U.S. Army Induction Center (Lamartine St. School, Worcester, Mass.) 3, 18
U.S. Army K-9 Corps 154, 156
U.S. Army Ordnance Department 60, 91
U.S. Army Quartermaster Corps 123, 146–147, 154–158, 161
U.S. Army Quartermaster Remount Service 127, 155, 156
U.S. Coast Guard Headquarters, New York, N.Y. 120, 121
U.S. Coast Guard operations 1, 99, 111, 113, 115, 117–121, 127, 139, 141, 145, 155, 160, 161, 162, 165–166, 173, 175
U.S. Coast Guard Station, Napeague Bay, L.I. 120
U.S. Naval Air Station, Brunswick, Maine 150
U.S. Naval Air Station, Sanford, Maine 150
U.S. Naval Headquarters, Portland, Maine 168, 169, 170
U.S. Navy Eastern Sea Frontier Headquarters, New York, N.Y. 120
U.S. Navy operations 1, 99, 113, 127, 145, 150, 155, 161, 162, 168–170, 175

Upton State Forest (Upton, Mass.) 62

VI Army Corps war games *see* Fort Devens maneuvers
Vinton, 2nd Lt. Russell W. (CO, G-181) 116, 133
Vitone, Orlando (H-181) 80, 141
Voellings, John J. (B-181) 101, 126, 139, 159

WAGS 156
Waldoboro, Maine 165, 170
Warwick, R.I. 115
Washburn, Arnold M. (H-181) 33, 73
water supply problems 63, 81, 85
weather conditions 20, 29, 33, 34, 36–37, 62–63, 80, 85, 94, 110, 127, 146–148, 173–174
Webster, Mass. 17
Weekapaug (Westerly, R.I.) 101, 126
Welch, Robert (L-181) 114
Welcome, Clifford P. (F-181) 6–7, 34, 36, 56, 101, 111, 134, 139, 140, 142, 144, 145, 146–7, 150, 152, 156, 158–159, 161
Westerly, R.I. 101, 113, 115, 159
Westport Point, R.I. 101
Wetkowiecz, Frank (M-104) 26
Whalen, Pvt. John (181st) 56
Whalom Water and Amusement Park (Lunenburg, Mass.) 64
Wheaton Square (N.G.) Armory (Worcester) 14
Whitney, Col. Walter E., Ret. (L-181) 110
Wilson, Leona (USO) 53
Winchell, Walter 128
Winston-Salem, N.C. 88
Wiscasset, Maine 165
Wonalancet, N.H. 160
Woods Hole, Mass. 100
Worcester, Mass. 3, 4, 12, 13, 14–17, 18, 19, 40, 52, 54–58, 64, 86
Worcester County 3

Yankee Doings newsletter (YDVA) 2, 6, 60
York Harbor, Maine 134

Zapustus, Stanley J. (F-181) 101
Zerby, Barry L. (NARA) 126
Zmuda, Jan (Roseland Ballroom, Taunton, Mass.) 51
Zuckerman, Lee (H-181) 73